ADULT AND CONTINUING EDUCATION
Theory and Practice

PETER JARVIS

ROUTLEDGE

First published 1983 by Croom Helm
Reprinted 1988 by Routledge
Reprinted 1990, 1992
11 New Fetter Lane, London EC4P 4EE

© 1988 Peter Jarvis

Printed in Great Britain by
Biddles Ltd, Guildford and King's Lynn

British Library Cataloguing in Publication Data

Jarvis, Peter
    Adult and continuing education.
    1. Adult education
    I. Title
    374   LC5215

ISBN 0-415-01862-5

CONTENTS

Contents

Contents

Contents

FIGURES

Figures

TABLES

To
Mother and Jack with gratitude
and
in memory of
my Father

ACKNOWLEDGEMENTS

Few books can be written without the encouragement, inspiration and, even, provocation of friends and colleagues. This book has all of these origins and without them it would have been the poorer. There are, however, some who deserve especial mention and to whom I am greatly indebted: Miss Sheila Gibson, Dr Alan Chadwick and Dr Colin Griffin have read all or part of the book in draft form and their comments have enriched the text considerably; the post-graduate students in the Department of Educational Studies at the University of Surrey have continued to help me to clarify some of my ideas in our teaching and learning sessions; Mrs Hilarie Hall has undertaken the responsibility of transforming my handwritten draft into a camera ready typescript with expertise and efficiency.

I would like to express my gratitude to those who have given me permission to quote or reproduce from other writings: the Cambridge Book Company, New York, to quote Roby Kidd's 'Ten Commandments', Dr Colin Griffin has allowed me to summarise most of the points he raised in his paper on continuing and recurrent education in table 8.5; Holt, Rinehart and Winston have allowed me to reproduce Professor Dennis Child's diagram of Maslow's hierarchy of needs and Professor Robert Gagné's diagram of the relation between phases of learning and events of instruction; Jossey Bass have granted me permission to reproduce two diagrams from Professor C Houle's *The Design of Education*.

Once again, I must gratefully acknowledge the help and encouragement of my wife, Maureen, and children, Frazer and Kierra, who have encouraged me to write, even though it has resulted in them under-taking additional family responsibilities.

Many people have, obviously helped me to

produce this text but, like every writer, the final responsibility for what has been produced must rest with me.

P. JARVIS
University of Surrey

INTRODUCTION

The study of adult education is growing in significance as the training of educators of adults is
being undertaken more frequently in the United
Kingdom and elsewhere. But there are few text-
books that seek to introduce students to a broad
sweep of the field, so that this text has been prepared with this aim in view. It is hoped that
students of the education of adults on ACSET I, II
and III, Certificate, Diploma and Degree courses
might find it a useful volume. In addition, it is
hoped that other practitioners in the field of adult
and continuing education will find much in this book
that is relevant to their work.

With this aim in mind, the book has been very
fully referenced so that readers can follow up any
of the points that interest them and can also refer
to the original sources. Further reading is
suggested at the end of each chapter, so that ideas
from each chapter might be developed by interested
readers. The contents of the book are wide enough
to introduce students and practitioners to a
variety of contemporary issues in the study of the
education of adults. The aspects discussed in this
book reflect the purpose from which it has been
written, so that a great deal of it is devoted to
the teaching and learning transaction. These have
been divided into different chapters in the book for
reasons of clarity but in reality such a division
is frequently artificial.

The text attempts to combine the theoretical
with the practical and it is hoped that those who
read it will find it informative, relevant and,
above all, useful.

Chapter One

TOWARDS A RATIONALE FOR THE PROVISION OF
EDUCATION FOR ADULTS

Education, it is generally agreed, is a good thing
so that during the past century it has assumed an
important place in policy making at both the levels
of local and national governments and, consequently,
a proportionate amount of the total public expenditure has been directed towards it. Kumar (1978:
248) suggested that in the 1980s it is anticipated
that 8% of the Gross National Product would be
claimed by education. Yet examine that expenditure
and clearly the greatest amount is directed towards
the education of the young. Indeed, it has been
estimated that 85% of all expenditure on education
by public authorities goes on initial education and
that only about 1% of the Gross National Product is
devoted to the education of adults. (ACACE Report
1982a:58). If the amount of money expended on
vocational education and that spent by industry and
commerce on education is included in these statistics, then the figures are underestimates of the
real figure (see Woodhall, 1980). Nevertheless, it
is clear from these estimates that adult education
is the 'poor cousin' (Newman 1979) of the education
world. They reflect the idea that education is something that happens predominately to the young - 'a
front-end' conception of education rather than regarding it as a lifelong process. While 'lifelong
education' may be a relatively new term the idea of
lifelong learning is far from innovatory: Plato
expected that the philosopher-kings should divide
their time equally between the affairs of state and
study after the age of fifty years. But this education of the elite has gradually been extended to
the masses; initially under the influence of
Christianity when 'education for salvation' (Kelly
1970:1-3) became a feature of British life in the
first Elizabethan period and, by the nineteenth

1

century, adult schools, mechanics institutes and
university extension classes were established in
Britain and lyceums, library societies and cultural
societies in America (see Kelly 1970, Peers 1958).
By the second Elizabethan period the education of
adults has become widely accepted. Additionally,
many recreational associations have introduced educative components to their activities and occupations and professions generally devote a considerable proportion of their resources to the education
and training of their personnel. Legge (1982) documents a vast array of providers of education for
adults in the United Kingdom, while Boone et al
(1980) indicate something of the range of provision
in the United States. Throughout the world the education of adults is occurring and, gradually, a
study of comparative adult education is emerging
(see Charters 1981, Harris 1980, Kulich 1982a,
Titmus 1981) which indicates that the breadth of
provision is wide enough for scholars to develop the
study of this sphere of education. It would, therefore, be quite false to assume that the education of
adults is a marginal or insignificant branch of education; rather it is one that is quite crucial to
any comprehension of the concept of education and
basic to its practice. This opening chapter, however, offers a justification of the education of
adults based upon the nature of contemporary
society and upon the nature of the individual: it
is divided into two main sections, starting with
contemporary society, and demonstrates that education should be provided for people throughout the
whole of their life span. It must be borne in mind
throughout that this division is quite arbitrary
since the individual and society are dialectically
inter-related and interdependent, so that any
changes in society will affect individuals but
people can and do cause transformation in society
and its culture.

THE NATURE OF CONTEMPORARY SOCIETY

Any discussion about the nature of society inevitably assumes certain theoretical perspectives but
this brief one does not seek to enter any sociological debate about the structure of the social
system. Rather it assumes that society is a complex
social system in a state of continuous change and
that change is the norm rather than the exception.
It also recognises that the educational institution

is both the recipient of the pressures for change
exerted by other institutions in society, especially
the technological and the economic, and a source of
pressure on other institutions. Finally, it is
recognised that the individual is moulded by the
forces that are exerted upon him as he seeks to discover his place in society but that the human being
is more than a passive recipient and processor of
social pressures, he is able to act back upon his
world and become an agency of change.
     Every society produces its own culture which
is carried by human beings and transmitted through
interaction but, more recently, this culture is also
being stored in audio and video cassettes, in
computers,etc. Culture, in this context, refers to
the sum totality of knowledge, values, beliefs, etc.
of a society. Because of its apparent commonality
among members of a society, culture seems to be a
phenomenon external to the individual and objective.   Actually, this objectivity is more apparent
than real since each individual has internalised
aspects of his culture. Consequently, it may be regarded as 'objectified' rather than 'objective' and
the manner in which an individual acquires that
culture, after having been born into a society, may
be simply illustrated by the following diagram.

Figure 1.1:   The Process of Internalisation
              of 'Objectified' Culture

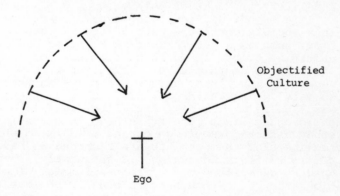

Objectified
Culture

Ego

Every individual has the culture of his society
'transmitted' to him through interaction with other
people. The arrows in the above diagram indicate
the direction of the transmission in every interaction between 'ego' and 'alter'. Hence it may be
seen that there is a sense in which every interaction is a process of learning and teaching. Every
time an individual learns something as a result of
being exposed to any of the media, the same process
of learning is occurring. It is the process of
socialization. There is a sense in which some
facets of education may be regarded as a part of the
process of socialization, although the former is
usually viewed as a more formal process than the
latter. However, it is possible to understand
precisely how Lawton (1973:21) can regard the
curriculum as a selection from culture within the
context of this discussion. Obviously, the process
of acquiring culture is very significant during
childhood, both through socialization and through
education. However, sociologists regard sociol-
ization as a lifetime process having at least two
aspects: primary socialization is 'the first
socialization an individual undergoes .... through
which he becomes a member of society. Secondary
socialization is any subsequent process that inducts
an already socialized individual into new sectors of
the objective world of his society' (Berger and
Luckmann, 1967:150). Similarly, education may be
regarded as a lifelong process and further reference
will be made to the concepts of lifelong learning
and lifelong education below.

It is not difficult, however, to realize that
in a society where the rate of social change is very
slow, such as a pre-industrial European one or a
primitive tribe, it would be feasible for an individual to learn most of the cultural knowledge
necessary for him to assume his place in that
society during childhood. In such societies, it
was, and still is, only the elite, eg. Plato's
philosopher-kings, the priesthood, who continue to
study esoteric knowledge during adulthood, while the
remainder of the populace are regarded as having
completed their education. Consequently, it is not
hard to understand why a front-end model of education emerged, although it is equally obvious that
such a model has a little relevance to a society
whose culture is changing rapidly. From the onset
of the Industrial Revolution, with the introduction
of more sophisticated technology, the rate of social
change increased. Indeed, change is endemic to

4

technological societies. This means that the learning process should not cease at early adulthood.
New knowledge, new ideas, new values and new
practices all have to be confronted. Hence, a growth
of educational provision occurred in the eighteenth
and nineteenth centuries and the people were encouraged to learn more. Both children and adults
were provided with additional educational opportunities and it is frequently claimed that the
reason for this new emphasis on education was because a need existed to produce a competent and
literate work force. Clearly this was so. Yet education, once introduced, had functions of a non-
educational kind. Quoting one of Her Majesty's
Inspectors for Education in London during the late
nineteenth century, Kumar (1978:248f) writes: 'If
it were not for her 500 elementary schools London
would be overrun by a hoade of young savages'.
Perhaps education is still being used to keep
people 'off the streets', but now the subjects are
a little older! Education is used for many purposes
but, clearly, it is an important agency in preparing
individuals to respond to the rapid social change
that is occurring. Because change is so rapid, it
is necessary for individuals to keep learning, so
that they should not become alienated from the
culture that engulfs them.

Max Scheler (cited Merton 1968:520f) focused
upon the effects of change on knowledge as early as
1926, when he realised that some types of knowledge
alter faster than others, the fastest being technological knowledge. He called this 'artificial'
because it is a form of knowledge that does not
persist over time and he classified knowledge into
seven types, based upon their degree of
artificiality: myth and legend; knowledge implicit
in the natural folk language; religious knowledge;
basic types of metaphysical knowledge; philoso-
phical-metaphysical knowledge; positive knowledge
of mathematics, natural and cultural sciences;
technological knowledge. Irrespective of the
validity of Scheler's classification, he highlighted
an important phenomenon about knowledge - that
different types change at varying rates. Hence the
more a person's knowledge becomes outdated the more
new knowledge he has to learn if he is to remain in
accord with his culture. The more technologically-
based the society, the more easy it is for individuals to become alienated, for all are affected
by the changes in technology, as evidenced by the
introduction of the pocket calculator, the digital

5

watch and the micro-computer. Hence the individual
needs to learn new knowledge to prevent the onset of
alienation or anomie and lifelong learning, even
lifelong education, may help him to adjust to the
cultural changes prevalent in contemporary society.
   This phenomenon is even more common in the
sphere of employment, with many occupations and
professions being based upon knowledge that occurs
at the artificiality end of Scheler's spectrum. For
instance, the Advisory Council for Adult and
Continuing Education's report (1982b:9) states:

> In recent years the obsolescence of knowledge
> has been most marked in the professions. Many
> professional bodies now encourage, and some-
> times require, their members to undertake
> regular courses of continuing education and
> professional development. The need for
> regular updating will broaden across much
> more of the working population.

Continuing education has become a reality in the
professions (see Houle 1980). Additionally, some
more traditional occupations have declined whilst
others have disappeared, leaving many to seek new
forms of employment and industrial training.
Government re-training schemes have become a relatively common phenomenon in recent years in the
United Kingdom and many forms of vocational education appear to be increasing and expanding. Indeed,
Woodhall (1980:22) estimates that in 1978-9, in the
United Kingdom, a figure of £3,000 million was spent
on all forms of vocational training, equivalent to
one-third of the total expenditure on education and
equal to about 3% of all wages and salaries.
   Not only have technological innovations led to
unemployment, recent monetarist policies in Western
Europe, especially the United Kingdom, and in the
United States have resulted in increased unemployment and also in a gradual lowering of the age of
retirement. This has resulted in more leisure time,
even though it is enforced and often unwanted. In a
society dominated by a work ethic, in which it has
been regarded as good to work but evil to be idle,
leisure has always been regarded as a mixed
blessing. Consequently, it is being recognised that
values about leisure will have to adapt or they will
be changed which, incidentally, illustrates a way
by which values respond to social pressure. But
some people have to learn how to use their leisure
and Parker (1976) has drawn a useful distinction

between education for leisure and education as leisure.

That some people have to learn how to use this leisure may appear to be surprising initially but it is less surprising when it is realized that many who are now entering enforced unemployment, at an earlier stage of their lives than they originally anticipated, were brought up with the expectation that they would work until they approached the end of their lives and that not to work was regarded as malingering. Hence,the expectation of having to work for the greater part of their lives has meant that many people have not really learned how to use non-work time as constructively as they might. Yet it may actually be wrong to tell people what to do with their leisure but correct and beneficial to provide them with the opportunity to consider how they employ creatively the additional freedom that technological changes and specific economic policies have produced. One aspect of preparation for un-employment that has occurred recently has been pre-retirement education (see Coleman 1982, Jarvis 1980, 1983b,interalia) in which programme time is frequently devoted to the use of leisure.

By contrast, education as leisure has trad-itionally been undertaken by more educated people because many, especially those from the working classes who were unsuccessful during their initial education, have tended to shun the formal provision of leisure time education once they had completed their initial and, perhaps, their vocational ed-ucation. The history of liberal adult education is a long and honourable one, being enshrined in the university extension movement and other types of provision, such as the Workers Educational Association, and the demand for it appears to be unabating (ACACE 1982b). This may be demonstrated from the many people who attend the university extension classes, local education authority classes and courses organized by other commercial and voluntary agencies. Additionally, the creation of the Open University has demonstrated the tremendous attraction that academic study has for many people who do not possess the traditional, formal qual-ifications for university entry. Similar movements exist in many parts of the world (Rumble and Harry 1982) and in America with its Free Universities movement (Draves 1980) and the provision of part-time degree education throughout the life span. More recently, education and the elderly has assumed increasing significance: in America, there are the

7

elderhostels (Zimmerman 1979:10 and 22f); in
France, l'université du troisième age; in the
United Kingdom there are endeavours currently being
undertaken to create a University of the Third Age.
Many of these new educational movements have already
shown that leisure time education does not necessarily result in any lowering of academic standards; indeed, the academic standards may be lifted
in some instances. Hence leisure time education is
more than hobby type education,which is often be-
littled. Yet the provision of this latter form of
education ia also of great importance since it provides opportunity for life enrichment and reflects
a positive attitude on behalf of the learner to the
acquisition of new knowledge and skills. Parker
(1976:99) quotes Jary with approval when he concludes that 'the leisure centredness of liberal
adult education ought not to be hidden or apologised
for. It should be recognised and its gratifications
elaborated. It should be seen as a highly distinctive form of leisure.'
     If adult education can help people to relate
more easily with contemporary culture, if it can
help them to use their leisure time in a creative
manner, if it can enrich the lives of many who undertake it, then it would appear to be quite ludicrous
to relegate it to the margins of the world of education and, clearly, its provision will become
even more important since more people are living
longer. Hence they have more actual time in their
lives to learn things. But 'what is the use of
learning new things when a person is old?' is a
question frequently posed. Yet if learning is life
enriching, as it is for many people, then the
elderly have as much right as anyone else to enjoy
the fruits of learning. Dewey (1916:51) wrote that
since 'life means growth, a living creature lives as
truly and positively at one stage as another, with
the same intrinsic fullness and the same absolute
claims. Hence education means the enterprise of
supplying the conditions which insure growth, or
adequacy of life, irrespective of age'. But another
objection that is often raised is that "you can't
teach an old dog new tricks". Yet is this adage
true? Recent research (see Allman 1982, Sherron
and Lumsden 1978) has indicated that the elderly
can and do learn effectively, even if their methods
of learning may be slightly different. Old dogs can
be taught new tricks!
     Indeed, people of all ages are realizing that
they either want, or need, to return to studying

later in their lives. This has led to the growth
of another important sphere of education: return to
study courses. Two major types have emerged:
firstly, a skill-type course in which students are
actually taught how to study effectively and numerous books have been written on this subject, such
as Richardson et al (1979) and Gibbs (1981). The
latter is student-centred and adopts many of the
perspectives of an educator of adults. Secondly,
courses have been provided to enable adults to
change the direction of their lives and to have a
new opportunity (see Hutchinson E and E, 1978).

Thinking people are much more able to play a
part in the wider life of society, democracies need
people who are not only able to think but who are
also knowledgeable about areas of social and political life. Only by having a thinking and educated
populace can a democratic society be achieved, even
if the ideal of democracy is only an ideal - it is
a goal to strive towards! Lengrand (1975:30), one
of the most influential writers on lifelong education, suggested that modern democracy 'in its
political, social, economic and cultural aspects
can only rest on solid foundations if a country has
at its disposal increasing numbers of responsible
leaders at all levels, capable of giving life and
concrete substance to theoretical structures of
society'. Few would want to dispute this claim and
it may be through the educational process that some
of these responsible leaders emerge.

As a result of major changes in society,
culture is changing and adult education provision
can assist people to understand the processes that
are occurring and help them to adapt and take their
places in a constantly renewing society. People
require the provision of adult education classes to
help them in their work, in their leisure and, indeed, in enriching the whole of their lives. With
the provision of education for adults, one condition
exists that is a necessary foundation stone for the
creation of a democratic society. Yet people are
not really only the passive recipients of the
culture of society, as Figure 1.1 depicts, so that
it is now necessary to examine the second facet of
this argument: the nature of the individual.

THE NATURE OF THE INDIVIDUAL

At the start of the preceding section it was
suggested that one element in the inter-relationship

between the individual and his society is that he is
the recipient of its culture. Even so, it was
stressed that there is another aspect to this
process and this is exemplified in the following
diagram.

Figure 1.2: The Nature of the Individual
in relation to 'Objectified'
Culture

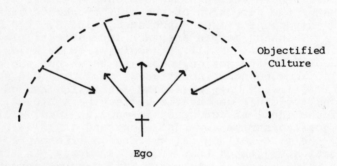

Objectified
Culture

Ego

The human being is not a passive recipient of his
cultural heritage, he does not have it imprinted
upon a 'tabula rasa' type of mind; but he receives,
processes and externalises. The arrows demonstrate
that all social interaction is both a teaching and
a learning process. During the process, he accepts
some aspects of culture, modifies others and even
rejects some of the information with which he is
presented. But he does more than merely processing
what he receives, he is frequently active in pursuit
of the knowledge, ideas, values and beliefs enshrined in objectified culture.

The nature of man has occupied the minds of
philosophers and theologions for centuries and it is
not the purpose of this section to encroach upon
their deliberations, nor even to attempt to summarise their arguments. It is intended, however, to
suggest that the human being is an active participant in the learning process throughout the whole of
life and that the reason for this lay both in his
nature and in his relationship with the wider
society. Initially, this section is designed to
demonstrate that man is a lifelong learner and,
thereafter, it will be shown that man is by nature a
meaning-seeking animal; it is claimed here that
this endeavour to understand himself, his society
and his universe lay at the root of the learning

10

process. Finally, it is concluded that the provision of education for people of all ages is
essential because it helps to facilitate this quest
to understand,which is at the heart of humanity
itself.

Man as a Lifelong Learner: Lifelong education, it was
claimed earlier, is not a new concept but the
rapidly changing social conditions of contemporary
society have provided impetus for a wider acceptance
of the idea.   In recent years the stimulus has been
strengthened by a considerable number of publications and an increasing amount of research has also
been devoted to the topic.   Organizations, such as
UNESCO, have adopted it and have thereby brought it
into the political arena.   However, adult educators
have, generally, been a major force in drawing
attention to the practice of lifelong learning. One
such writer on the subject has been Ronald Gross
(1977) who records some of the stories of lifelong
learners.   Quoting from one of these, Cornelius
Hirschberg, he (1977:27) writes:

> I am stuck in the city, that's all I have.
> I am stuck in business and routine and
> tedium.   But I give up only as much as I must;
> for the rest I live my life at its best, with
> art, music, poetry, literature, science,
> philosophy and thought.   I shall know the
> keener people of the world, think the keener
> thoughts, and taste the keener pleasures as
> long as I can and as much as I can.

In case this sounds too idealistic to be practical,
Hirschberg read on the subway to and from work each
day, and during his lunchtime,for most of his
business life.   He estimated that he had undertaken
some ten hours of serious reading each week for
about two thousand weeks - enough reading time to
get at least five college degrees!   His university
was the world of books and the opportunity to think
about the ideas he acquired from them.
  Libraries, then, and museums are important ad-
juncts to human learning.   Their existence is an in-
dication that man seeks to learn from numerous
sources.   Recently, adult educators have taken considerable cognizance of their significance to lifelong education and a number of studies have been
published in this field, eg. Chadwick, 1980;
Dadswell, 1978;   Dale, 1980;   Surridge and Bowen,

1977. Additional learning facilities are provided
by the media. Groombridge (1972:27ff) regards
television as a liberal educator because it makes
people aware of what lies beyond their milieu, it
helps them to understand each other and it provides
a rich diet of imaginative experience. As long as
it is recognised that what is seen and heard is
actually a distillation of reality through the media
process, then these claims are valid. Indeed, the
British Broadcasting Corporation's charter specifically states that one of its functions is to educate.
In a totally different context, Moemeka (1981:104)
suggests that in African countries local radio can
'provide a continuous flow of educational information and messages on all aspects and endeavours
that affect the lives of rural communities, and so
arouse their awareness and stimulate them ...'.
Travel is another medium through which individuals
learn, so that many adult education institutions,
schools and colleges, organize visits and study
tours both in the United Kingdom and abroad as part
of their programme of learning activities. The arts,
museums, libraries, radio and television all cater,
in one way or another, for something in man that
drives him to learn more about the universe in which
he lives and about the people with whom he inhabits
this planet.

  Hence the people about whom Gross was writing
may not be exceptions, rather they may be much more
common that it is generally believed. In a survey
conducted by the National Institute of Adult
Education (Hutchinson 1970:52f) it was suggested
that '40 per 1000 of the adult population may be
enrolled in adult education classes in any one year'
and that this did not include those adults attending
universities, polytechnics and all colleges of
further and higher education. More recently, it has
been estimated (ACACE 1982a:46) that allowing 'for
double counting, the number of adults engaged in
some form of education or training in any one year
is more likely to be about 16% of the adult population, giving a figure of about 6 million in
England and Wales'. Obtaining accurate ·statistics
about the participation rate of adults in education
is a very complicated undertaking and, therefore,
in the end an estimate is all that may be obtained.
The same is true in the United States. For instance,
Johnstone and Rivera (1965:33) calculated that between June 1961 and June 1962 there were at least

2,650,000 adults in full-time education, 17,160,000
in adult classes and some 8,960,000 undertaking
self-education, but they recognised that these
totals were no more than approximations. Nevertheless, their research highlighted the prevalence of
the autodidact and they (1965:37) wrote that 'the
incidence of self-education throughout the adult
population is much greater than we anticipated'.
They had discovered millions of lifelong learners
who were not using the educational services, people
who wanted to learn and understand through their
own direction.
    Not long after Johnstone and Rivera published
their monumental study another seminal research
report highlighting the lifelong learner appeared.
Allen Tough (1971- 2nd edition 1979) reported research into adult's self-directed learning projects
and he suggested that self-directed education is
even more common than Johnstone and Rivera indicated.
He (1979:1) writes that it ' is common for a man or
woman to spend 700 hours a year on learning projects.
Some people spend less than 100 hours, but others
spend more than 2000 hours in episodes in which the
person's interest to learn or to change is clearly
his primary motivation'. Tough was not concerned
merely to count the odd hours of enquiry in which
an individual might indulge since he considered
that these could not be described as learning projects. Rather he (1979:6) defined a learning project as 'a series of related episodes, adding up to
at least seven hours'. Tough, and his fellow
researchers, interviewed sixty-six people in depth
in their initial research and discovered that all
but one of them had undertaken at least one learning project during the year prior to the interview,
that the median number of projects was eight and
that the mean time spent on learning projects was
816 hours. A participation rate of 98% was discovered - far higher than Johnstone and Rivera
would have anticipated from their research. But
Tough and his colleagues employed a more intensive
interview technique than Johnstone and Rivera and
this method of research was one reason for the
higher statistics. Additionally, Tough acknowledges
that his sample was not random, so that it is not
technically correct to claim that 98% of the population of Canada, nor even of Ontario - where the
research was conducted, undertake at least one
seven hour learning project per annum. Indeed, his

statistics may be a considerable over-estimation, although they might actually be correct, but they do suggest that people have a need to learn, know and understand. These various research statistics may all indicate that the human being has a basic need to learn, a need that may be as basic as any of the needs identified by Maslow in his well-known 'hierarchy' of needs.

Man and the Need to Learn: Maslow's 'hierarchy' of needs is usually represented as in Figure 1.3a. Child (1977:40ff) suggested that the need to know comes at the top of the hierarchy, but in the third edition of his text he (1982:43) has adapted this slightly and omitted the highest stratum. At the same time he has continued to highlight the significance of knowledge and understanding. Maslow (1968:60ff) certainly considered the need to know but claimed that knowledge has a certain ambiguity about it, specifying that in most individuals there is both a need to know and a fear of knowing. However, the fear of knowing may be the result of social experiences rather than being basic to the person. The need to know may be a fundamental need, even if the consequences of that knowledge may be dangerous. If this is the case, then Child's suggestion does require further consideration. Does the need to know actually occur at the apex of the hierarchy? Is there a progression through the hierarchy which occurs only when the more preponderant needs are satisfied? Is it even a hierachy? Argyle (1974:96f) suggests that the main supporting evidence for the hierarchy comes from the lower end but that there 'is not such clear evidence about the upper part of the hierarchy'. Houston et al (1979: 297) claim that the order of needs is itself arbitrary and that the exact order is not particularly important. If the order is unimportant, then both Maslow's and Child's construction of a needs hierarchy is open to reconsideration.

Child may be correct when he suggested that the intellectual pursuit of knowledge is a higher

Figure 1.3a: Maslow's 'Hierarchy' of Needs

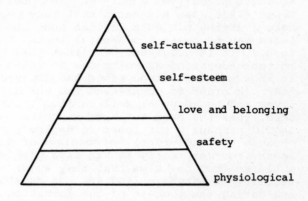

Figure 1.3b: Maslow's 'Hierarchy' of Needs
as represented by Child
(1977:41)

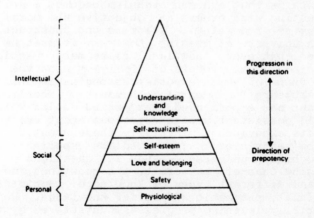

order need but this may only be true for the
academic pursuit of knowledge. But the fact that
Tough (1979) has suggested that many people undertake learning projects implies that the need to
learn may be quite fundamental to the human being.
Indeed, it is suggested here that this need is
better understood as being one to learn rather than
to know and understand since the individual needs to
learn in order to comprehend the world in which he
lives and to adapt himself to it. If this is the
case, then the need to learn is quite basic and
should perhaps occur lower in Maslow's hierarchy
because the individual is conscious of the need to
learn from very early in his life, as is manifest in
children from the time that they acquire the
facility of language (and ask the question 'why?')
and during the process of the formation of the self.

Elsewhere (Jarvis 1983c:20-23) this theme has been
expanded a little in the context of the religious
development of the individual. Without seeking to
rehearse that argument some of its conclusions are
summarised here because of their significance to
this discussion. It is suggested that the processes
of the formation of the self and of beginning to make
sense of the objective world occur simultaneously
during early childhood. Indeed, Luckmann (1969:50)
maintains that a human organism becomes a self, constructing with others an 'objective and moral
universe of meaning'. Prior to the construction of
this universe of meaning, however, it must be recognised that every individual poses many questions of
meaning. This process of focusing upon the
'unknowns' of human experiences begins in childhood
and appears fundamental to humanity. Nearly every
parent has experienced that period during which the
child persistently asks questions about every aspect
of its experience. Initially these questions appear
to be restricted to its immediate experience but as
the child's universe expands its questions of
meaning change. Answers to the questions, however,
demand different types of knowledge: empirical,
rational, pragmatic and belief knowledge. Hence,
initially learning progresses, unfettered by the
boundaries of the disciplines, as a result of a
process of questioning at the parameters of the
child's experiences. As the questions are answered
and the child acquires a body of knowledge, so the
learning need is receiving some satisfaction.
During early childhood these questions are overt and

the learning experience explicit. When children attend school, however, teachers (and other adults) sometimes attempt to provide information that bears little or no relation to the questions being posed at that time and, therefore, the knowledge being transmitted may appear irrelevant to the recipient. Unless the teacher is able to demonstrate its relevance and create a questioning attitude there may be little internal stimulus to learn what is being transmitted. (This does not mean that the child does not want or need to learn, only that the child may not want to learn what is being transmitted). However, by the time the child matures into an adult answers to many of the questions may have been discovered and the adult has been socialized into the objectified culture of society. The adult appears to ask fewer questions. But during periods of rapid social change the questioning process is evoked. During traumatic experiences the accepted internalized body of knowledge may not be able to cope with the situation and the questioning process is reactivated. Schutz and Luckmann (1974:8) write: 'I only become aware of the deficient tone of my stock of knowledge if a novel experience does not fit into what has, up to now, been taken as a taken-for-granted valid reference scheme'. In other words when an individual's biography and his current experience are not in harmony, a situation is produced in which the individual recommences his quest for meaning and understanding. Indeed, for the most part, these questions are raised intermittently throughout life, about differing aspects of life's experiences, so that the process is never really complete. Perhaps, as Tough has implied, questions are asked much more frequently than adult educators have generally assumed, so that the learning need is ever prevalent.

Before progressing further with this discussion it is necessary to recall Maslow's original 'hierarchy' of needs and Child's adaptation of it. Maslow suggested that there are five basic areas of need: physiological, safety, love and belonging, self-esteem and self-actualization. Child suggested that understanding and knowledge should be added to the pinnacle of the hierarchy. But it was suggested that the needs do not actually form a hierarchy and it has been argued here that the need to learn is quite fundamental to humanity and that it manifests itself during the process of the formation of the

self, so that in any formulation of human needs
the learning need should be specified. Hence,it is
suggested that Maslow's hierarchy should be adapted
and seen as a taxonomy.

Figure 1.4: A Taxonomy of Human Needs
            - following Maslow

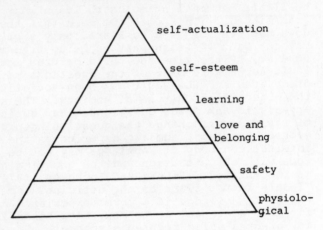

self-actualization

self-esteem

learning

love and
belonging

safety

physiolo-
gical

This is clearly not a hierarchy but a process
through which a child passes during early maturation.
All the needs exist in individuals and, wherever
possible, human beings seek to satisfy them. Hence,
the provision of education throughout the whole of
the life span may help the learner to satisfy a
basic human need, especially in a rapidly changing
world in which the individual may be posing many
questions of meaning. Herein may lie one theoretical
base of andragogy, a point to which further reference will be made below.

Some of the ideas that occur in the above
argument are similar to those adduced by Mezirow in
his discussion on 'perspective transformation'. He
(1977:157) claims that:

to the degree our culture permits, we tend to
move through adulthood along a maturity
gradient which involves a sequential re-
structuring of one's frame of reference for
making and understanding meanings. We move
through successive transformations towards
analysing things from a perspective increasingly removed from one's personal or local
perspective.

18

Mezirow has certainly raised some very significant points about the process of adult learning, to which further reference is made later, but he implies that this 'maturity gradient' is inevitable and sequential and that it relates to development and ageing rather than to the individual's response to the world, so that it is not totally similar to the position adopted here and it cannot be utilised as a rationale for the provision of education for adults.

However, it might be objected that if human beings have a basic need to learn, there is no need to provide education since they will seek to satisfy their learning needs in any case. However, this argument contains no substance because education, the provision of libraries, museums etc. have all emerged as means by which individuals may learn answers to their questions of meaning. Yet it must be recognised that education per se is only one of a number of ways through which the learning need can be satisfied. Another answer to the objection may be posited in the form of an analogy: if safety is a need that is always going to be satisfied then there would be no reason for legislation about health and safety at work and yet today there are probably very few people who would dispute the need for the existence of such an Act of Parliament.

SUMMARY

In this chapter it has been argued that the provision of education for adults is necessary because of the nature of contemporary society and the nature of man. It was suggested that there are various features in society that have to be taken into consideration, including: rapid social and cultural change; the obsolesence of technical knowledge resulting in the need for individuals working with such knowledge to keep abreast with developments; an increase in the amount of leisure time and an increasing number of people living into old age; the need to work towards a democratic society. Additionally, it has been argued that man has a basic need to learn and that he is a lifelong learner, so that the provision of education is one means by which he can satisfy this basic need.

However, it was recognised at the outset that these two aspects are not discrete entities but that there is an inter-relationship between the individual and society, and that this division was only made for ease of analysis. One approach without the

other is to present a false picture of reality, so
that a rationale for the provision of education for
adults must always contain a combination of both
sets of reasons proposed here.

Thus far the concepts employed have gone unde-
fined and undiscussed, so that it is now necessary
to explore some of the many concepts that are
discussed in the literature about the education of
adults.

SELECTED FURTHER READING

*ACACE Report : Continuing Education : From Policies to
Practice (1982a)*

An important report from the Advisory Council for
Adult and Continuing Education in which it makes a
case for a comprehensive system of continuing education to be introduced into England and Wales and
provides considerable information about the scope
and cost of the provision of education for adults in
Britain. It presents an overview of the present
situation.

*ACACE Report: Adults: The Educational Experience and Needs
(1982b)*

This research report was published after this
chapter had been written otherwise some of the data
from it would have been included. The report contains data from a national survey of 2460 interviews
in England and Wales and is based upon the idea of
participation in continuing education rather than
adult education. It is a very important research
report about adult and continuing education.

*Serving Personal and Community Needs Through Adult Education
Boone et al (1980)*

The Association of Adult Education of the United
States of America (now part of the American
Association of Adult and Continuing Education) has

issued a series of eight handbooks, all of which are quite significant studies. This is a symposium of seventeen chapters providing information about a wide range of developments in the United States in various aspects of adult education.

Education and Democracy   *J Dewey (1916)*

This is a classical study in the field of education which should be read by all who are involved in the education of adults because Dewey grapples with many of the problems that concern them. In a sense, this book contains the foundations of a philosophy of lifelong education.

The Lifelong Learner   *R Gross (1977)*

This is a small book that introduces readers to the concept of lieflong learning and to the idea that life is an invisible university. Stimulating and enjoyable reading.

Adequacy of Provision   *(ed) E M Hutchinson (1970)*

This report is now mainly of historical interest since it has been surpassed by the more recent ACACE (1982b) report. Nevertheless, it does contain valuable material about participation in adult education in England and Wales.

Volunteers for Learning   *J W C Johnstone and R J Rivera (1965)*

This is a seminal study of Americans attending adult education: it is a large study, twenty chapters containing data about the educational experience of Americans between June 1961 and June 1962. While the study is rather dated it remains an important reference.

An Introduction to Lifelong Education   *P Lengrand (1975)*

The author of this book has been at the forefront of the movement to promote lifelong education in Europe. It is an easy book to read but it raises quite succinctly many important issues.

The Adult's Learning Projects   *A Tough (1979-2nd edition)*

This is a most important study containing the report of Tough and some of his research colleagues into self directed learning. Not only is the book a research report but it also raises significant issues relating to theory and practice in the education of adults.

Chapter Two

AN ANALYSIS OF CONTEMPORARY CONCEPTS APPERTAINING
TO THE EDUCATION OF ADULTS

Many ideas were raised in the opening chapter without any of them being rigorously defined, so that it
is now necessary to examine some of them. It is
intended to analyse the concept of education and
then to apply the analysis to some of the terms in
contemporary usage that relate in some way to the
education of adults, during which the underlying
philsophies will become more apparent. In addition,
it will become clear that the same terms are employed in different ways while on occasions,
different terms are used to convey the same meaning.

THE CHANGING CONCEPT OF EDUCATION

In the opening chapter, reference was made to the
so-called 'front-end' model of education and it was
claimed that while this model was appropriate for
less technological societies it is no longer relevant to contemporary society. However, such a
claim requires further discussion, but before this
is undertaken it is appropriate that this particular
model is examined. Perhaps the simplest way to
illustrate the concept is diagrammatically and an
adaptation of Boyle's (1982:8) diagram is used for
this purpose

Figure 2.1:   The Front-End Model of Education

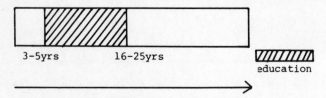

lifespan

This clearly demonstrates the idea that education occurs only during the formative years and that when social maturity, or adulthood, is achieved then education ceases.   This idea is reflected by many writers on the subject of education.   John Stuart Mill, for instance, claimed that the content of education was to be found in 'the culture which each generation purposely gives to those who are to be their successors' (cited in Lester-Smith 1966:9). Emile Durkheim (1956:71), a French sociologist and educationalist, regarded education in a similar manner: for him it was 'the influence exercised by adult generations on those who are not yet ready for social life'.   But by the beginning of the twentieth century it was becoming more apparent that an inter-generational perspective was not adequate to describe the educational process.   John Dewey (1916:8), for instance, was forced to add a pre-fix to the term education in order to express the same sentiments as those specified by Mill and Durkheim, stating that formal education was necessary if society was to transmit all its achievements from one generation to the subsequent one.   Today, formal education refers to teaching method rather than to the structure of the educational provision and the term most likely to be used to convey the same idea is initial education.   This has been described as:

> going to school, including nursery school, but it could go on full or part-time into the mid-20's.   After compulsory schooling, 'initial' education takes a wide variety of forms: full-time study in sixth form, university, college, polytechnic, medical school, military academy and so on;   part-time day release, evening classes and correspondence courses; on the job training in the factory.
> (ACACE 1979:9-10)

The idea underlying initial education is that at a
given stage in the life span the individual has
stored away sufficient knowledge and skill to serve
him for the remainder of his life, so that his education is then complete.

Such a model of education is also implicit in
the writings of the well known English philosopher
of education, R S Peters, who makes a clear distinction between education and the educated man. Peters
(1972:9) regards being educated as a state which individuals achieve (the educated man), whilst education is a family of processes that lead to this
state. However, it might be advantageous to this
analysis to enquire whether the educated person is
an end-state. Peters'writings tend to suggest that
he considers it as such for he (1972:7) claims that
education 'was not thought of (previously) explicitly as a family of processes which have as their outcome the development of an educated man in the way
in which it is now'. While this seems to imply that
Peters considers that the educated man is an end-
state, it is possible to regard it as a social
status in contrast to the uneducated person,since it
is an achievement. Yet even if it is an achievement
is it possible for the educated person to undertake
more education? Of course it is - but to where does
the additional process lead? If it is regarded as a
status, then that status remains unchanged. Peters
rightly claims, to be an educated man is not to have
arrived but to travel with a different view
during life. Hence the educated person is
being educated throughout the whole of his life
Indeed, it might be that if the state of educated man were achieved then the process must continue or else the state would be lost. Hence it is
maintained here that the process is significant,
perhaps more significant than the state or the end-
product. Therefore, it is claimed, no initial nor
intergeneration aspect may be considered intrinsic
to the concept of education and that since the educated man should always be in the process of being
educated, the implications of having achieved a
state of having been educated are misleading.

It may, therefore, be concluded that education
is about a learning process and, as such, it may be
seen as a response to the basic learning need in man
that was discussed in the previous chapter. However,
not all learning is educational. Few people would
deny, for instance, that indoctrination is a learning process but they would almost certainly wish to
deny that it is an educational one,so that specific

criteria need to be adduced in order to ascertain
whether any learning process is educational. Elsewhere (Jarvis 1983a), this has been worked out in
some detail, so that it would be repetitive to do
more than summarise that discussion here.

Peters (1966:23ff), following Wittgenstein,
claims that education like many other phenomena is
too complex to define but he suggests that there are
a family of similar phenomena that may be regarded
as education. He puts forward three sets of
criteria for consideration as a basis of education
but they were not regarded as totally satisfactory,
so that other criteria were suggested: education
must involve a learning process; the learning
process should not be a single event; the process
should be planned rather than haphazard; education
is essentially a humanistic process because knowledge is humanistic and because the process involves
human beings as learners and, also, maybe as teachers; learning has to involve understanding, which
is essentially a quality of critical awareness.
Before a definition is offered it is necessary to
examine the term 'humanistic' within this discussion.
Dewey (1916:230) claims that knowledge is essentially 'humanistic in quality not because it is about
human products in the past, but because of what it
does in liberating human intelligence and human
sympathy'. He goes on to suggest that any specific
matter that does this is essentially humane, so that
in this context humanistic has two facets: it
is concerned about the welfare and humanity of the
participants and it is humane. Hence this makes
claims that the educational process is normative and
idealistic. Education may now be defined as 'any
planned series of incidents, having a humanistic
basis, directed towards the participants learning
and understanding'. (Jarvis 1983a:5). This definition is very broad since it is the common factor
in the multitudinous branches of education and it is
possible to modify and adapt it, so that the definition may reflect the meaning added to the basic
idea when a pre-fix is placed before the term education, eg. lifelong education requires only that
'and which may occur at any stage in the life span'
added to the end of the definition. Hence it may be
seen that this basic definition of education does
not restrict education: to any specific learning
process; to any time in life; to any specific
location; to any specific purpose. It is, therefore, maintained that the front-end model of education, depicted in Figure 2.1, is only one branch of

education rather than being the total educational
process. It is recognised, however, that it is
difficult to change people's attitudes towards education and that this front-end model of initial
education is equated with education per se in many
people's minds, so that the education of adults is
still often viewed as an optional extra added after
education has actually been completed, so that it
remains marginal to the instituion of education in
society.
    This definition will be considered in relation
to the various branches of education that are relevant to the education of adults but, prior to em-
barking upon this, it is necessary to clarify the
relationship between teaching, learning and education.

TEACHING, LEARNING AND EDUCATION

Tough (1979) demonstrated that many of the adults'
learning projects were completely self-directed and
that neither a teacher nor an educational institution were necessary to their successful implementation
Yet it would be difficult to claim that many of
these projects were not educational. It might be
more true to claim that the more self-directed the
project the greater the likelihood that the learner
can respond to his own learning needs and also self-
actualise in the process, thus demonstrating the
humanistic nature of education itself. Consequently,
it may be seen that while the learner is an essential element in the educational process, the teacher
is not. Learning may, and often does, occur without
teaching but the extent to which teaching can occur
without learners and learning is much more debatable.
A teacher may claim to have taught his subject and
say that nobody learned anything - but would the
claim actually be correct? If nobody had learned,
had the teacher actually taught or had he only tried
to teach but had not succeeded? Teaching, it is
claimed here, is dependent upon learning, but the
converse is not true.
    Teaching may be regarded as the intention to
bring about learning (Hirst and Peters 1970:78),
but if it is unsuccessful it may be viewed as an
unsuccessful attempt to teach rather than unsuccessful teaching. Unsuccessful teaching may occur when
some learning has resulted from the teaching but
when all the intentions have not been achieved.
Learning is often defined in behavioural terms and

27

Hilgard and Atkinson (1967:270), for instance,
define it as 'any more or less permanent change in
behaviour which is the result of experience'. However, the acquisition of new knowledge need not
result in behavioural change, but learning has
occurred. Hence this definition is not accepted
here. It will be recalled from the last chapter
that learning was put into the context of the
acquisition of culture and it is, therefore, proposed to regard learning as any process of receiving
and assessing any aspect, or aspects, of culture.
This will be discussed further in the next chapter.
    Many different learning processes occur during
the human life span, but not all of them may be considered educational, since it must be borne in mind
that any definition necessarily excludes those
phenomena that are not in accord with it. Hence the
definition adopted above includes many aspects of
learning but it does not incorporate them all. Self-
directed learning, for instance, may always be considered to be educational but others may never be so
regarded, eg. indoctrination. However, there are
other learning processes, ie. learning through being
instructed, that might be considered educational in
some instances but not in others. Learning may
occur in some instructional situations which may
not be considered educational since the quality of
interaction between instructor and learner was such
that the latter failed to self actualize or because
he no longer felt that he was esteemed or accepted
by the instructor. Clearly there are some teaching
techniques that rarely allow for the learner's own
humanity and experience to surface and when these
techniques are employed some questions must be
raised about the extent to which the learning
process is educational. (see Jarvis 1983a: 80-93 for
further analysis).
    From this brief discussion it may be seen that
because education is regarded here as a humanistic
process, it is seen as one in which the value of the
human being and the quality of interaction between
teachers and learner, when it occurs, are paramount
to it. Where these high ideals are not manifest in
the learning process then the extent to which it is
educational is open to doubt. Nevertheless, it must
be borne in mind that this humanistic analysis is
only of value if the process is one in which planned
learning and understanding occurs.

ADULT EDUCATION AND THE EDUCATION OF ADULTS

At first sight the terms appear to mean precisely the same and Hostler (1977:58) seems to employ them synonymously but, because of the history of the former term, there is a considerable difference between the two which will become apparent in the following discussion.

The term 'adult education' carries specific connotations in the United Kingdom which imply that it is specifically liberal education, and this also has a stereotype of being a middle class, leisure time pursuit. Underlying this implication is the idea that the adult's education has been completed and, during leisure time, the adult can indulge himself and improve or broaden his knowledge or skill or hobbies. Hence, these implications reflect a conception of a front-end model of education and, perhaps, because of the prevalence of this perception of education it is hardly surprising that adult education is regarded as marginal. Obviously much adult education, especially that provided by Local Education Authorities, University Extension, etc., will occur during leisure time, but leisure need not be equated with only the pursuit of the creative arts or physical or domestic skills. Leisure time activities do not preclude any form of learning, whether aesthetic, athletic or academic, but they may have been undertaken for the sheer enjoyment of learning rather than for a vocational purpose. Hostler (1978:134) rightly states that 'one quite common error is to imagine that because liberal education is not undertaken for the sake of results, it does not *have* (his italics) any results'. Clearly it often does have results. The existence of the Open University in the United Kingdom, and similar institutions in other parts of the world, bears witness to the fact that leisure time education for adults can and does produce results - in the learner, in the academic work produced (even research projects for higher degrees) and in the award of academic degrees. In the first instance, then, it must be recognised that the term 'adult education' has a social definition as being a form of liberal education undertaken by those people who are regarded as adults. Even so, it must be recognised that this is a social rather than a conceptual definition and that this is why it is important to distinguish between adult education and the education of adults. However, the definition of adult still complicates this discussion.

A number of major differences occur in the analysis of the term and it is necessary to summ-- arise them here. Wiltshire (1976) suggested that adult education might also be understood as an educational process conducted in an adult manner. Taken to its logical extreme this interpretation would allow for children in schools to be regarded as participating in adult education if the process in which they were engaged was conducted in an adult fashion. However, Wiltshire was aware of this possible interpretation and suggested that an adult also has to be mature, experienced and over twenty years of age, a figure that appears to be somewhat arbitrary. Even though it is possible to agree with Wiltshire that adulthood also implies maturity and experience, it is harder to accept that these are either absolute or discrete, or that they occur at a specific biological age. Hence, it is necessary to pursue this discussion about adulthood a little further and to return to the matter of an adult learning environment in a subsequent chapter.

Paterson (1979) discusses the concepts of adult, education and adult education but since he regards education as the process of developing learners as persons, he is a little restricted in his analysis of adult education. Nevertheless, he views adult- hood as a status, involving certain responsibilities, entered into at a specific age. He (1979:1) claims that people are deemed to be adults because of their age but, although they are not necessarily mature, they are expected to behave in an adult manner. Adult education is, therefore, different from other forms of education because of the nature of its students and this may be an answer to Legge's (1982: 3) question about whether there is a need to have a sharp dividing line between child and adult. That the term is employed may be an even more significant reason why it requires analysis. By contrast to Paterson, Knowles (1980:24) suggests that the basis for treating people as adults is that they behave as adults and that they perceive themselves to be adults. Like Legge, he does not regard the dis- tinction between adulthood and childhood to be ab- solute, recognising that during the individual's life span the process of transition is both gradual and continuing. However, it might be ob- jected that Knowles' subjective approach is rather circular and to some extent this is since he defines 'adult' by 'adult', so that the conception of social maturity might be employed here. When an individual is regarded as having reached a level of social

maturity in which he can assume a responsible
position in society he may be regarded as an adult.
Knowles goes on to state that clarification of the
term 'adult education' is more difficult because it
is used with at least three different meanings: the
process of adults learning; a set of organized
activities carried out by a variety of institutions
to achieve specific educational objectives; a field
of social practice. Knowles (1980:25) describes the
last of these three, a combination of the other two,
as bringing 'together in a discrete social system
all the individuals, institutions and associations
concerned with the education of adults ....'

It is clear from this brief discussion that in
any analysis of the terms 'adult education' and
'education of adults' the definition of the term
'adult' is deceptively difficult. In a sense, it
might be easier to employ the term 'post-compulsory'
education to overcome this problem but this term
does not convey the same wealth of meanings as does
the word 'adult'. Hence, it is suggested here that,
following Knowles, adulthood refers to the fact that
both an individual's own awareness of himself and
other people's perception of him accredit him with
a level of social maturity accorded to the status of
an adult in that society. The education of adults,
therefore, refers to those learning processes undertaken by people who have achieved the status of
adult. At the same time it has to be recognised
that there is also an institutionalised adult education service and that on occasions, the words
are used to refer to it.

At this stage it is possible to draw some conclusions about the two terms under discussion in
this section. In the United Kingdom 'adult education' is used within a liberal education framework,
sometimes carrying with it implications of a front-
end model of education. For these reasons, it is
more desirable to employ the term 'education of
adults' because this may refer to any educational
process undertaken by adults, whether liberal,
general or vocational, and located in the spheres of
adult, further or higher education or outside the
institutional framework entirely. This terminology
also implies that education is not completed at any
stage in the lifespan and, indeed, that the education of adults may begin in the period of initial
education and, for some people, it continues into
post-compulsory sectors. Additionally, it will be
recognised that the term has some overlap with the
idea of continuing education, which will be referred

to later in this chapter. However, the term education of adults is a broad term and one that encourages the development of a separate sphere of study
within education, a point to which further reference
will be made. Clearly this latter usage is very
similar to the American use of the term 'adult
education', so that the different implications in
the terminology should be borne in mind when reading
the literature from either country. While these
differences are unfortunate, they do reflect the
differing historical traditions of the two countries.

LIFELONG EDUCATION

Once the front-end model of education is rejected
the way is open to formulate other approaches to the
subject, one being that the process of education begins in childhood and continues throughout the lifespan. Whilst lifelong education as an ideal has
recently been adopted by the United Nations Educational, Scientific and Cultural Organization
(UNESCO) it is not really a new concept for Dewey
(1916:51) wrote:

> It is common place to say that education
> should not cease when one leaves school. The
> point of this common place is that the
> purpose of school organization is to insure
> the continuance of education by organizing
> the powers that insure growth. The inclin-
> ation to learn from life itself and to make
> the condition of life such that all will
> learn in the process of living is the finest
> product of schooling.

While not everyone would agree with Dewey's understanding of the purpose of the school organization,
they may well agree with the sentiments expressed in
the remainder of the quotation. Later in the same
passage, Dewey (1916:51) continues:

> Since life means growth, a living creature
> lives as truly and positively at one stage as
> at another, with the same intrinsic fullness
> and the same absolute claims. Hence educa-
> tion means the enterprise of supplying the
> conditions which insure growth, or adequacy of
> life, irrespective of age.

For Dewey, education is one of the major foundations

of a rich life but it is a foundation that need not
be laid at the beginnings of life or in childhood,
it is one that may be laid at any stage of life and
then built upon. While Dewey has not been particularly relevant to a great deal of thinking about
adult education in the United Kingdom, his influence
has been far greater in the United States. Among
his disciples   was Lindeman - author of 'The
Meaning of Adult Education (1961, first published
1926) - whose own influence continues to be extended
through existing practitioners in the field.

Soon after Dewey's influential book, from which
these quotations have been drawn, appeared in
America, an important document about adult education
was published in Britain. A L Smith, chairman of
the committee that produced the famous 1919 Report,
wrote:

> That the necessary condition is that adult
> education must not be regarded as a luxury
> for the few exceptional persons here and there,
> nor as a thing which concerns only a short
> span of early manhood, but that adult education
> is a permanent national necessity, an insep-
> arable aspect of citizenship, and therefore
> should be both universal and lifelong.
> (Introductory Letter to 1919 Report -
> para xi:5)

This far-sighted statement, like many others in the
Report, was loudly acclaimed but never implemented,
so that the idea of lifelong education remained an
ideal. Yeaxlee (1929:31) returned to the subject
and claimed that 'the case for lifelong education
rests ultimately upon the nature and needs of the
human personality in such a way that no individual
can rightly be regarded as outside its scope, the
social reasons for fostering it are as powerful as
the personal'. Here, then lies an argument for
lifelong education, very similar in substance to
that produced earlier in this study, yet this case
was made in the United Kingdom over a half a century
ago but the concept has remained dormant for many
years.

It was not until after the 1939-45 World War
that the term gained prominence again and then this
was because organizations, such as UNESCO, adopted
it, influenced by such writers as Lengrand (1976).
Thereafter many publications, emanating from UNESCO,
have developed and expounded the concept. The
Faure Report (1972) advocated that education should

33

be both universal and lifelong, claiming that education precedes economic development and prepares each person for a society that does not exist but which may do so within his lifetime. The Report claims that education is essential for man and his development and, therefore, the whole concept of education needs to be reconsidered.

In 1976, lifelong education appeared to have 'come of age' when the "Lifelong Learning Act" was passed into law in the United States. This law authorised the expenditure of forty million dollars annually between 1977 and 1982 on lifelong education. (Peterson et al 1979:295). However, Peterson and his associates (1979:423) were forced to conclude that while 'lifelong education and learning policies are gaining favour in numerous foreign countries, notably Scandinavia, there are at the moment signs of slackening progress' in America. Despite this rather gloomy assessment there are signs of innovation in lifelong education in America, in such institutions as elderhostels (eg. Zimmerman 1979).

Higher education is also gradually changing its direction and beginning to practise policies of lifelong education, although this process is extremely slow. Kulich (1982b) documents how Canadian universities are moving in this direction, but Tight (1982) shows that, with the exception of the Open University and a few other institutions based mainly in the south-east of the United Kingdom, potential part-time students have little or no possibility of gaining access to higher education. Williams (1977) actually claims that lifelong education is the new role for institutions of higher education but, unfortunately, it is one that they have been slow to assume in the United Kingdom.

Having briefly reviewed some of the main developments in lifelong education, it is now necessary to formulate its definition. Dave (1976:34) regards lifelong education as 'a process of accomplishing personal, social and professional development throughout the lifespan of individuals in order to enhance the quality of life of both individuals and their collectivities'. Lawson (1982:103) has tried to show that such a wide conception of education 'fails' to distinguish between the general mass of formative influence that shapes us or between the general learning which an intelligent being undergoes in adapting to circumstances'. He pleads for a more careful analysis of the claims that are made on behalf of lifelong education. While Lawson is clearly right to criticise Dave's approach,

since it offers no real definition of education,
Lawson himself does not offer an alternative. Even
so, in his discussion Lawson does seem to be in
danger of including the content of what is taught
and learned in the educational process, rather than
regarding the actual content as incidental to the
process. It seems, therefore, that a *via media* between the too limiting approach of Lawson, on the
one hand, and the too broad approach of Dave, on the
other, is required and it is suggested that a modif-
ication of the definition of education offered
earlier fits into this category. Lifelong education
is, therefore, any planned series of incidents,
having a humanistic basis, directed towards the
participants learning and understanding that may
occur at any stage in the lifespan.

Lifelong education is, therefore, a concept and
an ideal which remains rather meaningless unless it
is actually implemented. This has occurred in
different ways and in various places and each different approach contains within it its own philosophy.
Three major perspectives have occurred; continuing
education, recurrent education and community education. Each is examined in turn and, finally, the
concept of the learning society is discussed.

CONTINUING EDUCATION

This term is so close in meaning to lifelong education that, in the United Kingdom especially, it has
tended to be employed synonymously. Indeed the
symposium,organized by Jessup in 1969,was published
as 'Lifelong Learning -- a symposium in Continuing
Education' and the discussion paper published by the
Advisory Council for Adult and Continuing Education
states:

> Continuing education has long been a popular
> idea among some people concerned with the
> education of adults. It has gone under a
> variety of names in different countries:
> education permanente, lifelong education,
> recurrent education.
> (ACACE 1979a:7)

This Report is clear that continuing education
should not be regarded as further education in the
manner that this currently exists in the United
Kingdom. However, the above quotation actually
raises at least three major questions: to what

extent is continuing education conceptually different from lifelong education?; is continuing education actually synonymous with further education?;
what is the relationship between continuing and recurrent education? The last of these three questions
is discussed in the following section, but the first
two are explored here.

Venables (1976:19) defines continuing education
as 'all learning opportunities which can be taken up
after full-time compulsory schooling has ceased.
They can be full-time or part-time and will include
both vocational and non-vocational study'. But
MacIntosh (1979:3) disagrees with this definition,
suggesting rather than continuing education refers
to post-initial rather than post-compulsory education. The logic of this suggestion is quite clear
from the previous discussion on the education of
adults: initial education may continue for longer
than compulsory education, so that if continuing
education followed compulsory education it would
actually commence during initial education for
many people. Hence, it may be concluded here that
continuing education is post-initial education, but
that it is not synonymous with lifelong education.
Lifelong education makes no distinction between
initial and post-initial education whereas continuing education refers only to the latter part of
lifelong education and is, therefore, only one branch
of education.

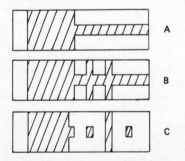

Figure 2.2 indicates that continuing education may
take a number of forms: (a) suggests some form of
continuous part-time education and is less frequent
than other forms; (b) suggests that continuous education can be both full-time and part-time, this is
even rarer than (a); (c) is the most realistic as it
implies that continuing education is intermittent
rather than continuous. There are similarities between this concept and that of recurrent education,
which will be discussed later in this chapter.

Continuing education, however, is not the same
as further education for a number of reasons:

further education is post-compulsory but not necessarily post-initial; further education tends to
imply a specific level of study whereas continuing
education does not; further education is usually
pre-vocational, vocational or academic while, conceptually continuing education need not be directed
towards any course assessment or award.

From this discussion it is clear that continuing education differs slightly in its conceptualization from any of the previous terms that have
been thus far elaborated upon. Yet the name of the
Advisory Council linked together adult and contin--
uing education; this same coupling occurs in a
number of national organizations, such as the
American Association of Adult and Continuing Education, so how does it differ from adult education?
It was pointed out earlier that adult education has
connotations of hobbies and skills in part-time
leisure education and that this is much narrower and
more specific than the education of adults. Continuing education embraces aspects of personal, social,
economic, vocational and social education (Venables
1976:23-4) and may actually equate to the concept of
the education of adults rather than to adult education. Indeed, the Advisory Council issued two
reports, one on adult education (1981) and another
on continuing education (1982a), so that it is clear
that in the Council's thinking the specific connotations of adult education, as already discussed,
were seen separately from those of continuing education. However, it is quite significant to note
that when the Venables Committee reported back to
the Open University its proposed division of continuing education did not include the undergraduate
programme, which tends to suggest that the Committee
still included elements of the liberal education
framework of adult education within its consideration of continuing education. This also implies
that continuing education is being used to refer to
specific types of post-initial education, despite
claims to the contrary.

Having accepted the implications of McIntosh's
definition it is now necessary to explore these in
further detail. The first significant point is that
the concept appears to be a politically neutral one
making no reference or criticism of the initial
education system nor implying any form of evaluation
of the total contemporary educational system.
Perhaps its apparent neutrality may be taken to incorporate a conservative bias, thereby making it a
politically acceptable term. But because the term

appears neutral it is acceptable to people of all
political persuasions, which may be a reason why
Sockett (1981:5) was able to claim that in 'the last
five years. Continuing Education has gradually
worked itself up the national education agenda only
to be stopped in its tracks by economic factors'.
While it is certainly true that some forms of continuing education have been harshly treated as a
result of the recent economic depression, the
British government has certainly financed a considerable amount of continuing vocational education
and pre-vocational education under the auspices of
the Manpower Services Commission. However, this
support seems to be provided in response to recurrent crises in the level of unemployment rather
than because of a national comprehensive plan of
continuing education is being implemented, something
advocated by the Advisory Council (ACACE: 1982a).
Hence, the social definition of continuing
education appears to be restricting it to work-
related education.

Continuing education is, therefore, a term
which refers specifically to post-initial education,
but since its parameters are being restricted in the
general use of the word it has assumed especial
significance in the professions (Houle 1980). While
the conceptual definition of profession is debatable,
professions are occupations based upon a circum-
scribed area of knowledge and since that knowledge
base is likely to be artificial, in the sense used
in the opening chapter, it is necessary for each
profession to ensure that its practitioners keep
abreast with the latest developments in the field.
Hence, Apps (1979:68f) cites the definition of continuing education provided by the Accrediting
Commission of the Continuing Education Council of
the United States as:

> ... the further development of human abilities
> after entrance into employment or voluntary
> activities. It includes in-service, up-
> grading and updating education. It may be
> occupational education or training which
> furthers careers or personal development.
> Continuing education includes that study
> made necessary by advances in knowledge. It
> *excludes* (my italics) most general education
> and training for job entry. Continuing educ-
> ation is concerned primarily with broad
> personal and professional development. It
> includes leadership training and the

improvement of the ability to manage personal,
financial, material and human resources. Most
of the subject matter is at the professional,
technical and leadership training levels or
the equivalent.

Hence, in the United States, and to some extent in
the United Kingdom, the term continuing education
tends to be restricted to post-initial education in
the vocational sphere. Clearly professional continuing education contains many similar ideas to those
discussed earlier in this section and while it may
be unwise to limit the term to vocational education,
the combination of adult and continuing tends to
encourage this interpretation to be adopted. One of
the few apparent advantages of this combination of
concepts is that it might produce an enhanced recognition of the fact that education in the professions is as much a part of the study of education as
it is an element in the professions. Such a realization might produce outcomes advantageous to both
education as a whole and to education in individual
professions.

Professions clearly provide their members with
many updating programmes in continuing education but
this has led to considerable debate about the extent
to which the professions should make it mandatory
for their members to attend such courses. Additionally, universities, polytechnics, colleges of
further and higher education, business schools and
the professions themselves are all offering continuing education provision for the professions, so
that unless a national policy is actually drawn up
and implemented problems and disputes might occur.
Alford (1980) highlights how some of these problems:
of competition between educational providers; of
finance; of the political nature of accreditations;
etc.; are occurring in America. These are all
issues that have to be confronted in the United
Kingdom, unless the 'law of the jungle' is to become
manifest in continuing education (see Stephens 1981:
138). Yet there is a danger that a national policy
might restrict innovations, so that too tight a
control might be as damaging as no control at all to
the development of continuing education.

Continuing education may, therefore, be seen to
be a continuation of the educational provision beyond initial education, especially in the vocational
sphere, and it is also a concept that implies no
criticism of the present system. Indeed, its major
concerns seem to focus upon the provision of

vocational continuing education, access to it and
extension of it. However, its presence by virtue
of offering no criticism of the current structure of
education actually serves to re-inforce the status
quo, so that it is inherently conservative. No such
claims may be legitimately made about the next form
of education strategy to be discussed in this
chapter, for recurrent education has certainly had
some radical claims made on its behalf.

RECURRENT EDUCATION

If UNESCO has adopted the term 'lifelong education'
then 'recurrent education' is the concept espoused
most frequently by the Organization for Economic
Cooperation and Development (OECD). Brought to the
attention of a wider audience in the late 1960s by
Olaf Palme, it gained currency through the publications of OECD and, in the United Kingdom from
the mid 1970s through the discussion papers and
other documents produced by the Association of
Recurrent Education. There is some agreement about
the definition of the term, which is perhaps summarised by the following, rather tautologous
suggestion that recurrent education is 'the distribution of education over the lifespan of the
individual in a recurring way' (OECD 1973:7). This
is a little broader than an earlier definition proposed by OECD that recurrent education 'is formal,
and preferably full-time education for adults who
want to resume their education, interupted earlier
for a variety of reasons'. (OECD 1971, cited by
Kallen 1974). These two definitions have been
selected because they indicate two conceptions of
recurrent education, which may be illustrated in
the below manner, following (Boyle 1982.8):

Figure 2.3: Alternative Models of
Recurrent Education

(a)

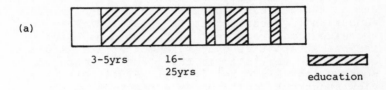

3-5yrs   16-
                25yrs

education

(b)

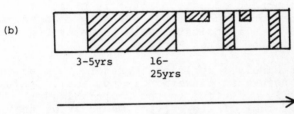

3-5yrs   16-
                25yrs

lifespan

In the first diagram it may be seen that the education is full-time but in the latter it is either
full-time or part-time and it may be recalled that
continuing education might also assume a full-time
or a part-time form, so that it would be legitimate
to ask whether these two terms are synonymous.

One of the most significant features of recurrent education is that the individual is regarded
as having a right to a specified amount of formal
education during his lifetime and that this need not
all be taken during the formative years, within the
period of initial education. Indeed, Gould (1979)
not only regards this as a moral argument about the
equality of educational opportunity but he also relates it to a wider perspective of equality of occupational opportunity. It is, therefore, regarded
by some exponents as a radical, moral strategy for
lifelong education. Unlike continuing education
which appears to occur in a piecemeal manner in response to expressed or perceived needs etc., recurrent
educationalists regard their approach to be a 'comprehensive alternative strategy for what are at present
three unrelated sectors: a) the conventional post-
compulsory educational system ... b) on-the-job
training of all kinds ... c) adult education: (OECD
1973:25).

Houghton (1974:6) has claimed that recurrent
education 'is the first new idea in education this

century ... It represents one of those very rare
shifts in the framework of thinking which Kuhn has
described. Its emergence marks the beginning of the
end of the dominant apprenticeship paradigm in
education'. Clearly this is a massive claim but, at
the same time, recurrent education does offer a
radical alternative system, one that its exponents
claim to be realistic in the light of contemporary
society (eg. Flude and Parrott 1979). Others may
view recurrent education as a reaction to the technological innovations in society rather than a
radical alternative idea. However, not all exponents of recurrent education actually expect the
whole education system to be radically changed, as
Cantor (1974:6-7) indicated when he described its
emergence in the United Kingdom.

> It is hardly surprising therefore to discover
> that recurrent education is not of all system-
> atically organized in the United Kingdom;
> indeed many of its critics would argue that
> there is as yet little official recognition
> of the need to make systematic provision for
> it. However, education in the United Kingdom
> does contain elements of recurrent education
> upon which to erect a more systematic
> provision.

Obviously Cantor thought that a system would emerge,
perhaps with a few policy decisions to aid it on its
way. Indeed, this type of presentation reflects a
less radical approach to recurrent education and
seems to co-incide with a continuing education perspective; this approach is also reflected in some
of the later OECD publications (eg. OECD 1977).
 Since some exponents of recurrent education
tend to present a more radical approach to education
and others have embraced the more moderate continuing education perspective, it is not surprising
that some theorists have extended this distinction
to other respects of the curriculum. Griffin (1978),
for instance, has focused upon the main aspects of
teaching and learning in the curriculum: aims,
content and method. He suggests that recurrent
educationalists will tend to be more student centred,
have a more integrated approach to content and,
generally have a more romantic curriculum perspective while those who had adopted a continuing education approach will have a more classical perspective
on curriculum issues. While he has tended to polar-
ize continuing and recurrent education, he admits

that he has undertaken a tentative exercise. However, he has raised many valuable points about these
two forms of education, and this might have been even
more insightful had he also sought to incorporate
some of the other philosophical issues espoused by
many adult educators.

One of the main practical features in recurrent
education is the idea that full-time education may
be embarked upon later in life by some people and
this entails some form of paid educational leave.
This was recognised in some of the early OECD
literature (OECD, 1973:70-2),where discussion
occurred about the extent to which paid educational
leave should be a statutory right or whether it
should be the result of negotiations between employers and employees. By the time that the OECD
had actually published this document, France had
already introduced legislation which allowed for up
to 2% of a firm's labour force to take leave of
absence at any one time and for 1% of the wage bill,
rising to 2% by 1976, to be spent on employee education (OECD 1975:35). Other European countries were
also introducing similar legislation and the
International Labour Organization called for each
member state to formulate and apply a policy of paid
educational leave (Convention 140:1974). Killeen
and Bird (1981) investigated the extent to which
paid educational leave exists in England and Wales
and concluded that between 15% and 20% of the total
work force received some paid, or assisted, educational leave in the year of the study, 1976-7,
which approximated to six days per person for
courses organized by the employing organization and
twelve days per person attending courses mounted by
other organizations. They noted that this educational leave is not evenly distributed, younger
workers being more likely to be released than older
ones, and that the courses tended to be vocationally
based and had a qualification as one of its end-
products. Bryant (1983) reports a similar research
project in Scotland in which he records the same
type of picture as that discovered in England and
Wales.

Killeen and Bird (1983:38ff) demonstrate clearly the conceptual confusion surrounding the education of adults since they refer to paid educational
leave as part of the system of continuing education.
Their emphasis reflects the fact that the term
'continuing education' has greater currency in the
United Kingdom than does recurrent education, even
though it might not be quite so refined conceptually.

43

Since continuing education is a much more nebulous
concept, having no undertones of radicalism, it is
hardly surprising that it has gained so much support
and that it is incorporating elements of recurrent
education within it. It is perhaps also significant
to note that the term 'recurrent education' has
appeared less prominently in some of the later OECD
publications (OECD 1977).

Recurrent education, then, has two major stands:
a more radical one that regards it as a strategy for
the reform of the whole educational system and perhaps also the wider society, while the more conservative stand is less ambitious in its claims
preferring rather to regard it as a reformist
approach to implementing lifelong education. There
is, therefore, a marked difference in the philosophy
of the two stands and yet they both recognise that
while education may not be continuous after initial
education it should be lifelong, a right that all
people should receive and that sufficient provision
should be made for them to do so.

COMMUNITY EDUCATION

Occasionally a word appears in the English language
that becomes ideologically acceptable for a period
of time: 'community' is such a word and it was
widely accepted in the United Kingdom in the 1960s
and 1970s as representing something intrinsically
good and right. Perhaps this was because a certain
nostalgia was present in society at that time for a
world that was past. Hence the idea of community
education appeared to be accepted with almost the
same uncritical appraisal as the term 'community' was
received. This process was aided and abetted by the
fact that it is a confused and multifarious concept.
In order to begin to appreciate some of these facets
it is necessary to understand the use of the word
'community'.

In sociology the main meaning of the word stems
from the work of the German sociologist, Toennies
(1957), who wrote in the last century about social
change. He recognised that a change in the type of
human relationships was occurring from one which may
be seen as personal and longlasting (community) to
one that was formed by association. Hence, the term
'community' assumed a distinctive meaning in sociology referring both to personal relationships and to
the fact that they should be established within a
specific locality. Toennies actually considered

that these personal, longlasting relationships were disappearing as society became more urban and its members more mobile. Thus it is not surprising that the term assumed an ideological significance in an increasingly impersonal and individual society, especially in the period that it did, when stress was being placed upon human values and the value of humanity in general.

A second, but quite similar, use of the term refers to those groups of people who live together in a specific place, eg. a monastry, and where the value of the community life is extolled. Here people interact in a personal manner in a specific locality but the boundaries of the community are even more tightly drawn. Thirdly, the word is sometimes used without reference to the personal relationships, when it refers only to the locality, eg. the people of such-and-such a community. This is perhaps the most common use of the word, although there is one other that is employed very frequently; in this instance it refers to 'extra-mural' in its widest sense, so that a community nurse, for instance, is one who cares for her patients outside the walls of the hospital, etc.

Consequently, it is easy to comprehend how difficult the term 'community education' is to under-stand, since all of these meanings of community are interrelated and confused in the diverse educational processes that are often classified as being a part of community education. It is, therefore, not sur-prising that an analytical philosopher, such as Lawson (1977), should point out this conceptual con-fusion and raise doubts about the phenomenon. However, other adult educators, eg. Kirkwood (1978), considered that Lawson's approach, while valuable, was rather conservative and not entirely correct. Perhaps it would be true to say that generally new forms of adult education arise in response to ex-pressed needs or demands and that in their initial stages they are not classified in any manner, so that Lawson's analytical approach is a necessary reflec-tion upon the innovations that are occurring within the education of adults.

From the above discussion it is possible to distinguish at least three different types of educa-tion which might be labelled community education: education for action and/or development; education in the community; extra-mural forms of education. It is now necessary to explore each of these three different forms.

45

Education for Community Action and/or Development: Perhaps
the most well-known exponent of this position is
Paulo Freire, who maintains that education can never
be neutral. He formulated his ideas in Latin
America, against the background of illiteracy and
poverty, and his thinking reveals the synthesis of
Christian theology,existentialism and Marxism that
has been quite dominant amongst certain groups of
intellectuals in Latin America over the past two or
three decades. While his ideas developed in a third
world situation, they are relevant to the United
Kingdom and America, as London (1973) shows. Even
though much of Freire's work has been written in
Portuguese, it is widely available in English (see
bibliography). He emphasized that education should
make the learners critically aware of their false
consciousness and of their social condition. In
becoming aware, they should reject many of the myths
erected by the ruling elite that prevents them (the
learners) having a clear perception of their own
social reality. Having undergone a process of
demythologization, learners should act upon the
world to endeavour to create a better society.
Clearly Freire's radical, but moral, approach is one
that many will criticize, especially those who for
varying reasons wish to see education as a neutral
process.

Freire is not alone with this perception of education although few other writers have formulated
it in such a sophisticated manner. Among those in
the United Kingdom whose approach to education is
similar to Freire's is Lovett (1975, 1978, 1979,
1980, etc) who has worked both in inner-city
Liverpool and, more recently, in Belfast in Northern
Ireland. Lovett (1975:155) suggests that some adult
educators see 'the role of adult education in
community action ... as ... providing the working
class with an effective educational service so that
they can take full advantage of the educational
service *and* (his italics) make the best use of their
individual talents and abilities'. But should adult
educators be involved in the action in the community?
Newman (1973:26) suggests that there are conditions
under which the adult educator 'should not try to
stop short of involvement in community action' but
by contrast, other adult educators consider that
while they should be prepared to teach activists
what to do, they should not actually be involved in
the action. (Flude 1978:163). Flude's position
shows that one who adopts a more radical position

in the continuing education/recurrent education
debate may be a little less radical in the community
action/community development discussion. Clearly,
however, there are legitimate differences in approach
on this issue and it would be quite unwise to
attempt to draw conclusions about the extent to
which educators of adults should, as part of their
teaching, be involved in community action.

At the same time, it is clear that education is
an essential tool in the process of community development. Fordham et al (1979) document a project,
undertaken by the University of Southampton, in
which they were involved in seeking to establish and
strengthen adult education provision in an informal
educational setting in a working class housing
estate in Havant. Here the educators were concerned
to develop adult education for the sake of the whole
area rather than as a response to the demands of
potential students. In this instance, the educator
is taking the initiative rather than merely publishing a prospectus and awaiting enrolments. It would
be quite possible to record a multitude of community
development projects in which adult education has
played a major role but perhaps it is wiser to note
here that the journal of the International Council
of Adult Education *Convergence* usually carries
reports of a number of these enterprises from developing countries and, recently, The International
Journal of Lifelong Education has also published
similar studies.

Education in the Community: Perhaps the earliest formal
education of this type stemmed from the work of
Henry Morris, who was responsible for the establishment of community colleges in Cambridgeshire
before the Second World War (see Jennings, no date),
and whose ideas were influential in their introduction in Leicestershire shortly afterwards
(Fairbairn 1978). From these beginnings have grown
the larger urban educational and social complexes,
such as the Abraham Moss Centre in Manchester and
the Sutton Centre in Nottinghamshire. One of the
central ideas of these schemes is that the school
should be the focal point of the community, in a
similar manner to that of the parish church in
medieval times, and that adults should be able to
attend classes in these centres. As a result of
Midwinter's work in Liverpool, he (1975:99)
concludes that:

Education must no longer be open to caricature

as a few hours at school for a few years
in... pre-adult life. It must be viewed as
a total, lifelong experience, with the home
and the neighbourhood playing important parts,
and everybody contributing to and drawing on
this educative dimension of the community.

However, he does not specify all the advantages of
comprehensive schools including adults among their
learners but Mary Hughes (1977:226-232) sees many
advantages in allowing adults to attend community
schools at the same time as children, not the least
being that it is education on the cheap. In
America, the community college concept has also been
implemented and comprehensive programmes are offered
for younger and older students who wish to study.
(Yarrington 1979:86-94).

Fletcher (1982), who conducted a five year research project at the Sutton Centre, shows how a
multi-purpose centre can be beneficial to all the
participating organizations, how the school children
are able to participate in adult classes and how
adults are enabled to join with children in learning
during the day. He shows how this approach can be
beneficial to all concerned provided that there is
some adaptation in the way that the initial education is organized. These large urban educational
complexes have also been introduced in other parts
of the United Kingdom and a similar community school
complex established in the suburbs of Grenoble, in
France, was also influenced by these developments.

Adult Education beyond the Walls: Extra-mural adult education is a term usually restricted to university
adult education extension classes where staff from
the universities teach in the community, or the
university employs part-time staff to teach liberal
adult education classes under its auspices in the
wider community. Recently, the term has assumed some
significance with other educational institutions
organizing educational classes in their local
communities. However, these forms of educational
outreach are rarely regarded as community education,
even though they are examples of education 'beyond
the walls' of the educational institution. By contrast, Head (1977) records how he, with the aid of
a social work student on placement, was able to work
in an informal manner with older, single men in a
day centre teaching them how to write letters and
how this exercise developed into a wider educational
exercise. Head was involved in an endeavour that

some adult educators might classify as community
education while others might regard it as adult
basic education since the learners were the end-
product of the educational exercise.

This point might be further demonstrated since
it will be recalled that Tough's research suggested
that many individuals undertake learning projects
during the course of a year and that these are
frequently undertaken outside of the normal educational institution. In addition, Brookfield (1979)
records how he discovered a leaderless discussion
group which met to learn more about specific subjects
and how he was able to provide material for the
group although he never attended it. Other adult
educators will also be aware of the existence of
similar groups and even, perhaps, have been involved
in helping establish such groups without necessarily
attending them. Certainly since the advent of the
Open University an increase in the number of such
groups will have almost inevitably occurred as students
meet together informally to discuss their studies.
Perhaps the development of educational technology
has resulted in an increase in the number of auton-
onous learning groups, but it is to be doubted
whether this form of education beyond the walls
would be regarded as community education.

Having reviewed a number of different types of adult
education that might be classified under the heading
of community education, taking the various usages of
the term 'community', at least two questions remain
to be answered: is there any theory of community
education and is there anything distinctive about
it?

Fletcher (1979:67) suggests that there are
three premises in community education:
- the community has its needs and common
  causes and is the maker of its own culture
- educational resources are to be dedicated
  to the articulation of needs and common
  causes
- education is an activity in which there is
  an alternative between the roles of student,
  teacher and person

He goes on to argue that certain implications follow
from this in terms of centre or periphery activities,
formality and informality and democratic control.
This, in turn, results in active and reactive processes. However, perhaps Fletcher is guilty of re-
ification of the concept of community in the first
of these premises and he might have argued that

there are groups and categories of persons in the
locality who have common causes who may be helped by
the allocation of educational resources, eg. the
underprivileged. Then the philosophy underlying the
theory would be one of responding to certain forms
of social inequality in order to produce a less
unequal society in which more people interact on an
interpersonal basis, so that the locality begins to
generate its own community ethos. It would, therefore, be a matter of social policy and educational
commitment to divert educational resources to the
underpriviliged and, as such, it would reflect the
philosophy that led to the creation of educational
priority areas in initial education. However, this
argument still fails to differentiate between
community education and other forms of education of
adults, such as adult basic education or educational
programmes for immigrants etc? How does community
education differ from these? This is one of the
more difficult questions, and community education is
not distinct unless it is seen to be an educational
response to social inequality. But if it is only a
response of this nature, adult basic education could
be equated with it. Hence the intended outcome of
the response might be important, so that community
education might be regarded as a response to social
inequality, the aim of which is development in the
location or action in order to improve the standard
of living, the quality of the environment, etc. in
the vicinity. If this argument is accepted then the
sociological concept of community which involves
both the quality of human relations and a specific
locality is that which forms the basis of community
education. Indeed, this position is reflected in
Fletcher's (1979:7) own definition of community education as 'a process of commitment to the education
and leisure of all ages through local participation
in setting priorities, sharing resources and the
study of resources'. Another approach would be by
extending the definition of education offered
earlier in this chapter to include the sociological
concept of community, so that community education is
any planned series of incidents, having a humanistic
basis, directed towards the people in a specific
locality learning and understanding how to enrich
the quality of human relationships and social living
in that area. Such a definition allows for both
community development and community action.

This argument leads to the logical conclusion
that the second and third types of education described in this section, ie. education in the

community and adult education 'beyond the walls' are
merely innovations in lifelong education and should
not really be classified as community education,
since its distinctive feature is the community in
which the learners will be involved rather than the
development of the learners for their own ends. The
alternative position would be for any form of education that relates to any of the definitions of
community with which this section commenced being
regarded as community education. If this were to be
accepted, then the parameters of community education
would be broadened to include many forms of adult
and lifelong education that have been discussed here,
so that the result would be that the term would not
be distinctive and would therefore become meaningless. Consequently, it is suggested that a number
of types of education of adults often regarded as
community education are wrongly classified.

THE LEARNING SOCIETY

Community education refers to special categories of
person living in a specific locality but the final
concept discussed in this chapter sets its boundaries much more widely. The learning society is a
futuristic concept, an ideal, that draws together
many of the ideas and ideals raised in this chapter.
Although it is futuristic, it may be possible to
detect its emergence as rapidly changing levels of
technology provide people with the social conditions
necessary for, and make people aware of, the opportunities to extend their learning throughout the
whole of their lives. However, unless the provision
of the facilities exist   as well as the social
conditions and the awareness the end result would be
one of frustration and disatisfaction, so that it is
important that a comprehensive policy for lifelong
education should be formulated by different societies
in the world. Hutchins (1970:134) wrote that it 'is
a society in which everyone has begun a liberal education in educational institutions and is continuing liberal learning either in such institutions
or outside them, a society in which there are true
universities, centres of independent thought and
criticism is one in which values may be transformed'.
Indeed, he (1970:134) offers a vision of the ideal:
'A world community learning to be civilized,learning
to be human .... Education may come into its own!'
      Thus it may be seen that at the foundations of
the learning society are values accorded to learning

as being 'normal and commonplace' and education is regarded as an 'inherent human right of all its citizens' (Boshier 1980:1). The learning society, it must be recognised, is learner based, has no barriers of access and provides a flexible but life-long system of education. It is society organized in such a manner as to make all kinds of learning available to everyone on a full-time or a part-time basis. Hence Boshier (1980:1-2) claims that a learn-ing society cannot emerge through additional learn-ing programmes being grafted on to existing pro-vision, rather it requires a deliberate policy and definite changes in curriculum aims especially in initial education.

While a learning society might be emerging, a number of major constraints exist to inhibit its progress, including: the idea that education should have an aim other than learning for its own sake; the prevalence of the idea that education is only initial education; the understanding of leisure as being something which is uncreative and of little value, so that it is only malingers who have it. It is perhaps interesting that 'leisure' should no longer be related to 'education' since the word 'school' is derived from a Greek word *'skhole'* which means 'leisure spent in the pursuit of knowledge'. (Collins English Dictionary 1979). Perhaps a re-discovery of the original meaning of the word 'school' is necessary in a learning society. But Tough, Brookfield and other researchers have all shown how people do use their leisure in learning, so that it may be necessary to understand the fact that people do use their leisure in this way and emphasize this more frequently than do educators at present. However, the front-end model of education remains a constraint to the emergence of a learning society which means that the concept of education learned by trainee teachers should include a life-long rather than an inter-generational perspective, and that they should see a major function of the school in society as being an institution which helps children discover the joy and skills of learn-ing so that they can spend much of the remainder of their lives so doing. Indeed, Husen (1974), among others who have written on this subject, suggests that schooling has to change considerably to accomm-odate the learning society.

SUMMARY

This chapter has sought to illustrate some of the
philosophies and concepts apparent in the current
discussions about the education of adults. Initially,
the front-end model of education was discussed and
it was suggested that such an approach is not particularly relevant for education in contemporary
society, so that a humanistic definition of education was offered, ie. that education is any planned
series of incidents, having a humanistic basis,
directed towards the participant(s) learning and
understanding. Education is seen, therefore, as an
idealistic process in which the humanity of the
participants is paramount.
     The education of adults was seen to be any ed-
ucational process in which those who regard themselves and are regarded as socially mature participate while adult education was seen to contain
connotations of liberal education. Not that liberal
education was, consequently, devalued since it was
later seen to be at the heart of the learning
society in which individuals are encouraged to learn
in order to help develop their own humanity. The
learning society has, above all, one conception of
education as its basis: that education is a lifelong process of learning and developing - which is
an ideal at which to aim. Three strategies for implementing lifelong education were discussed:
continuing education tends to be gaining wide acceptance but it is a conservative concept that casts
no aspersions on the present system; recurrent
education seems to be being incorporated into the
continuing education system but it is a more radical
conceptualization, especially among some of its
exponents, which implies that the current system
needs radical reform so that everybody may receive
an equal entitlement of education at some stage
during his life; community education was also shown
to be a rather confused concept and it was suggested
that the concept should be restricted to those educational processes in which the learners intended
to use their learning to improve the quality of life
in a specific locality, while other forms of education generally classified under this heading might
be better regarded as other innovations in lifelong
education.
     This chapter has, therefore, endeavoured to
clarify some of the contemporary concepts and to
show in the process some of the underlying philosophies and trends in current society. Having

examined these concepts it is now necessary to examine the adult learner and adult learning, a subject that forms the basis for the next two chapters.

SELECTED FURTHER READING

Foundations of Lifelong Education   *(ed) R H Dave 1976*

This book consists of eight papers, by seven authors, on lifelong education. Each is written from the perspective of a different academic discipline and provides a wealth of ideas about lifelong education.

Learning to Be   *E Faure (chairman) 1972*

UNESCO's important report on lifelong education. This is a very important document and one that all who are involved in the education of adults, especially in the vocational sphere, should be familiar.

Cultural Action for Freedom   *P Freire 1972a*

This short book encapsulates many of Freire's most significant ideas. The book is difficult to read, unless the reader has a sociological background, but the ideas that Freire discusses are very important and they repay the hard work of careful study.

A Future for Lifelong Education (2 vols)   *E Gelpi 1979*

These two volumes could easily be a single book but they bring together many of the ideas of Ettore Gelpi, who is the head of the Lifelong Education Unit at UNESCO. The chapters cover a variety of topics from a worldwide perspective and they focus especially upon lifelong education in relation to the working classes and industrial society.

Recurrent and Continuing Education – a curriculum model approach   *C Griffin 1978*

This is a short discussion paper, published by the Association of Recurrent Education, which seeks to distinguish between these two concepts. While the distinction drawn may be too polarized it clearly demonstrates some of the differences in philosophy and perspective between the two approaches.

Recurrent Education   *V Houghton and K Richardson (eds) 1974*

This symposium demonstrates clearly the differing perspectives which may be discovered among those who support this policy. It is, perhaps, the only single collection of papers to cover the whole spectrum

Continuing Learning in the Professions   *C O Houle 1980*

This book has rapidly assumed importance in the sphere of continuing education as a major work. It is not only a book about the concept, it is a practical book about the application of continuing education in the different professions. Houle is one of America's foremost theorists of adult education and, if for no other reason, it is well worth educators in the professions being aware of the ideas it contains.

The Learning Society   *T Husen 1974*

This distinguished Swedish scholar introduces the concept of the learning society and places it clearly within a futuristic orientation. It is a valuable book which raises many important issues.

Adult Education, Community Development and the Working Class
T Lovett 1975

This is a report of a community education project in which the author was involved in Liverpool. Many elements of the project are fully described and the implications of the work discussed fully. It is a good example of the problems associated with outreach adult education.

An Analysis of Contemporary Concepts

Recurrent Education: A Strategy for Lifelong Education
OECD 1973

This is a clear statement of OECD's policy on recurrent education.   The report discusses the concept, sets the scene of recurrent eduation and
highlights important points.

Chapter Three

THE ADULT LEARNER AND ADULT LEARNING

Earlier in this study it has been argued that learning is a basic human need, so that the process of
learning is manifest in most people throughout much
of their lives. Hence, it is maintained that life--
long education should be regarded both as a human
right and as a fundamental necessity in any civilized society in order that every individual is enabled to respond to his learning needs, fulfil his
potential and discover a place within the wider
society. For too long education has been regarded
as 'something done to children' and at some stage in
adolescence, or soon after, it is completed - except
for the minority who continue to attend educational
institutions. Even though the many may never darken
the doors of an educational institution again in
their lifetime, it does not mean that they have
ceased to learn and, therefore, some continue in the
process of self-education, even if the learning that
they provide for themselves might not always be
quite so enriching as they may have received had they
availed themselves to the wider educational provision. Much of this learning may have been covert
and, despite the work of Tough and similar research
projects (see Tough 1981 for a recent bibliography),
the actual amount of learning per adult remains unknown and, perhaps, unknowable. However, in these
past two decades an increasing emphasis has been
placed upon the adult learner and his learning and
many studies have appeared, to which reference has
already been made. Consequently, this chapter
focuses upon these aspects and contains two main
sections: the adult learner and the adult learning.
In the following chapter some of the writers about
adult learning are examined.

THE ADULT LEARNER

Previous discussion highlighted the problem of de-
fining the term 'adult' and concluded that adulthood is reached when the individual is treated by
others as if he is socially mature and when he considers himself to have achieved this status. However, such an approach does not really appear to enrich the debate about the adult learner a great
deal, neither does it contribute much to the theory
of adult learning, so that it is necessary to pursue
this discussion a little further at this point.

The Self: It was noted in the first chapter that the
self concept is quite significant to the early
learning process and this acts as the starting point
for this discussion. Luckmann (1967:48-9) argues
that during the early years the individual self becomes detached from its immediate experience in the
interaction with other persons. This detachment
leads to an individuation of consciousness and
permits the construction of schemes of meaning since
these respond to the learning needs that the evolving
self develops. This, in turn, results in the self
integrating the meanings that have evolved in response to the learning questions which have arisen
from previous experience. Hence, ultimately, a self
is formed that integrates the 'past, present and
future in a socially defined, morally relevant biography'. There is, therefore, a sense in which the
self transcends its biological body, reaching out to
the socio-cultural environment and responding to
pressures from it in a dialectical relationship in
order to create a sense of meaning, as was illustrated in the opening chapter.
    This discussion raises philosophical questions
about the nature of man that cannot be avoided in
any consideration about the adult learner, however,
it will not be pursued much further here since it is
beyond the scope of this particular study. Suffice
to note that, if this argument is accepted, the
person has two major components: the self and the
physical body in which the former is contained. This
is an important conclusion since the ravages of time
clearly have their effect on the physical body, but
what of their effect on the self? Following
Luckmann's argument, it may be seen that every new
experience is interpreted by the self and has a
meaning given to it which is then integrated into
the meanings of past experiences stored in the mind.
This ultimately results in a system of meaning or

a body of knowledge that helps the person in-
terpret 'reality'. But what if the physical body
and even the brain itself begin to deteriorate
during adulthood? Does it not affect the ability of
the self to process these experiences in a meaningful way? Luckmann might respond in the negative to
this, at least until such time as the brain ceases
to function efficiently or at all. In recent years,
psychologists have tended to support this conclusion.

Until fairly recently it was thought that when
the human being achieved biological maturity he
reached a plateau and, after a few years, deteriora-
tion set in. Thorndike (1928), for instance, concluded that the ability to learn 'rises until about
twenty, and then, perhaps after a stationary period
of some years, slowly declines' (cited from Yeaxlee
1929:41). However, this argument has come under
some criticism in recent years and Allman (1982)
summarises some of these later research findings.
She records how Horn and Cattell have suggested that
there are two forms of intelligence: fluid, which
stems from the biological base and, crystallized,
which is capable of growth through the major part of
life since it is influenced by the social processes
that the individual experiences. In the same paper
she (1982:47) points to Birran's 'discontinuity
hypothesis' which states that 'the biological base
ceases to be the primary influence on behaviour
after physical maturation is complete and as long as
the biological base does not enter into a hypoth-
esized critical range of pathology, it will not re-
gain supremacy of influence'. From these and other
studies, she concludes that since adulthood is not
the end-product of childhood and adolescence,life-
long education becomes a means of facilitating
future adult development. In a similar fashion, one
of the foremost investigators of education and ageing, Gisela Labouvie-Vief (1978:249) concludes that
'much of what we now know about the educability of
adults is in need of revision' as a result of recent
research on the topic. Therefore, the old adage
that 'you can't teach an old dog new tricks' is not
only misleading but it is also inappropriate since
older people can and do learn new things.

The physical capabilities of the adult, however,
do decline after they have reached a peak in late
adolescence or in early childhood. Verner (1964:18)
summarises these as including: sensory decline;
loss in strength; lengthening of reaction time;
decline in sexual capacity; changes in skin texture,
muscle tone and hair colour; and a gradual decline

in overall energy'. He suggests that there are a few physiological losses that are very significant in the process of adult learning: loss in visual acuity, loss in audio acuity, loss of energy and the problems of homeostatic adjustment. Since these all affect adult learning and, therefore, adult teaching, they need to be taken into consideration. However, these physiological changes may induce an adult to underestimate his powers to learn and so re-inforce the perception that education is something that occurs early in life.

Nevertheless, irrespective of the conditions of the physical body, the individual self continues to interact with others within the same socio-cultural milieu enabling the person to continue to construct a universe of meaning. If other people are withdrawn then that dynamic tension between the self and the wider society, which is at the heart of learning, disappears and the person may begin to doubt himself, suffer senility, anomie, etc. But does the adult always learn when he is interacting with others? Clearly many situations are familiar, so that the individual does not have a traumatic experience in every interaction and the amount of new knowledge gained may be minimal and it may merely re-inforce that which is already known. But on other occasions the discrepancy between what the individual knows and the meaning that he gives to his experience is greater and then the learning experience becomes more explicit. Schutz and Luckmann (1974:8) state:

> In the natural attitude, I only become aware of the deficient tone of my stock of knowledge if a novel experience does not fit into what has up until now been taken as a taken-for-granted valid reference schema.

Thus it may be argued that given specific social situations every adult is a learner, whereas in familiar experiences the knowledge gained merely reinforces that which the individual already has. Yet there is a sense in which this argument suggests that the motivating force for learning is a discordant experience between the self and the socio-cultural environment, but it would be unwise to suggest that this is the only reason for undertaking such an activity. Tough (1979:44-62) shows how complex these reasons are and it would not do the sophistication of his argument justice to attempt to reproduce it here: suffice to note that Tough discusses many reasons, among which are: pleasure, esteem, desire to employ what is learned, satisfying curiosity, enjoyment gained from the content of what is learned, completing unfinished learning and social benefits.

Characteristics of the Adult Learner: It may thus be asked, who is the adult learner? Clearly Tough's finding of 98% of his sample, discussed earlier, appeared to be rather high and that might be accounted for by his methodogy. Yet Peters and Gorden (1974), in a similar piece of research, discovered that 91% of their sample of 466 had also conducted learning projects. Other research has supported these findings, so that it does appear that the majority of adults actually undertake learning projects and that, from the above argument, every adult is a learner.

However, the adult who learns and the one who learns through joining an educational institution in order to continue his education may not be quite the same. It is much more difficult to discover the statistics for and the characteristics of the latter type of person than it might appear on the surface. Chanley et al (1980:7) suggest that about 16% of the adult population of England and Wales attend post-secondary education in any one year. However, their statistics for vocational education appear to be incomplete, so that this figure is probably an under-estimate. By contrast, Johnstone and Rivera (1965) report that over 20% of the American population attended education in the year commencing June 1961, but this figure included full-time students and those whom they classified as self-directed learners. Cross (1981:51), reporting the statistics from the National Center for Educational Statistics in America, suggests that some 12% of the American population over the age of 17 years were engaged in some formal, organized adult education, but this excluded those studying for an academic qualification. ACACE (1982b:15) discovered that 47% of the sample interviewed claim either to have taken part at some time or to be currently engaged in some form of post-full-time education or training, 12% were engaged in a study at the time of the research and another 10% had been during the three year period prior to it and that 'large numbers of the population are interested in using their (leisure) time actively rather than passively in a wide variety of ways'. (ACACE 1982b:27). Killeen and Bird (1981:20) calculated that between three and four million people received some sort of educational leave during

61

1976-6 but this was not always on a full-time basis.
However, from these varying figures it is clear that
accurate statistics are difficult to obtain and that,
since the social provision of education is changing
rapidly any statistics discovered in one year may
have little relevance a few years later. Research
into who joins tutorless discussion groups and into
those who attend voluntary organizations in order to
learn is still in its infancy and it might be unwise
to estimate numbers, although Verner (1964) suggests
that the same type of people participate in formal
community life as those who participate in adult education.

It is, therefore, necessary to try to summarise
some of the findings about the type of person who
actually participates in adult classes. Charnley et
al (1980:37) conclude that:

> ... the adult education service has attracted
> a variety of students, but the student body
> is not distributed in a way which reflects
> the class structure of the population as a
> whole. The exceptional case of extensive
> working class participation is adult literacy
> where special funds were made available. The
> tendency (is) for the higher socio-economic
> groups .... to take fuller advantage of the
> provision.

Two specific and recently reported studies demonstrate the validity of this conclusion. Sidwell
(1980:309-317) conducted a survey of sixty-three
evening and nine day classes in modern languages for
adults in Leicestershire between November 1978 and
May 1979. 1139 students were sent a questionnaire
and a response rate of 41.7% was achieved. Women
outnumbered men, over 75% of the respondents could
be classified as coming from the non-manual socio-
economic classes and 71.5% had already studied a
language during their initial education. The modal
age group was between 30 and 34 years. Jarvis
(1982b), studied a small adult education centre in a
Surrey village during the academic year 1979-80 in
which 477 students registered. Of the 368 respondents to a questionnaire, 87.8% were women and many
classified themselves as houswives. Of the remainder, the great majority were from non-manual backgrounds, 62% were in the age group 22-45 years and
only 5.7% of the respondents were over 65 years. The
Advisory Council survey also discovered that women
students outnumbered men, but only slightly, and that

the adult student body is predominantly under the
age of 45, and that its social class is concentrated
heavily in the Cl grouping, which is lower middle
class. Statistics from American research also point
to similar findings: higher participation rates
among women, among the 17-34 years age group, among
the more wealthy and the better educated. (Cross
1981:54). Cross concludes that the amount of formal
schooling is the one variable most significantly
correlated to educational interest and participation
in adulthood. This conclusion is in accord with the
phenomenological argument of Schutz and Luckmann
(1974) who write that individuals are likely to
repeat their past successful acts because it enables
them to act upon the world in a confident manner.
Support for such a position would also come from behavioural psychology since repetition of past successful acts may be interpreted as a re-inforcing
action.

It would be difficult to specify the type of person
in professional occupations who attends in-service
continuing education. However, some evidence may be
found in the work of Rogers (1962) who discovered
that those professional practitioners most likely to
introduce innovations to their practice were those
who were better educated and who kept up with recent
developments by reading the professional journals
and attended professional association meetings and
conferences. Hence the place of the professional
journal and the regular conference assumes a significance that the educator of adults has to take
into consideration. For other occupations, Killeen
and Bird (1981) suggest that young male workers are
more likely to receive paid educational leave than
any other category of the work force, which provides
additional evidence for the current feminist argument.

Few mature people enter the field of higher
education as full-time students although many more
study part-time, especially with the Open University.
Hopper and Osborn (1975) investigated mature
students in three universities and one polytechnic
and discovered that there were more men than women
and that they had, on the whole, received more than
the basic minimum education required by law but that
many of these students had been socially downwardly
mobile since leaving school, so that they re-
entered the educational system from socio-economic
class III (non-manual). By contrast, those who had
been upwardly socially mobile tended to enter it
from socio-economic class II. They also noted that

many of the students had a low sense of personal
self-esteem and that they tended to experience a
sense of marginality. More recently, Roderick et al
(1981) have conducted a similar study in Sheffield
and they also discovered that more men than women
were mature students and that the median age of male
students was lower than that of the female students.
However, they also noted that a surprising number of
the mature students were either separated or
divorced. They (1981:53) suggest that 'in cases
where marriages run into difficulties, some women
become alarmed at their lack of qualifications and
consequent inability to earn enough to support themselves and their children' so that they return to
full-time education. However, it would be a feasible
interpretation to suggest that the marriage break-
down also frees some people to return to full-time
education. They also record data from 520 mature
students who applied to one of the universities of
Birmingham, Leeds, Liverpool, Manchester and
Sheffield for the years 1977 and 1978: 69% were
men, 49% were under 30 years of age and only 11%
were over 40 years; 48% were married but only 6%
were separated or divorced; 25% were already in
the professions and a further 20% were in clerical
employment.

In the past decade the Open University has
enabled many mature students to study part-time for
a degree whilst remaining at home and continuing in
their employment. Throughout the period of its
establishment it has maintained and published full
statistical reports about its students. McIntosh
(1974) noted that in the early years of its establishment there was a downward shift in the age of
those who registered, that school teachers predom-
inated amongst the first students although there
was an increasing number of student without any
formal educational qualifications in the first few
years. However, she (1974:59) pointed out that only
8% were objectively working class although 15%
classified themselves as such and she considered
that many Open University students are upwardly
socially mobile. Rumble (1982) recorded how the
proportion of school teachers studying in the Open
University has declined as teaching in the United
Kingdom has moved towards an all-graduate entry. He
showed how each year between 1970 and 1980 more men
than women have applied to study with the Open
University but that the overall trend has been for an
increasing number of women to apply. However, the
male applicants classified as either in a skilled

trade or other manual occupations has never exceeded
10% of the total number of applications nor has the
number having no formal education qualifications
ever exceeded 12%. The majority of those applying
for the Open University are under 40 years of age,
with less tha 1% of the total number being over the
age of 65 years.

Thus it may be concluded that the majority of
adult students tend to come fron non-manual occupations, to have been relatively successful in terms
of examinations in their initial education and to be
under 45 years of age. Men predominate in vocational courses and in full-time higher education but
women are more likely to attend classes that do not
lead to a qualification* However, the proportion of
women entering the Open University does appear to be
approaching that of men.

Motivation to Study: The question remains, however,
about the reasons why mature people wish to attend
educational institutions and many pieces of work
have investigated this topic, indeed research into
participation is among the most established areas of
investigation in adult education. Courtney (1981)
claims, quite correctly, that research in this area
has been rather sporadic in Britain although there
were two very early pieces, ie. Hoy (1933) and
Williams and Heath (1936). The National Institute
of Adult Education's report *Adequacy of Provision*
records that "the two main reasons for going to
classes were 'work' and 'know more about the subject/
learn the correct way' " (Hutchinson 1970:59). The
Advisory Council research discovered that:

> Men attach more importance to the idea that
> education is a means to getting on in the
> world: women give rather less emphasis to it.
> Such a difference is not large - a matter of
> 7% less agreement in the case of women - but
> it confirms what has been said elsewhere in
> this report about the contrast between the
> male and female view of continuing education.
>   (ACACE 1982b:41-2)

Hence it is clear from this research that men tend
to have a slightly more instrumental attitude towards education than do women. In contrast to this
work, the research in the United States has been
much more consistent and elaborate (see Houle 1979,
Courtney 1981, Cross 1981). Cross (1981) indicates
that four main methods have been employed to

investigate this phenomenon: in-depth interviews, motivation scales, questionnaires and, what she calls, hypothesis testing. Space forbids a full account of all the work published but a brief résumé of some of the findings are included here. Houle (1979:31-2) draws the general conclusion that participation in any type of educational activity is usually undertaken for a variety of motives rather than a single one, and that these usually re-inforce each other. Houle (1961) himself formulated an early and useful typology within which to classify these motives: goal-orientated learners, activity-orientated learners and those whose main orientation is learning for its own sake. Within each of these classifications a number of different motives can be specified. This typology has formed the basis of a number of analyses but Johnstone and Rivera (1965:46) classified the motives of their sample in the following manner: prepare for a new job; help with the present job; to become better informed; spare-time enjoyment; home centred tasks; other everyday tasks; meet new people; escape from daily routine; other or none - a miscellany of unclassifiable responses. They go on to show how motives to partici-pate vary with different subjects studied and with the age, sex and socio-economic position of each respondent. They (1965:159-160) conclude that:

> there are very pronounced ways in which the uses of adult education differ across the range of social classes. At lower socio-economic levels adult education is used primarily to learn skills necessary for coping with everyday life ...
> As one moves up the social class, ...
> they shift .... to getting ahead .... In general, there is an overall shift away from learning for the purpose of basic life adjustment .... (to) enrichment of spare time.

Other research projects have subsequently employed different typologies to these and yet the overall findings do not differ greatly. Burgess (1971),for instance, indentified seven basic orientations to adult education, which were a desire: to know; to reach a personal, social or religious goal; to take part in a social activity; to escape; to comply with formal requirements. Morstain and Smart (1974) highlighted six clusters of reasons: social rela-tionships, external expectations, social welfare,

professional advancement, escape/stimulation and
cognitive interest.   In a more recent piece of research, Aslanian and Brickell (1980) interviewed 744
adult learners by telephone and discovered that 83%
of them specified a life transition as the motivating factor that caused them to start learning, eg.
a change in employment. While their research method
might have biased their response, it does point to
the significance of analysing the life-world of
learners in order both to understand their motivation and their approach to learning.
     It is quite clear from all of these research
findings that most of the main reasons for participating in adult education classes lie in a cluster
of orientations that are quite similar, despite the
fact that different researchers employ their own
terminology. The reason for participation does not
always lie within the learner but in the dynamic
tension that exists between the learner and his
socio-cultural world. Yet if there is a need to
learn and if most people actually embark upon learning projects there must be reasons why so few people
appear to attend formal educational provision. Carp,
Peterson and Roelfs (1974) suggest three sets of
factors which inhibit participation: situational
barriers, institutional barriers and dispositional
ones. They suggest that cost and time are the major
hurdles and this is in accord with Charnley et al
(1980:37) who also focus upon fees as a major issue
in leisure time education, but they also suggest
other factors, such as a lack of flexibility in the
adult education service which prevents some people
from attending. The Advisory Council's research
(1982b) noted that some 15% of their respondents
had not participated in any form of post-initial
education nor did they wish to do so in the future
but that there were others who have not participated
in the past but wish that they had or who wish to do
so in the future. In addition, there were some 15%
of the sample who wished that they had participated
in the past, hoped to do so in the future, but who
had never actually been involved in any form of
post-initial education. Hence this research, while
not specifying why non-participants had not actually
been involved in post-initial education suggests
that it would be unwise to assume that non-participants are all opposed to any participation in education. Some innovative developments in adult education, eg. Hutchinson and Hutchinson (1978), demonstrate the validity of this conclusion and the
journal *Adult Education* published quarterly by

the National Institute of Adult Education, usually carries a section in which it reports interesting or significant developments showing how the adult education service has responded to specific demands.

This section has attempted to draw together a wide range of material to describe the adult learner: it claimed that every adult is a learner but that there are definite characteristics of and types of person who attend the variety of educational provision that exists. Clearly adult learners who join educational institutions are younger and tend to be middle class but this does not mean that the remainder of the population do not learn or that they may not want to join in formal educational provision. Having looked at the adult learner it is now necessary to examine adult learning.

ADULT LEARNING

A theory of adult learning has been implicit in much of the previous discussion but it is now necessary to make this explicit. It will be recalled from the opening chapter that the learner was placed within his socio-cultural framework and that both the learner and the socio-cultural milieu have to be taken into consideration when constructing any theory of learning. The socio-cultural milieu may itself be divided into two distinct elements: the objectified culture of a society and the means by which it is transmitted to individuals. But the individual may also be regarded as a duality of the self and the physical body in which it is located. Hence, there are at least four factors that need to be taken into consideration when framing any theory of learning.

Implicit in Figure 1.2 (chapter one) is a learning cycle and this may be demonstrated in more detail.

Figure 3.1: A Learning Cycle Implicit
in the Individual in his
Socio-Cultural Milieu

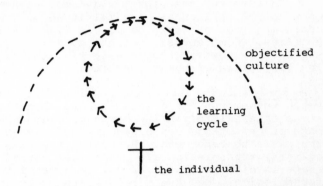

objectified
culture

the
learning
cycle

the individual

Thus it may be seen that the dialectical relationship
between the individual and his culture illustrated
in Figure 1.2 may be regarded as a learning cycle in
Figure 3.1 and that learning occurs when there is a
dynamic tension between the individual and the
agencies of transmission of the culture of the
society, but before this is discussed in greater detail it is necessary to clarify each of the elements
in the process.

Culture: In sociological literature this term refers
to the sum total of knowledge, beliefs, ideas,
values, practices, etc. prevalent in a specific
society. Yet culture is neither static nor objective but it is a dynamic phenomenon affected by the
pressures of changing technology, the forces of
economics, political ideology, etc. etc. Scheler
(1926), as was shown earlier, demonstrated quite
clearly that the elements of culture change at varying paces, so that while it is depicted here as a
rather static homogeneity it is actually more like a
patchwork quilt with each little element altering at
a different rate to every other. This means that
there is always new knowledge, values, beliefs, skills
etc. for the learner to acquire and, at the same
time, it may also result in the learner having to
unlearn old knowledge and skill, etc. in order to
remain in harmony with his cultural environment.
Many people, especially among the elderly, find it
difficult to keep abreast with all the changes and
the anomie that they experience is sometimes manifest in such phrases as, 'I don't know what the
world is coming to these days' etc. Yet only a

selection of culture (a curriculum) is ever transmitted to or acquired by individuals because of its
extensiveness and complexity, so that there are always new things to learn.

Culture is, therefore, a dynamic phenomenon
open to the influences of a multitude of pressures,
including that of individuals, as Figure 3.1 illustrates. Comprehension of the dynamic nature of
culture is, however, quite essential to understanding the nature of human learning.

Agencies of Cultural Transmission: Culture is not a thing
but a phenomenon, it exists nowhere objectively but
it is internalized in the human mind and the raw
data of culture is contained in the printed word,or
the cassette tape, etc. Hence the agencies of
cultural transmission are themselves varied and operate in different ways and since some of these are
technological, eg. the wireless, the television, it
is possible for the learner to utilise these means of
transmission to select for himself those elements of
culture that he wishes to learn and in this way he
becomes a self-directed learner.

Whenever a person interacts with another there
is usually a two-way process of transmitting and receiving individual interpretations and analyses of
some aspects of culture.

Figure 3.2:   The Two-Way Transmission
of Individual Interpre-
tation of Selections from
Culture

Ego ————————————————————▶ Alter

Thus in almost every interaction ego and alter are
both teachers and both learners and their interaction may be interpreted as a negotiation of their
differing understandings of the aspect of culture
which impinge upon their meeting. This is a significant feature in the education of adults since
both teacher and student bring to the human interaction their own experience and their own analyses
of the culture within which they interact. A number
of writers in the education of adults highlight this
point although it is perhaps most explicitly discussed by Freire (1972b:53). However, it is rare
for any human interaction to be on perfectly equal
terms, so that the direction of the flow is more
likely to be in one direction than the other. Hence,

if ego is a pupil and alter a school teacher, it
might be claimed that the lower arrow, in Figure 3.2
above, would be the more prevalent because the child
has more to learn from the teacher than the teacher
has from the child. While this claim is perfectly
valid it is, perhaps, much more debatable than
it appears! However, the interaction in some forms
of teaching and learning may be depicted, as in
Figure 3.3:

Figure 3.3:   A Unidirectional Transmission
              of Culture

alter

ego

The above form of interaction occurs when ego is
unable to communicate with alter, eg. when alter's
status is much higher than ego's, in some forms of
instruction, in the formal lecture, or when the mode
of cultural transmission is via technological media.
Even in these situations, ego processes the information that is received rather than having it merely
imprinted on the mind, although it might be argued
that in many instances there is insufficient
critical awareness, so that a form of imprinting
actually occurs.

The Self: The self is that detached individuation of
consciousness that expands as its experiences increase in number, so that it evolves into a sophisticated, complicated, but often fragile phenomenon. Hilgard and Atkinson (1967:481-3) suggest that
there are four aspects of the self that should be
noted: it may be an agent; it is continuous;
self-perception is largely dependent upon the extent
to which others accept, or reject, the individual;
it is the embodiment of values and goals. Kidd
(1973:126), by contrast, specifies four other

aspects of the self: what the person actually does and says; how a person feels and perceives his own behaviour; how a person is perceived by others; the ideal self, constant but changing throughout the whole of life. More recently, Lovell (1980:115) has suggested that the self includes three main elements: self-image, ideal self and self-esteem. From the above, it may be seen that different writers are focusing upon a number of similar aspects from their differing perspectives and, in addition to all of these features, the self processes and assesses all the ideologies, beliefs and meanings that have emerged in reflection upon the experiences of living.

The concept of self is rather complex but ill-defined and yet the self is most significant in playing both the role of teacher of adults and that of an adult learner. To be a teacher is an adult role but it is much less clearly defined in relation to other adults. Additionally, since the learner's role is designated by modern society to be one per-formed by young people an adult learner's self-perception may be in opposition to the way that he understands that his role should be performed (see Harries-Jenkins, 1982:19-39). Hence comprehension of the concept of self is quite crucial to both the theory   and the practice of teaching adults.

The Physical Body: The human being may be perceived as both body and self and the former reaches its physical peak during late adolescence, or in the early twenties, and after a period it begins to decline. Certain physical abilities, such as sight and hearing, become less efficient during later life and this affects the adult's efficiency in receiving the elements of culture that are being transmitted to him, so that it is most essential that awareness of this should be taken into consideration when de-signing any premises for adult education or any teaching and learning programme for adults.

Having discussed these four elements in the process of learning it is now necessary to turn to the process of learning itself, so that the next section of this chapter expands upon the learning cycle illustrated in Figure 3.1.

The Learning Cycle: The significance of each of these factors to the process of adult education is apparent from the above discussion and each of these elements will be referred to frequently in this and subsequent chapters. However, it must be recog-nised that everybody's experience is unique and as individuals grow older so their uniqueness is even more apparent. This is not to deny each child is unique but merely to state that since adults have had more experience of life the more likely they are to manifest their differences. Hence generalizations only seek to convey a sense of the norm rather than specific situations.

It will be recalled from Figure 3.1 that in the process of learning there appears to be a cyclic relationship between the individual and his object-ified culture as he both processes and interalizes the culture and also as he externalizes it in his relations with other people. Hence, it is now poss-ible to develop a learning cycle, taking into con-sideration the foregoing discussion.

Figure 3.4: A Learning Cycle

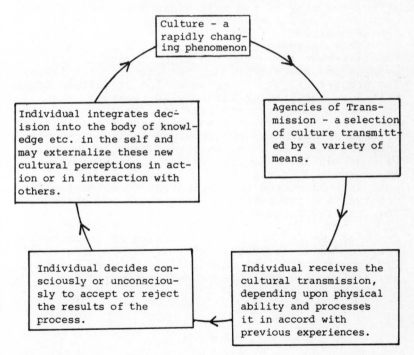

Thus learning may be regarded as a process of re-ceiving and assessing any element of culture, by whatever means it is transmitted. Such a definition is much wider than those frequently cited by learn-ing theorists: learning is 'a relatively permanent change in behaviour that occurs as a result of

73

practice (Hilgard and Atkinson, 1967:270) or learning is 'any more or less permanent change in behaviour which is the result of experience' (Borger and Seaborne, 1966:14). Both of these definitions emphasize a change in behaviour as being an element of learning but this is too restrictive because it would necessitate the exclusion of the acquisition of new cognitive knowledge unless it resulted in behavioural change. The definition offered by Brundage and Mackerarcher (1980:5) is much closer to that suggested here; they state that adult learning 'refers both to the process which individuals go through as they attempt to change or enrich their knowledge, values, skills or strategies and to the resulting knowledge, values, skill, strategies and behaviour possessed by each individual'. However, this is a rather cumbersome definition, so that while it conveys many of the main ideas suggested in this section it does not actually capture the totality of the argument.

This learning cycle represents a process and it is clear that there are two major facets to the process and these represent the teaching and learning processes: there is a selection of culture transmitted to the learner that may be regarded as an approach to teaching and this will be discussed subsequently and there is also the learner's selection of culture which may be perceived as student-centred learning and this is quite significant in the education of adults. However, before these approaches are discussed it must be recognised that not all that is transmitted to the learner is automatically received and processed and that there are phases in the learning process itself.

Phases of Learning: Within the context of teaching and learning Gagné (1977:284-286) has developed a model for understanding the relationship between learning and instruction and this is re-produced in the following diagram.

Figure 3.5: Relations between Phases of Learning and Events of Instruction according to Gagné (1977:285)

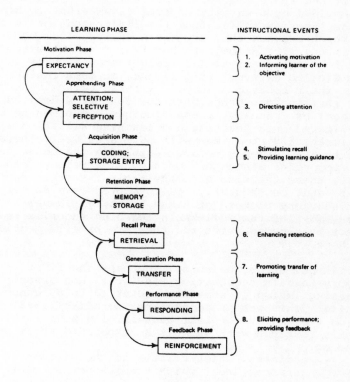

The above diagram clearly demonstrates a relationship between teaching and learning and this is developed in the fifth chapter from a more specifically adult education perspective. However, the above diagram is included here to demonstrate that the learning cycle may be sub-divided in a slightly different manner and that the learning process is more complicated than may appear from Figure 3.4.

It is now necessary to examine theories of learning and this is undertaken in the next two sections of this chapter. the first examines some of the basic learning theories and the second examines the ideas of reflection and experience.

Basic Learning Theories: Many of the psychological theories of learning reflect the model of teaching, described above, in which the individual is shaped or moulded by a variety of sources external to him. These theories suffer from the limitations of this approach because they have been derived from experiments with animals rather than research with human beings. Animals are taught and learn by responding to external stimuli and, in some instances, have their behaviour shaped by human beings rewarding them in accordance with the teacher's desired objectives. Because these findings can often be replicated in a teaching and learning situation with children, and sometimes with adults as well, there has been a tendency to over-emphasize the behavioural approach. Since they omit consideration of the self, these theories are inevitably less than complete and, consequently, fail to produce a totally satisfactory picture of human learning. Nevertheless, most of the well-known learning theories reflect this perspective and they are briefly mentioned here.

'Trial and Error' Learning: Perhaps the first theory to gain recognition was 'trial and error' learning, which is sometimes referred to as connectionism. This was propounded by Thorndike (1928) towards the end of the last century, and as a result of his research with animals he expounded three laws, that of:
- readiness, which relates to the circumstances under which the learner is satisfied, annoyed, etc.,
- exercise, which refers to the process of strengthening the connection discovered between stimulus and response by practice,
- effect, which relates to the process of strengthening, or breaking, any connection as result of the consequences of any action.
Basically, this theory propounds a quite fundamental way of behaving: that if the learner discovers some act or explanation to be effective or valid it will be repeated until such time as the consequences of the action no longer produce the desired or expected results. By virtue of starting with the learner it is hardly surprising that Thorndike was able to pursue his work into adult learning.

Conditioning: In contrast to Thorndike, the following two theories commence with the teacher. Perhaps the most well-known of all psychological research into learning is that of Pavlov (1927) who proposed the theory of classical conditioning. Briefly stated, this theory asserts that the learner learns (is conditioned) to associate the presentation of a reward with a stimulus that occurs factionally prior to it. Thus Pavlov's dogs salivated at the sound of a bell since they had been fed when this had been rung on previous occasions. Operant conditioning, however, occurs when the response is shaped by the reward, so that after every action that approaches, approximates or achieves the desired behaviour the learner receives a reward. This form of conditioning is expounded by Skinner (1951) who has more recently argued that 'man is a machine in the sense that he is a complex system behaving in lawful ways, but the complexity is extraordinary'. (Skinner 1971:197). Throughout this latter book Skinner suggests that conditioning can explain all learning and that the exciting possibilities for the future lie in what man will make man into. Skinner has grappled with the philosophical problems of behaviourism but he may not be able to convince everyone that his perspective is quite so all-embracing as he suggests. Even so, there is a great deal of research evidence to support many of the claims of the behaviourists. Not all conditioning may be intentional, nor is it all conscious, but it certainly occurs during the process of the education of adults. Lovell (1980:35), for instance, suggests that classical conditioning has occurred when students choose an evening class or a subject because the tutor had created a warm, friendly atmosphere. By contrast, the process of grading within assignments or praising a reticent student for contributing to a group discussion are both aspects of operant conditioning.

Gestalt Theory: Another theory of learning that has been based upon research with animals has emerged with Gestalt psychology. The word 'Gestalt' actually means 'shape' or 'form', and as early as 1912 Max Wertheimer postulated that the individual did not perceive the constituent elements of a phenomenon but that he perceived them as a totality. He formulated the 'Law of Prägnanz' in which there are four aspects of perception: similarity, proximity, continuity and closure. Similarity refers to the fact that people group phenomena by their similar

salient features rather than by their differences:
proximity refers to the fact that individuals group
phenomena by their closeness to each other rather
than by their distance from one another; continuity refers to the fact that objects are often
perceived in relation to the pattern or shape that
they constitute in their totality; closure refers
to the fact that there is a tendency to complete an
incomplete representation so that the whole is perceived rather than the incomplete parts (see Child
1981:73-4). From the holistic perspective Köhler
(1947) suggested that solutions to problems appear
to come abruptly, as by a flash of insight, and that
they are achieved because the insight emerges from
the perception of the relationship between the different factors rather than in response to separate
stimuli. Whilst this theory has a number of attractive features, especially since it is recognised
that some people are holisitc learners, the idea of
insight or intuition, almost demands that it should
be rooted in an earlier process, either socialization or an earlier learning experience, so that it
would be unwise to regard all learning in such an
inspirational manner.

Reflection and Experience: In recent years, especially
among adult educators, much more emphasis has been
placed upon the learner than upon the teacher. For
instance, when the learner is in his socio-cultural
setting, it may be seen how he is either aware that
he is in harmony with his environment or that he is
out of phase with it. When the learner actually
experiences a discrepancy between his expectations
and his perception of the ethos of the wider society
then an imbalance is produced in the individual-
social system and the learner may need to recreate
the equilibrium. Hence, a motivation to learn is
located within this awareness of a learning need.
The learner's response to the balance may not be
mindless and mechanical but may emerge as a result
of the individual reflecting deeply upon the situation before deciding how to act. Reflection is
quite crucial to the human being and it may be that
this facility is one of the major ways in which
humans differ from other animals. It is, therefore,
one essential component in any learning theory.
Freire (1972a:55-6) emphasizes the significance of
reflection in the learning process in order that individuals should become conscious of their social
situation before they decide to act upon the world
and thereby participate in the process of creation.

Reflection is a major part of that aspect of the learning cycle (Figure 3.4) referred to as 'processing the stimuli that the learner receives from the wider culture' and perhaps needs to be emphasized more in Gagné's phases of learning, so that much human learning starts from the experiences of the learner rather than from the teacher's selection of culture. Experience is a significant element for many theorists of adult education and this will become evident in the next chapter. However, Kolb and Fry (1975) have devised a learning cycle that emphasizes the individuals experienced and this is illustrated in Figure 3.6.

Figure 3.6: An Experiential Learning Cycle

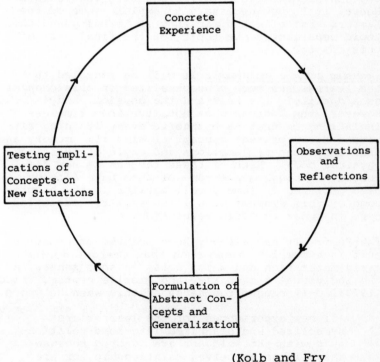

(Kolb and Fry
1975:33-7)

Kolb and Fry claim that the learning cycle may begin at any stage and that it should be a continuous spiral. It will be noted that there are elements of previous theories in this cycle, which is quite understandable since no one theory of learning is

79

able to explain the complexity of the many forms of
learning that occur. Additionally, it may be quest-
ioned as to whether there is an implicit behavioural
definition of learning contained within this cycle.
Nevertheless, it does raise significant issues about
learning from experience. In addition, Kolb and Fry
suggest that the movement in the vertical axis represents a process of conceptualization while that
on the horizontal axis represents the variation between active and passive manipulation. They claim
also that each quadrant represents a learning style.

The emphasis on this learning cycle is rightly
upon concrete experience but it must be recognised
that individual learners perceive phenomena differently and that some of those variations in perception are related to differences in the learner.
Hence, it is now necessary to explore some of the
factors that effect efficiency in learning and this
topic constitutes the topic for the final part of
this chapter.

Learning and the Individual: It will be recalled that
the learner has been conceptualized in this chapter
as a duality: the self and the physical body.
However, the learner does not live in a timeless
isolation, so that he brings to every learning situation his: present concept of himself; memory and
past experiences; emotions and style of learning;
physical body. Each of these factors is now discussed, although since some of them have already
been explored in some detail earlier in the chapter
some of this discussion will be a little curtailed
here in order to avoid repetition.

The Self: It has already been pointed out that the
self is a complex phenomenon that emerges during
early maturation and which acts, in some senses, as
the individual's cognitive and emotive centre. Kidd
(1973:130-1) caught the sense of this when he wrote:

> All new experiences for the learner are
> symbolized and organized into some relation-
> ship with the self, or are ignored because
> there is no perceived relationship, or are
> denied relationship, or given distorted
> meaning because the experience seems incon-
> sistent with the structure of the self.

The individual adult brings to the learning situation his store of knowledge and experience and he is
more likely to respond to a new learning situation

and learn effectively if he can organize his interpretation of that experience into the universe of
meaning that he has already constructed. Knox
(1977:433) recognised that this store of knowledge
itself helps to determine what is learned as effective 'adult learning typically entails an active
search for meaning and discovery of relationships
between current competence and new learnings'. However, severe difficulties are presented to the learner if he is unable to integrate his new knowledge
with that which he has already, so that he may develop an attitude that suggests he is reluctant to
change. But Katz (1960) points out that one of the
major functions of attitudes, such as this, is to
protect the self against the harsh realities of the
outside world.

However, the self is not merely the processor
of received knowledge, it is an active phenomenon
which has the ability to reflect upon its own processes. Hence the learner has a conception of himself, he may also have developed an idealized self-
concept and he will have also developed a measure of
self-esteem. All of these factors affect the individual's response to every learning situation. If
the learner, for instance, has a highly developed
sense of self-esteem and a positive conception of
himself, he is less likely to feel threatened by new
learning experiences but one who has neither of
these is likely to be un-nerved by the situation.
Clearly, when this occurs it may be the result of
his experience in initial education and it is a sad
reflection upon the school system that some adult
educators are aware that some adults have developed
such a deep suspicion of education (Rogers 1977:52),
so that the adult educators attempt to create a non-
school, adult ethos in which they hope to overcome
this perception. Belbin and Belbin (1972:84) illustrate how important it is for adult learners to
build a sense of confidence before they can acquire
specific skills.

The adult's idealized self may also affect the
direction that the learning will take for Brundage
and Mackerarcher (1980:26) declare that adults 'are
more concerned with whether they are changing in the
direction of their own idealized self-concept than
whether they are meeting standards or objectives set
for them by others'. While this may be true for
some adult learners more evidence would be required
before it might be accepted as a general principle.
Even so, the point is well made, that some learners
are concerned about conforming to their own idealized

self-concept in their learning experiences.

None of the factors under discussion are discrete or distinct, so that a degree of overlap is
bound to be evident in this discussion and this will
become apparent as the discussion progresses.

Memory and Past Experiences: The adult brings to
the learning situation himself and all the memories
and the interpretations that he has given to his
past experiences, which has both advantages and disadvantages to the learning. Thus it is intended to
discuss first the memory of the adult, then his perception of time and, finally, his experiences.

'I can't remember like I used to' is a common
expression among adults and one that many educators
of adults hear frequently from their students in the
teaching and learning situation. The expression
tends to give credance to the front-end model of
education, but is it correct? Obviously it reflects
an experience or else the person would not utter the
exclamation and yet Rogers (1977:59) points out that
'a young man and a man in his late fifties would both
be able to remember and repeat an average of eight
random numbers recited to them. But what does change
is that if the older man is asked to remember something else between the time he was first given the
numbers and the time he was asked to repeat them, he
is less likely to remember the original numbers than
the young man'. Yet older people do have many more
commitments than younger people and often study
part-time, so that additional information, etc.
might be given them from a variety of sources which
will make it harder to recall the information to be
learned. Hence, this means that teachers of adults
should provide opportunities during their teaching
and learning sessions, so that adults have time to
begin the process of storing the information that
they have gained. Additionally, it might not be
wise to discourage last minute revision when adult
learners are required to sit a traditional examination. Knox (1977:435) also points out that adults
are only more likely to retain information that they
receive if it is meaningful to them and able to integrate it into the store of knowledge that they
already have. All of these findings refer to what
is now called the short-term memory but once the
material is stored in the long term memory it can be
recalled and most people are familiar with the very
elderly being able to recall, from their long term
memory, information that they learned decades before.

The experience of time is another factor in the adult's learning process and one that is often forgotten in discussions about learning. Brundage and Mackeracher (1980:35-6) note a significant point when they state that children and young adults 'tend to measure time as "time from birth"; adults past 40 tend to measure time as "time until death"'. Hence, as time becomes shorter, so the learning needs focus more acutely upon the problems of the immediate present and previous experience becomes increasingly important to the older person. It may be,therefore, that certain subjects are more appropriate to the psychological orientations of different age groups: history, for instance, may be a more popular study for those whose orientation is already towards their past experiences than would be mathematics. However, more research is required to investigate the extent to which there is any correlation between preferred 'learning' topics, age and orientation towards time.

Throughout their lives adults accumulate a wide range of experiences that they store up in their memories and which they bring with them to every learning situation. Provided that the new knowledge can either be integrated into the stock of knowledge already stored or answers a specific learning need it presents no problems to the learner. However, if the new knowledge or skill involves unlearning previous experiences, then those previous experiences inhibit the efficiency of the learning. In a way this interference is similar to the problems encountered by the learner in recalling new information when other information has prevented the memorizing process from taking its natural course.

Adults bring to every learning situation a vast array of experiences from which they have learned to which they are able to give different interpretations. Clearly, some of these will make some new learning difficult but, by contrast, much of it may also be regarded as a resource to be employed in any teaching and learning situation, so that adults should be encouraged to utilize their wealth of experience rather than to disregard it when they embark upon any new learning project.

Emotions and Learning Styles: Adults who are under a great deal of stress, are over-stimulated or anxious do not learn as well as those who are stimulated to respond to their learning situation in a normal manner. (Brundage and Mackerarcher, 1980:26-32). They are much more likely to learn efficiently

when they are in a location in which they feel free
to express themselves without inhibition. It is for
these reasons that adults, returning to study, need
to be treated with the greatest consideration and
also why the first class of every adult session
requires careful organization by the tutor. Belbin
and Belbin (1972:168) record instances of individuals
undergoing in-service training who are so anxious
about passing the examination at the end of their
course, that they resign from their jobs rather than
to risk failure, since they consider that they would
lose face with their colleagues if the latter
occurred. Hence, teachers of adults need to be sensitive about the emotional state of their learners,
a facility that may be more significant in the educator of adults than many of the others generally
assumed essential to the teacher's role.

Teachers and learners should also recognise
that one of the features of adulthood is the uniqueness of each person. Hence as a result of all their
previous experiences, adults develop their own different styles of learning. Many publications record
these different styles (see Knox 1977: 443-449) and the
following list includes nine that are among the
most frequently mentioned:

Table 3.1: Learning Styles

Learning Style	Comment
Active versus Passive	It will be seen from the learning cycle that some learners may actively seek out information and these are self-directed learners, while others may be more passive in the receipt of information provided for them
Assimilator versus Accommodator	Kolb and Fry (1975:38-9) describe the assimilator as one whose dominant learning abilities are abstract conceptualization and reflective organization and the accommodator as one whose strength lies in active experimentation and learning from concrete experience.
Concrete versus Abstract	Some learners like to start with the concrete situation, such as the experience, while others, prefer to start from the abstract, theoretical

(Table 3.1 continued)

Learning Style	Comment
	idea. This is similar to the preceding type.
Converger versus Diverger	The converger is best at abstract conceptualization and active experimentation while the diverger's strengths lie in reflective observation on concrete experience. (Kolb and Fry 1975: 38)
Field Dependence versus Field Independence	Wilkin (1971:24) describes these as in the former mode 'perception is strongly dominated by the overall organization of the field, and parts of the field are experienced as "fused"'. In the latter mode 'parts of the field are experienced as discrete from organised background'.
Focusing versus Scanning	If learners have a problem to solve, focusers will examine it as a totality and generate hypotheses that will be modified in the light of new information, while scanners will select one aspect of the problem and assume it to be the solution, until subsequent information disproves it, when they have to recommence the task.
Holistic versus Serialistic	This approach reflects Gestalt psychology: some learners see phenomena as a whole while others string together the parts.
Reflection versus Impulsivity	This is similar to focusing and scanning and Kagan (1971:54-5), who undertook his studies among children, wrote that a 'child who does not reflect upon the probable validity of alternative solution sequences is likely to follow through the first idea that occurs to him. This strategy is more likely to end up in failure than one

(Table 3.1 continued)

Learning Style	Comment
	that involves reflection'.
Rigidity versus Flexibility	Some students are rigid in their approach to learning since once they have discovered a successful method they always seek to apply it. This creates its own difficulties, since problems emerge that cannot be solved by the normal approach.

It must be recognised that there is a tendency in the above to overlap but they are produced in this way to show the extent to which learning styles differ. This is a significant element in teaching adults that needs to be considered carefully by the educator. Few of the pieces of research demonstrate any relationship between learning style and learning effectiveness in adults since most of the research has been conducted with children.

The Physical Body: That the physical body declines once it has reached its peak is a self-evident phenomenon and, to some extent, the learner's ability to assimilate information and process it is related to the level of physical health. Knox (1977: 410) states:

> Physiological conditions and physical health can affect learning and cognition in various ways. Sensory impairment, such as poor vision or hearing loss, can restrict sensory input. Inadequate cerebral circulation or stress can impair memory. Ill health can restrict attention given to external events.

From the above it is clear that the educator of adults must be aware of these findings and ensure that the teaching and learning environment is such that any ill-effects of the physical condition are minimized. Additionally, it is known that as human reactions slow down it is more difficult for adults to sustain a high rate of learning and if they are expected to undertake learning at too fast a pace they experience stress and anxiety which leads to unsatisfactory situations in which learning is

either inhibited or prevented. But once adults are
enabled to learn at their own pace, when they feel
free and unpressurized adults of almost any age can
learn efficiently. Rogers (1977:62) records how
'training schools have found, literally to their
cost, that set training periods of perhaps three
weeks with formal examinations at the end produce
high failure rate'. Hence learning and teaching
methods have to be devised that allow the adult to
control the speed of his own learning.

SUMMARY

A theory of learning has been constructed in this
chapter in which the individual adult is located
within this socio-cultural milieu. The adult is
seen as a human being with a developing self but a
physical body in a gradual process of decline. When
the adult's experience of the wider world is
harmony with his understanding of it, then his
experience merely re-inforces that comprehension. By
virtue of the rapidly changing culture and a developing self this equilibrium is unlikely to be maintained for long and hence the adult realizes his
need to learn. However, in some instances, such
learning may not be embarked upon, especially in the
case of the elderly, and then anomie may be experienced. Yet other adults embark upon learning
projects, either of a self-directed nature or by
attending an educational institution. Those who
choose the latter option may have already been
successful in their previous experiences in educational institutions, they are more likely to be
under 45 years of age and have a middle class background. All people undertake some self-directed
learning, even if it is only reflecting upon
previous experiences, but research suggests that
many people actually embark upon learning projects,
some of which run into many hours duration.
     Having examined adult learners and adult
learning it is recognised that none of the theorists
of adult learning have been discussed in detail in
this chapter, so that the next one is devoted entirely to an analysis of the work of a number of
them.

SELECTED FURTHER READING

*Adult Learning Principles and their Application to
Programme Planning   D H Brundage and D Mackerarcher 1980*

This book has been prepared by the Department of
Adult Education of the Ontario Institute for the
Ontario Ministry of Education. It is a full synop-
sis of much of the literature about adult learning
and it applies some of the conclusions to planning
programmes for adults. It is a thorough study and
should be read by educators of adults.

Adults as Learners   K Patricia Cross 1981

This book raises many of the issues discussed in this
chapter, such as participation, motivation and facilitating learning: it is an academic study drawing
upon a great deal of the literature, mostly
American, but also producing a number of quite
original ideas. There is a great deal in this book
applicable to the education of adults outside of
America.

Adult Learning   M J A Howe (ed) 1977

A book of essays, many of which stem from the
University of Exeter. The book is psychologically,
rather than educationally, orientated, so that those
who do not have a background in this discipline may
find aspects of some of the papers rather academic.
Nevertheless, a wide spectrum is covered

How Adults Learn   J R Kidd 1973 (revised edition)

Written by one of the most well known of all adult
educators, this is a thorough, interesting and read-
able book. It displays a humanistic approach to
adult learning and reflects both the scholarship and
the commitment of its author.

Adult Development and Learning   A B Knox 1977

This is a massive study, much of it given over to
the adult, his development and place in the wider
world. Despite its size and the breadth of its
referencing it is a relatively easy book to read.

It contains one long and excellent chapter on adult learning.

Adult Learning   *R B Lovell 1980*

This is a concise text book, reviewing the research and raising questions about the findings and conclusions. It is precise, quite thorough and a good introduction to the subject.

Adults Learning   *J Rogers 1977 (2nd edition)*

Perhaps the most well known book on this topic in the United Kingdom, published as a paperback and easily obtainable. The book is well written, easy to read and full of good material. However, the topics covered are wider than adults learning and much of the book is in fact about teaching adults.

Chapter Four

ADULTS LEARNING - SOME THEORETICAL PERSPECTIVES

A P I &

Having developed an approach to adult learning in
the previous chapter it is now necessary to examine
the field of adult education more broadly and to
investigate some of the writings about adult learning that have been produced in recent years. This
chapter, which is closely linked to the previous one,
highlights the work of five major writers; each of
whom, in their various   ways, have examined different aspects of adult learning. Four of the
writers concentrate on adult education and the fifth
is an educational psychologist; three assume a
psychological and the remaining two a sociological
perspective. They are: Paulo Freire, Robert Gagné,
Malcolm Knowles, Jack Mezirow, and Carl Rogers; the
main works of each referred to here are listed in
the bibliography. These five have been selected
because, in their differing ways, they have contributed to the theoretical knowledge of adult learning
and their writings are examined here, comparing and
contrasting their ideas to those presented in the
previous chapters.

PAULO FREIRE

The writings of Freire are now very well known among
adult educators, even though some have confessed to
finding him difficult to comprehend. Freire's ideas
have emerged against the background of the oppress-
ion of the masses in Brazil by an elite, who
reflect the dominant values of a non-Brazilian
culture. His writings epitomise an intellectual
movement that developed in Latin America after the
Second World War, which is a synthesis of Christianity and Marxism and which finds its theological
fulfilment in the so-called liberation theology and

90

its educational philosophy is Freire's own work.
From this background, it may be assumed that at the
heart of his educational ideas lies a humanistic
conception of the learner but also a realization
that once the learner has actually learned he may
not remain passive but become an active participant
in the wider world. Hence,for Freire, education
cannot be a neutral process; it is either designed
to facilitate freedom or it is 'education for dom-
estication' (Freire 1973c:79), which is basically
conservative.

However, in order to understand Freire's thinking it is helpful to recall Figure 1.1 in which it
was suggested that objectified culture is transmitted
to the individual through the lifelong process of
socialization. Since the culture that is transmitted is foreign to the values of the Brazilian
people,who are its recipients, Freire claims that
this is the culture of the colonizers and implicit
in the process in the sub-ordination of the culture
of the indigenous people. He (1973c:50-1) illustrates this in the following manner:

> It is not a co-incidence that the colonizers
> refer to their own cultural practices as an
> art, but refer to the cultural production of
> the colonized as folklore. Similarly, the
> colonizers speak of their language, but
> speak of the language of the colonized as
> dialect.

Since construction of reality is contained within
language, the masses have a construction of reality
imposed upon them,which is false to their own
heritage. Thus the idea of a false self-identify
emerges, one that perpetually undervalues the indigenous culture and, therefore, the native person
sees himself as subordinate.Hence, the oppressed are
imprisoned in a cultural construction of reality
that is false to them but one from which it is difficult to escape, since even the language used by
them transmits the values that imprision them.
Through the process of literacy education
Freire, and his colleagues, were able to design
experiential situations in which the learners were
enabled to reflect upon their own understanding of
themselves within their socio-cultural milieu. It
is this combination of action and reflection that he
calls praxis (Freire 1972b:96). Herein lies the
difference between man and the other animals, man is
able to process his experiences and reflect upon

91

them. Through the process of reflection the individual becomes conscious of realities other than
that into which he has been socialized. Freire
(1971 cited 1976:225) writes that conscientization
'is a permanent critical approach to reality in
order to discover it and discover the myths that de-
ceive us and help to maintain the oppressing de-
humanizing structures'. He then expresses it slightly differently: conscientization 'implies that in
discovering myself oppressed I know that I will be
liberated only if I try to transform the oppressing
structure in which I find myself'. For Freire,
therefore, education is 'the practice of freedom' in
which the learner discovers himself and achieves his
humanity by acting upon the world to transform it.
In this latter proposition it is possible to detect
the ideas of Figure 1.2 (chapter 1) where the individual learner acts back upon his culture, so that
there is implicit in this some of the elements of
the learning cycle mentioned in the last chapter.

How do Freire's ideas differ from those suggested in earlier chapters? Fundamentally, there is
one major difference and some minor ones. In the
first instance, the socio-cultural background from
which his theory emerged has resulted in Freire de-
picting the objectified culture as being false and
hostile to the culture of the indigenous learner, so
that his approach is often viewed as being political
rather than literacy education. However, this interpretation of culture is not something that is
unique to Freire: many Marxist writers would concur
that the dominant cultural knowledge and values etc.
acquired by most members of a society are the cultural
perspectives allowed by an elite, so that some form
of cultural hegemony exists. (see Westwood, 1980 for
a discussion in which this approach is applied to
adult education and Bowles and Gintis, 1976, for
their analysis of American schooling from a similar
perspective). Thus, Figure 1.2 (chapter 1) actually
allows for such an interpretation to be assumed and,
indeed, teaching might even be viewed as an activity
that encourages it. Nevertheless, there is a significant difference between the model presented here
and Freire's thought: he incorporates two opposing
cultures into his understanding of the process -
that of the ruling elite and that of the oppressed.
Herein lies the crux of Freire's argument that no
education can be neutral since the culture of the
oppressed is in opposition to that of the elite.
Hence literacy education can only assume a political
perspective. The model produced earlier has not

sought to analyse the culture of the United Kingdom
in this way, although some sociologists and community educators might consider that such an analysis
is necessary and this will be discussed below in relation to the relevance of Freire's work for Western
Europe and the United States.

However, Freire places considerable emphasis on
the dialogue between the teacher-learner and the
learner-teacher and this is similar to the two-way
model of human interaction depicted in the previous
chapter. Freire recognises that the teacher may
facilitate the experience upon which reflection
occurs, which thus becomes a learning process.
Thus Freire regards the role of the teacher as a
facilitator who is able to stimulate the learning
process rather than as one who teaches the 'correct'
knowledge and values that have to be acquired. However, this does not differ significantly from the
model produced here since the teacher is regarded
here as either one who transmits cultural knowledge
or one who facilitates learning. This distinction
is discussed further in a subsequent chapter.

Freire's approach is a model for teaching
adults rather than necessarily one for teaching
children. It concentrates upon the humanity of the
learner and places great value upon the human being
but it is more structural and political in its emphasis,whereas the one discussed here is more phenomenological and individualistic. Herein lies a
slight difference in emphasis although not one that
is irreconcilable since both locate the individual
in his socio-cultural milieu and both regard the
learner as a recipient of information and experiences
transmitted from his culture and as an agent to act
upon that socio-cultural environment in order to
change it.

Having pointed to some of the apparent differences between Freire's approach and that discussed
here, it must also be recognised that there are many
similarities, including: his emphasis on the humanity of the learner; his concern that the learner
should be free to reflect upon his own experiences
and to act upon his socio-cultural milieu to transform it; his connection between the socio environment and the learner; his recognition that the
learner is an actor who is able to create his own
roles rather than one who merely plays the part for
he has been prepared, so that education cannot actually be a neutral process.

Out of the political condition of Latin America
has emerged a Christian-Marxist approach to

education that is both humanistic and radical. Yet the term 'radical' is often the 'kiss of death' to innovative approaches, as was seen with the concept of recurrent education. However, if there is not something radical about the educational process, the question needs to be posed as to how it differs from socialization? If education actually does provide the opportunity for the individual to process and reflect upon his experiences it must allow for him to place different interpretations upon those experiences and to choose whether, or not, he seeks to be a conformist.

Since Freire's ideas emerged in Latin America, do they have any relevance for contemporary Western society? This is a most important question to pose, since he could be dismissed as someone whose views are only of significance within the context in which they emerged. Yet this approach would be quite wrong, since many dominant ideas and values in contemporary society owe their origins to historical cultural milieu completely different from this one. London (1973:48-61) reflects upon Freire's work in the context of North America and he claims that in that society adult education has adopted a 'bland approach .... (a) non-controversial stance, and (a) safe and respectable perspective' (London 1973:59). But he maintains that a:

> central problem for adult education is to
> undertake programming that will raise the
> level of consciousness of the American people
> so that they can become aware of the variety
> of forces - economic, political, social and
> psychological - that are afflicting their lives.
> (London 1973:54)

Hence, it may be seen that London is sympathetic to the adoption of Freire's approach in North America. Perhaps his argument would have been even more compelling had he focused upon the different cultures and sub-cultures in America and examined whether a form of cultural hegemony actually exists. A great deal of what London has written might also be applied to some adult education that exists in the United Kingdom. Hence, it may be necessary, to enquire whether adult educators actually perceive their role in this way at all. Clearly, there is some evidence to suggest that community educators, such as Lovett (1975), Newman (1973, 1979), do actually adopt similar perspectives but, overall, it is doubtful whether the approach is regarded by many as

a significant element in their work. Yet it is
possible to argue that many people in the United
Kingdom are no more aware of the variety of forces
that afflict them, than are their counterparts in
the United States, so that it is an important ideal
for adult educators to try to raise their level of
consciousness. Thus Freire's ideas may be as significant to the United Kingdom as they are to the
United States of America.

ROBERT M GAGNÉ

Some of Gagné's work was used in the previous
chapter, so that that aspect of it will not be repeated here. Nevertheless, there is another element
of his work that is also significant to adult educat-
ion.and this is his types of learning. He has proposed eight types, seven of which he regards as a
hierarchy and the eighth may occur at any level.
These are: signal learning; stimulus-response
learning; motor and verbal chaining; multiple discrimination; concept learning; rule learning;
problem solving.
    He claims that signal learning may occur at
any level of the hierarchy and it may be understood
as a form of classical conditioning, which was discussed in the previous chapter. Clearly this
happens with both children and adults and it is no
doubt one of the ways in which everyone acquires
many attitudes and prejudices throughout the whole
of their life. The remaining seven types of learning are, according to Gagné, seven stages of a
hierarchy and they are now elaborated upon.
    Stimulus-response learning is the same as
operant conditioning in which the response is shaped
by the reward. The following two types of learning,
motor and verbal chaining, Gagné places at the same
level in the hierarchy: the former refers to skills
learning while the latter is rote learning. With
both, practice is necessary to achieve correctness
whilst re-inforcement is necessary to ensure that
the acceptable sequence is maintained. In multiple
discrimination learning, Gagné moves into the area
of intellectual skills; this, he suggests, is the
ability to distinguish between similar types of
phenomena, so that the learner is able to decide
which of similar types is correct for any specific
situation. In contrast to discrimination is the
ability to classify. Concepts are abstract notions
which link together similar phenomena so that, for

instance, friendship is a concept but individual
friendships are actual occurrences, education is a
concept but in actuality there are educational processes. Gagné suggests that the ability to learn
concepts is the next order of the hierarchy and it
may be recalled that developmental psychologists,
such as Piaget (1929), would claim that ability to
think in the abstract commences mostly during adolescence, so that it is necessary to recognise that
the education of adults may be different from the
education of children, since the levels of conceptual thought in the various learning processes are
different. This is a point implicit in Gagné's
hierarchy of types of learning but one that is important in relation to any consideration of andragogy. One particular type of classification is that
of rules and he maintains that the ability to respond to signals by a whole number of responses is
successful rule learning. At this level of thought
it is clear that Gagné perceives the individual to
be a little more free than some of the behaviourists
and this is quite fundamental to the understanding
of the education of adults.

Problem solving is the highest order of learning in Gagné's hierarchy and this occurs when the
learner draws upon his previously learned rules in
order to discover an answer to a problematic situation. It will be recalled that among the different styles of learning discussed in the previous
chapter was the dichotomy between the flexible and
the rigid learner, in which the former clearly has
the mastery of more sets of rules than the latter,
to assist in problem-solving. Problem solving is an
approach to learning and teaching used frequently in
the education of adults,so that the problem solving
sequence that he proposes is quite significant for
adult educators. He suggests, that the following
sequence occurs, in which the flexibility is
apparent: initially a learner proposes one or more
hypotheses concerning the problem and these are
based upon the rules that have already been learned.
These hypotheses are then tested against the actual
situation and once an answer has been discovered to
the problem the solution will be assimilated into
the learner's repetoire of rules, so that the next
time that a similar situation arises the learner will
not experience it as a problem. There are similarities at this point between Gagné's approach and
that of Schutz and Luckmann (1974) mentioned earlier.
Another psychologist whose analysis is similar to
Gagné's in this context is George Kelly (1955), who

claimed that all behaviour may be regarded as a form
of hypothesis testing to enquire whether the actual
world is really like the perception of it constructed by the individual. If it is, then the experience
merely reinforces the construct but, if it is not,
then the construct (hypothesis) has to be modified
in the light of experience. (see Candy 1981 for a
direct application of some of Kelly's ideas to adult
education).

The problem solving sequence has formed a basis
of many learning exercises in adult education and in
recent years a number of problem solving cycles have
been devised which are similar to the learning
cycles that were discussed in the previous chapter.
Figure 4.1 below depicts a problem solving cycle
that combines the sequence proposed by Gagné with
some of the ideas mentioned by Kolb and Fry (1975).

Figure 4.1: A Problem Solving Cycle

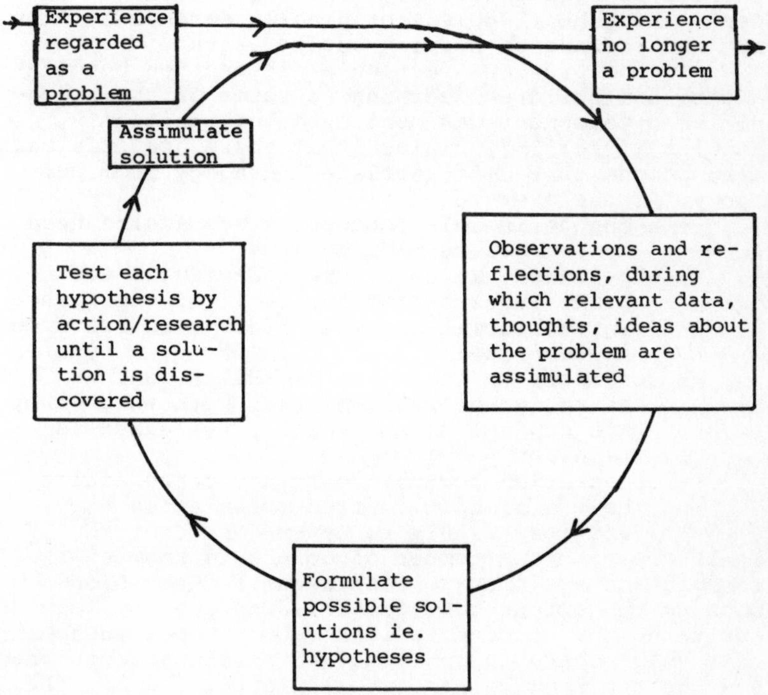

Thus it may be seen from the above figure that this
type of problem solving cycle actually relates back
to the learning cycle but it also highlights some of
the most important aspects of Gagné's hierarchy of

learning. It will be recognised, however, that since Gagné starts from a psychological perspective some of the wider cultural implications of learning, discussed in the previous chapters and in the work of Freire, are not so apparent. Yet the learning process that he has highlighted is significant for adult educators, since experience is frequently a basis for learning.

MALCOLM KNOWLES

Knowles may almost be regarded as the father of andragogy because, while he did not actually invent the term, he has been mainly responsible for its popularization. Indeed, the term derives from the Greek *'aner'*, meaning 'man', and it was first used in an educational context in Europe. Nevertheless, Knowles is most frequently associated with the concept, which he (1980:43) originally defined as 'the art and science of helping adults learn'.

In the previous section a distinction between adults and children learning in terms of their cognitive development was mentioned but, initially, Knowles (1978:53-7) claimed that there are four main assumptions that differentiate andragogy from pedagogy. These are:
- a change in self concept, since adults need to be more self-directive;
- experience, since mature individuals accumulate an expanding reservoir of experience which becomes an exceedingly rich resource in learning;
- readiness to learn, since adults want to learn in the problem areas with which they are confronted and which they regard as relevant
- orientation towards learning, since adults have a problem centred orientation they are less likely to be subject centred

It is clear that a number of points in Knowles' formulation are open to considerable discussion, such as the extent to which children are any less motivated than adults to learn about those phenomena that they regard as relevant and problematic to them and whether Knowles has actually specified all the relevant points in any discussion about the differences in adults and children learning. Indeed, when Knowles' work was first published in America it did stimulate considerable debate in the American journals about its validity. Initially, McKenzie (1977)

sought to provide Knowles' pragmatic formulation
with a more substantial philosophical foundation and
he argued that adults and children are existentially
different; a point with which Elias (1979:254)
agreed although he suggested that this was not necessarily significant since men and women are existentially different but no one has yet suggested that
'the art and science of teaching women differs from
the art and science of teaching men'. To which
point, McKenzie (1979) replied that the differences
between men and women, while pronounced, are not
significant when related to their readiness to learn
nor are they important in relation to their perspective of time. He also argued that andragogy is similar to but not precisely the same as progressivism.
Yet McKenzie did not really focus upon the point
that children might actually have the same readiness
to learn as adults, and indeed do, when they are
confronted with a problem the solution to which they
wish to know.

Another set of issues arose in the debate about
andragogy: Label (1978) suggested that the education of the elderly should be known as gerogogy,
since education should recognise the phases of adult
development; but are there only two phases in that
development? Knox (1977:342-350) would suggest
otherwise, so that to include gerogogy as a separate
element in the art and science of teaching would be
the 'thin end of the wedge' in a multiplication of
terms, which prompted Knudson (1979:261) to suggest
that all of these should be replaced by a single
concept of 'humanagogy' which is:

> a theory of learning that takes into account
> the differences between people of various
> ages as well as their similarities. It is a
> *human* (his italics) theory of learning not a
> theory of 'child learning', 'adult learning'
> or 'elderly learning'. It is a theory of
> learning that combines pedagogy, andragogy and
> gerogogy and takes into account every aspect
> of presently accepted psychological theory.

Perhaps Knudson's position is a logical outcome of
the debate but the term 'humanagogy' does not appear
to have gained a wide degree of acceptance and, in
any case, what makes humanagogy any different from
education? It appears that Knudson has merely in-
vented a new term for education, even though he has
emphasized one aspect of the process that is regarded as significant to this study: the humanity of the

participant.

In 1979, Knowles chose to re-enter the debate when he recognised that andragogy and pedagogy are not discrete processes and he (1979:53) claimed that 'some pedagogical assumptions are realistic for adults in some situations and some andragogical assumptions are realistic for children in some situations', and that the two are not mutually exclusive. However, since the debate was prolonged in America and as a number of questions were raised at the outset of this discussion it is worth enquiring whether Knowles' formulation is actually correct.

Knowles placed a tremendous emphasis on the self, something with which many adult educators would agree. Knox (1977) points out that the self undergoes development throughout the life span and that some aspects of that development may be related to physical age. But other scholars, such as Riesman (1950), have pointed out that some adults are 'other-directed', so that when they came to the learning situation they may seek to become dependent upon a teacher. While it may be one of the functions of an adult educator to try to help dependent adults to discover some independence, it must be recognised that this may be a very difficult step for some learners. But the fact that there are other-directed people suggests that Knowles' formulation is a little sweeping in this respect.

Knowles claimed that adults have an expanded reservoir of experience that may be emphasised as a rich resource for future learning, but do not children and adolescents also have some experience that may be used as a resource in their learning as well? Do adults only learn from their relevant problems? What of those adults who study with the Open University or attend university extension classes? Hence, it needs to be asked whether there are any foundations for his claims?

It does appear that while Knowles has focused upon something quite significant to adult learning, his formulation is rather weak, not based upon extensive research findings, nor is it the total picture of adult learning. Indeed, it is not a psychological analysis of the learning process, it does not describe why specific aspects of experience are relevant, nor does it generate a learning sequence for an adult, so that some of the claims that Knowles made for andragogy do appear to be rather suspect. It is not surprising, therefore, that in his later work he has made less all-embracing claims for this concept, nor is it surprising that even more recent

works have also been rather critical of it. Day and
Baskett (1982:150), for instance, conclude that:

> Andragogy is not a theory of adult learning,
> but is an educational ideology rooted in an in-
> quiry—based learning and teaching paradigm -
> and should be recognised as such .... It is
> not always the most appropriate or the most
> effective means of educating.
> The distinction between andragogy and peda-
> gogy is based on an inaccurately conceived
> notion of pedagogy

Yet despite its apparent conceptual weaknesses and
the many criticisms being levelled at the concept,
it is becoming a popular term in adult education;
so what are the strengths of the formulation that
have resulted in its gaining support? Day and
Baskett (1982) have perhaps located one of these
when they suggest that it is an educational ideology,
for clearly it is humanistic and this is a most
frequently expressed ideology among adult educators.
It also focuses upon the self-directed learner and
emphasizes the place of the self in the learning
process, which are very significant to learning
theory. Additionally, it arose in a period of
history in the twentieth century, which Martin
(1981) has characterised as romantic in which the
value of the individual was emphasized and the boun-
aries of the institutions of society were weak.
These boundaries resulted in an increased emphasis
on integrated approaches to academic study and a
wider acceptance of the ideological perspection of
progressive education. However, the late 1970s and
early 1980s have witnessed a reversal in this approach to knowledge, so that once again more emphasis
is being placed upon the academic disciplines and
'correct' knowledge. Hence, many of the points in
Knowles' formulation have mirrored the acceptable
ideals of that period and of many adult educationalists, so that some of its weaknesses were not
highlighted earlier.
    It may be concluded from this brief discussion
that, despite the claims sometimes made on its behalf, andragogy is not a theory of adult learning,
neither is it a theory of adult teaching even though
its humanistic perspective might provide some guidelines for an approach to teaching adults. Is it a
philosophy? Certainly, it includes within it an
ideological perspective that is both idealistic and

humanistic, so that it is not surprising that it has been found by many to be acceptable. However, andragogy might also be employed as a term to denote the body of knowledge that is emerging about the education of adults, in the same manner as pedagogy might be used to describe the body of knowledge about the education of children.

Knowles is, therefore, an important practitioner in the education of adults and some of the points that he has raised are based upon the humanistic ideals of education itself. It is significant that the points that he has raised are discussed within this theoretical context since, while andragogy is not a theory of adult learning, its implications are quite profound for the practice of teaching adults.

JACK MEZIROW

The work of Mezirow was cited in the opening chapter in order to illustrate how one writer's approach to learning was similar to the one being presented here. Mezirow (1977, 1981) draws upon the insights of a number of established disciplines and synthesizes them in a very original manner and this section summarises some of the ideas that he presents in two recent publications.

Mezirow starts from the assumption that everyone has constructions of reality which are dependent upon re-inforcement from various sources in the socio-cultural world. He calls these constructions of reality 'perspectives' and notes that they are transformed when an individual's perspective is not in harmony with his experience. In this situation of disjunction, the individual's construction of reality is transformed as a result of reflecting upon the experience and plotting new strategies of living as a result of his assessment of the situation. Mezirow notes that life crises are times when this occurs and his conclusion is both in accord with his own observations and those of Aslanian and Brickell (1980), who discovered that people tended to return to studying as a result of life crises. Hence, the crux of Mezirow's (1977:157) analysis is that when a 'meaning perspective can no longer comfortably deal with anomalies in the new situation, a transformation can occur'. He goes on to suggest that a learning sequence is established as a result of a discordant experience, which may be depicted in the form of a learning cycle.

Figure 4.2: A Learning Cycle
            - after Mezirow
            (1977:158)

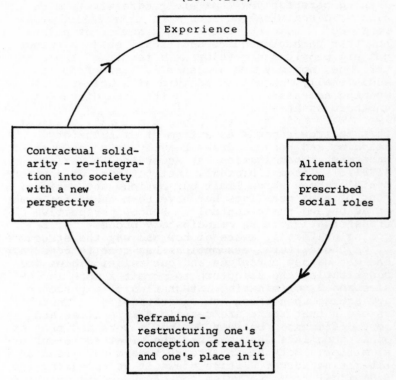

In a later work, Mezirow (1981:7) extends this cycle
to include the following ten stages:
1. a disorientating dilemma
2. self-examination
3. critical assessment and a sense of
   alienation
4. relating discontent to the experiences of
   others
5. exploring options for new ways of acting
6. building confidence in new ways of behaving
7. planning a course of action
8. acquiring knowledge in order to implement
   plans
9. experimenting with new roles
10. re-integration into society

The extent to which this is actually a sequence is
not clear since Mezirow also suggests that there are
two paths to perspective transformation - one sudden

103

and the other gradual. However, he (1977:159) regards these transformations as 'a development process of movement through the adult years towards
meaning perspectives that are progressively more in-
clusive, discriminating, and more integrative of experience'. However, there are a number of points
now that perhaps require additional evidence since
not all people may develop as a result of their experience, nor may they necessarily learn from it.
Additionally, should an individual's universe of
meaning necessarily change in the same direction to
another's as he ages?
     It is this movement along a maturity gradient
that Mezirow regards as a form of emancipatory
learning and here he draws heavily upon the work of
Habermas. Emancipation is, according to Mezirow
(1981:5), 'from libidinal, institutional or environ-
mental forces which limit our options and rational
control over our lives but have been taken for granted as beyond human control'. Hence, perspective
transformation is an emancipatory process 'of becoming critically aware of how and why the structure
of psycho-cultural assumptions has come to constrain
the way we see ourselves and our relationships, re-
constituting the structure to permit a more inclu-
sive and discriminating integration of experience
and acting upon these new understanding'. Thus it
is clear that there are certain similarities and
some differences between Mezirow's work and that of
other theorists who consider the wider socio-cultural milieu. Both he and Freire regard education as a
liberating force: Freire views it as releasing the
individual from the false consciousness in which he
has been imprisoned as a result of the dominance of
the culture of the colonizers but Mezirow regards
the freedom from a more psychological perspective;
both Freire and Mezirow focus upon the social construction of reality and regard learning as a method
by which this may be changed. Like a number of
theorists of adult learning, Mezirow focuses upon the
idea that learning occurs as a result of reflecting
upon experience, so that much of his work is relevant to understanding the learning process in socialization and in non-formal learning situations. However, he also suggests that there are different
levels of reflection and he (1981:12-13) specifies
seven of these, some of which he claims are more
likely to occur in adulthood:
     1. reflectivity: awareness of specific per-
              ception, meaning, behaviour
     2. affective reflectivity: awareness of how

the individual feels about what is being
perceived, thought or acted upon.

3. discriminant reflectivity: assessing the
    efficacy of perception, etc.

4. judgmental reflectivity: making and be-
    coming aware of the value of judgments
    made

5. conceptual reflectivity: assessing the ex-
    tent to which the concepts employed are
    adequate for the judgment

6. psychic reflectivity: recognition of the
    habit of making percipient judgments on
    the basis of limited information

7. theoretical reflectivity: awareness of why
    one set of perspectives is more or less
    adequate to explain personal experience

The last three of these, Mezirow maintains are more
likely to occur in adulthood and the final one he
regards as quite crucial to perspective transformation.

Hence, Mezirow has produced a comprehensive
theory about how the learner processes information
and data from his socio-cultural experiences. The
latter point is very similar to the phenomenological
approach suggested in the previous chapters; that
if a person's stock of knowledge is inadequate to
explain the experience, then the questioning process
is re-activated. Additionally, his emphasis upon
reflection is important since he has extended the
analysis quite considerably. Here his approach is
actually similar to that of Gagné but he concentrates upon reflection rather than learning. However,
his idea of progress and development during the
ageing process does require some further evidence
since it leads logically to the idea of the 'wisdom
of the elders' and to the notion that the self-
knowledge of the elders is always more mature than
that of younger people. Furthermore, the idea of
cultural change plays little part in Mezirow's
analysis. Nevertheless, his approach is both important and significant to understanding the process
of adult learning and, if the final three levels of
reflection actually do only tend to occur in adolescence and adulthood, then he raises some more significant points that need to be taken into consideration in the andragogy-pedagogy debate. Mezirow
locates his work within this framework and views it
as enhancing comprehension of andragogy as a professional perspective for adult educators.

105

CARL ROGERS

Carl Rogers is the final theorist to be discussed in this chapter: he is a humanistic psychologist who has expounded this psychological approach in the field of education. Having this theoretical perspective it is not surprising that he emphasises the self-actualization of the learner and he (1969:279-297) argues that the goal of education is a fully functioning person. However, this orientation reflects the therapist in Rogers and the distinction between education and therapy is occasionally blurred in his writings. Indeed he uses therapeutic techniques for educational ends. This fusion of these two distinct activities is highlighted by Srinivasan's (1977:72-4) discussion of the curriculum distinctions between self-actualizing and problem-centred education: emotional versus intellectual; involving the learning group in developing its own curriculum versus identification of appropriate subject matter; planning learning experiences so that learners can reassess their feelings versus building learning around a problem; support in active learning versus using prepared learning units; using a variety of audio visual approaches versus standardized printed materials and group discussion; using the group's spontaneity versus a programmed learning text; decentralized educational opportunities versus formal educational provision; participatory techniques versus teaching; assessing personal growth versus assessing learning gains. Clearly, Srinivasan has polarized the distinction since a number of the theorists mentioned in this chapter would focus upon the significance of some of the former elements in the dichotomies as significant aspects of their understanding of education. Certainly Rogers would not draw the distinction in quite the way that Srinivasan has and yet she has attempted to clarify an important conceptual issue. However, Rogers certainly comes close to Knowles in his empahsis upon the self and the need for self-development and self-direction. Knowles (1980:29-33) specifies fifteen different dimensions of maturation and he certainly regards maturity as one of the goals of education. Like Rogers and Knowles, it will be recalled that Mezirow was concerned about the maturation process of the learner, so it must be recognised that for a number of theorists this plays a significant part in the education of adults.

Unlike some of the other writers discussed here, Rogers records the results of his approach

106

to experiential learning within the context of graduate teaching in a university and he also records
incidents of others in a formal setting who have
attempted similar techniques. He suggests that experiential learning: has a quality of personal
involvement, both intellectual and affective; is
self-initiated, but he recognises that the teacher
has a facilitating role; is pervasive in as much as
it makes a difference to the leaner; is evaluated
by the learner in terms of whether it is actually
meeting his need rather than in terms of its academic quality; has an essence of meaning. It is perhaps significant to note, that while Rogers regards
experiential learning as self-initiated, he does not
actually dispense with the teacher, so that he is
describing a different learning situation from that
discussed by Tough. Nevertheless, Rogers (1969:103)
does claim that teaching 'is a vastly over-rated
function'.

Like Srinivasan, Rogers regards experiential
learning at one end of a spectrum but at the other
he places memory learning. He claims that experiential learning is typified by the following
principles:

1. human beings have a natural potentiality
   to learn;
2. significant learning occurs when the
   learner perceives the relevance of the
   subject matter;
3. learning involves a change in self-organ-
   ization and self-perception;
4. learning that threatens self-perception is
   more easily perceived and assimilated
   when external threats are at a minimum;
5. learning occurs when the self is not
   threatened;
6. much significant learning is acquired by
   doing;
7. learning is facilitated when the learner
   participates responsibly in the learning
   process;
8. self-initiated learning involves the whole
   person;
9. independence, creativity and self-reliance
   are all facilitated when self criticism
   and self evaluation are basic;
10. much socially useful learning is learning
    the process of learning and retaining an
    openness to experience, so that the pro-
    cess of change may be incorporated into
    the self.

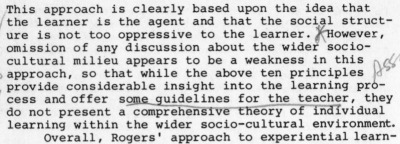

This approach is clearly based upon the idea that
the learner is the agent and that the social structure is not too oppressive to the learner. However,
omission of any discussion about the wider socio-
cultural milieu appears to be a weakness in this
approach, so that while the above ten principles
provide considerable insight into the learning process and offer some guidelines for the teacher, they
do not present a comprehensive theory of individual
learning within the wider socio-cultural environment.

Overall, Rogers' approach to experiential learning has much to offer and may provide inspiration
for the teacher, but it does not provide a comprehensive theory of adult learning.

SUMMARY

The work of five major theorists has been briefly
examined in this chapter and the intention has been
to highlight some of the similarities and some of
the differences between them. Both Freire and
Mezirow consider the socio-cultural milieu as a significant factor in the learning process in common
with the model presented earlier, although they
treat culture in rather different ways: Freire has
a two cultures model of society whereas Mezirow is
content to regard it as rather static and homogen-
eous. The process of reflection plays a significant
part in the work of a number of these theorists,
since they recognise that the human being is able to
sift and evaluate the external stimuli received from
his experiences. Experiential learning is quite
central to all of their considerations, since they
recognise that the adult learns most effectively
when the learning process is in response to a problem or a need. All of the writers, with the exception of Gagné, have placed considerable emphasis on
the self and, although it is most exemplified in the
works of Knowles and Rogers, it reflects the humanistic concerns of adult education. Even so, it is a
much more debatable point as to whether the aims of
education should be specified in terms of the development of the learner because the success of the educational process is then being evaluated by non-
educational criteria. Perhaps, therefore, the cognitive dimension of the learning process is insuff-
iciently emphasized in some instances, although
there is a danger of polarizing or over-emphasizing
formal education if Srinivasan's approach is adopted.
Clearly, the academic disciplines appear to be less

significant than the immediacy and relevance of problems and experiences, although there is a need of considerably more research into effective adult learning of the academic disciplines, which may occur as adults are gaining more opportunities to study for academic and professional qualifications on a part-time basis. For instance, there may be a relationship between experience and the disciplines being studied, etc. which requires more exploration. Most of the theorists focus upon the human need to learn, Rogers being the most explicit about it being basic to humanity but none of them sought to incorporate it into a comprehensive theory of learning needs, a point to which some reference has already been made. Mezirow and Freire have both developed comprehensive theoretical perspectives but Knowles' andragogical approach appears to have achieved the status of a theory, without having been systematically worked out. In all cases there are similarities with the model produced earlier in this study but in each instance the theorist has emphasized those elements that are most central to his own consideration, so that there are also a number of points of divergence.

In a sense it has been a little artificial to separate learning and teaching and to seek to extract from these writings only that which refers to the former, since learning and teaching are interrelated and intertwined. However, it is important to try to highlight and examine some aspects of adult learning prior to discussing teaching adults, but in the following chapter it is proposed to relate the discussion of these last two chapters to the teaching of adults.

SELECTED FURTHER READING

Pedagogy of the Oppressed   P Freire 1972

In this short book Freire works out his understanding of the influence of the dominant culture upon the oppressed. He discusses fully his 'banking' concept of education which is his criticism of the formal educational process and he claims that the outcome of the educational process is a freedom that enables individuals to enter into a creative relationship with their world.

The Conditions of Learning   *R H Gagné 1977 (3rd edition)*

This is an important study in which Gagné explores aspects of learning, including those discussed in the previous chapters. While it is not about adult education, or specifically about adult learning, much of what he has written is relevant to adult and continuing education.

The Modern Practice of Adult Education   *M Knowles (1980) -*
                                     revised and updated

This is a large book in which Knowles offers a guide to the theory and practice of adult education. Knowles has been a prolific author and this book contains many of his mature ideas. This edition is important since it includes his response to the andragogy-pedagogy debate that the publication of the first edition of this book stimulated.

A Critical Theory of Adult Learning and Education
                      J Mezirow 1981
                      (Adult Education Vol 32 No 1
                      Washington)

While Mezirow has written some important books, this paper deserves a wider audience. No doubt it will be republished in a symposium in the near future. However, it contains Mezirow's thoughts about perspective transformation and his theory of reflectivity. While the paper is difficult to read, the effort expended to do so should be richly repaid.

Freedom to Learn   *Carl R Rogers 1969*

This book has become a classic among adult educators, especially those who adopt the experiential approach. The ideas are not always presented in a systematic way and it contains many references of an autobiographical nature. Even so, it is important that educators of adults should be familiar with this approach to learning and teaching.

Perspectives and Non-Formal Adult Learning   *L Srinivasan*
                                                   1977

A short book containing references to a number of
adult educators including Knowles and Rogers. Additionally, it contains many case studies of where
non-formal adult education methods have been implemented. An easy book to read and a good introduction to this aspect of education.

Chapter Five

TEACHING ADULTS

Teaching may be an over-rated activity, as Rogers
(1969:103) maintains, but it remains at the heart of
the educational process, so that consideration needs
now to be given to it. Hirst and Peters (1970:78)
define it as the intention to bring about learning
and if this broad definition is adopted it may be
seen that any activity that is performed in order to
produce learning, however it is conducted, may be
considered to be teaching. Hence, it is clear that
Rogers and Hirst and Peters are perhaps using the
term in slightly different ways and it is, therefore,
essential to clarify its use at the outset. The
teacher can adopt a variety of approaches to the
performance of the role: didactic, socratic or
facilitative. If the teacher plays his role in a
didactic fashion, he expounds the knowledge to be
learned by the students; if he is socratic, he
leads the students towards a conclusion to their enquiry by shrewd questioning; if he is a facilitator,
he creates the conditions in which the learning can
occur but he does not seek to control the outcome of
the process once it has begun. Both the didactic
and the socratic approaches are teacher-centred and
may lead to the teacher's perception of reality
being accepted by the students, although the socratic is more likely to result in conclusions other
than those held by the teacher; whereas the facilitator has little control over the outcome of the
learning at all. Rogers was clearly condemning the
didactic approach and, maybe, the socratic one. By
contrast, the definition proposed by Hirst and
Peters is sufficiently broad to include all three of
the types mentioned here. Yet their definition is
not broad enough to include the informal and unintended teaching that may occur in the process of
human interaction, which was discussed earlier. This,

112

therefore, raises two major questions: to what extent is unintended teaching actually teaching and to what extent is the failure to produce learning, even though it was intended, actually teaching? It was suggested earlier that the failure to bring about learning should be regarded as an unsuccessful attempt to teach rather than unsuccessful teaching. If this conclusion is to be accepted, then teaching is not the intention to produce a learning outcome but it is the provision of any situation in which learning occurs. Hence, the teacher may be anyone who aids another person to learn, irrespective of whether he is part of the educational institution or whether he intended the learning to occur. But, clearly, this is too wide a definition within the context of the occupation of teacher. In this instance, a teacher may be defined as one who is employed to provide an environment in which learning may occur, so that within this framework the teacher will plan his teaching sessions with the intention to bring about learning, or with the intention of teaching.

Hirst and Peters acknowledge that teaching is not essential to education but claim that serious miseducation may occur if too much emphasis is given to this. However, it may be that this is a point at which Rogers would diverge from Hirst and Peters. They certainly do appear to place much more emphasis on the role of the teacher than many of the learning theorists discussed earlier might wish to. Learning can and does occur without a teacher but teaching is one way in which learning is facilitated and many adult educators would claim that one of the teacher's fundamental aims should be to help the learner to become independent. Hence, it might be claimed that teaching is one of the few occupations whose aim should be to make the client independent of the practitioner, a slightly different approach to that of first school teachers who try to dissuade parents from teaching their children until they are sent to school!

Learning, then, is considered to be the most significant element in education and it will be recalled that the definition of education adopted in this study broadened it to an intended process of learning rather than restricted it to the transmission of culture. Hence the position adopted here is quite different from that proposed by Peters (1966:25) who argued that one of the criteria for education is that knowledge of a worthwhile nature is transmitted to the learner. Rather, the

113

humanistic basis of education adopted here places
the learner at the focal point and it is, therefore,
the relationship between conditions of learning and
approaches to teaching that occupies the first
section of this chapter. Thereafter, the processes
of teaching and teaching techniques are examined in
some detail.

CONDITIONS OF LEARNING AND APPROACHES TO TEACHING

In the previous two chapters a number of points have
been raised about how adults learn effectively and
it is now necessary to draw many of them together
and to relate them to various approaches to teaching.
Table 5.1 summarises many of these conclusions.

Table 5.1:   The Conditions of Adult Learning
and Approaches to Teaching

Conditions of Adult Learning	Approaches to Teaching
Learning is a basic human need	Teaching is not essential to learning but may facilitate it
Learning is especially motivated when there is disharmony between an individual's experience and his perception of the world	Teachers and learners need to structure the process of learning together so that it may be relevant to the experience/problem that created the felt need to learn
Adult learners like to participate in the learning process	Teaching methods should be socratic or facilitative rather than didactic in many learning situations
Adult learners bring their own: - experiences to the learning situations - meaning systems to the learning situation	Teachers should use these experiences as a learning resource Teachers should try to build upon the meaning system, rather than seek to be contrary to it, so that

Table 5.1 (continued)

Conditions of Adult Learning	Approaches to Teaching
- needs to the learning situation	students may integrate their new knowledge with their old: methods should be used that enables students to use their previous knowledge as a resource Teachers should help students to be aware of the relevance of what they are learning; subject matter will be 'applied' rather than pure: learning will be individualized where possible
Adult learners bring to the learning situation their own: - self-confidence	Teachers need to be empathetic and sensitive to the humanity of the learner at all times and, when appropriate, always anticipate a successful learning outcome
- self-esteem	Teachers should 're-inforce' all 'correct' knowledge and understanding in order that students are enabled to maintain a high level of self-confidence and self-esteem. Teachers should provide opportunities for adult students to reflect upon 'incorrect' knowledge, so that they can 'correct' it for themselves, where this is possible
- self-perception	Teachers should encourage self-assessment

Table 5.1 (continued)

Conditions of Adult Learning	Approaches to Teaching
	rather than teacher-assessment
Adults learn best when the self is not under threat	Teachers need to create an ethos in which no adult feels threatened or inhibited - this is especially true at the outset of any new course of learning. Co-operation rather than competition should be encouraged
Adult learners need to feel that they are treated as adults	Teachers should not regard themselves as 'the fount of all knowledge' but they should attempt to create and facilitate a teaching and learning engagement between all the participants
Adult learners have developed their own learning styles	Teachers should recognise that different learning styles exist and encourage learners to develop effective and efficient learning. Hence, teachers, also need to be flexible and adopt teaching styles relevant to the teaching and learning transaction
Adult learners have had different educational biographies so that they may learn at different speeds.	Teachers should encourage adults to learn at their own pace
Adults have developed a crystallized intelligence	Teachers should not be influenced by previous academic record, especially that from initial education
Adults bring	Teachers should ensure

Table 5.1 (continued)

Conditions of Adult Learning	Approaches to Teaching
different physio-logical con-ditions to the learning situa-tion eg. declin-ing visual and/ or audio accuity less energy, failing health,	that the physical environ-ment in which the teach-ing and learning occurs is conducive to adult learning

In the above table it may be seen that the approach-es to teaching that have been suggested do not act-ually specify a particular teaching method, only a perspective that should be adopted. Clearly, there-fore, it reflects an ideological position, but then the definition of education adopted earlier in this study was normative. Knowles (1978:77-9; 1980:57-8) has developed a similar approach within the con-text of his discussion about andragogy, which again indicates the validity of the accusation levelled at it by Day and Baskett as an ideological paradigm. If they are correct, then the position adopted here is ideologically similar to that of Knowles: that since education is a humanistic process then the humanity of the participants is paramount in the learning process. However, this differs from Rogers, since the purpose of education is regarded here as being to bring about learning, and the de-velopment of the individual should be viewed as an additional bonus to be gained from participation in education. What, therefore, is the relationship be-tween learning and teaching apparent in table 5.1? Perhaps it may best be summarised by suggesting that both the teacher's role performance and the teaching methods he employs should never undermine, but al-ways seek to enhance, the dignity and humanity of the learner: to do less than this is a misuse of the teacher's position, immoral and falls below the high ideals of education.

Whatever links are drawn between the conditions of learning and the approach to teaching it is clear that the teacher of adults does not always stand in front of the class and expound the wisdom that he considers the students need to know (see the

exercise in Rogers (1973:82-4). This is not to
claim that there is no place for didactic teaching
but it does suggest an approach to teaching in which
exposition is less significant than it often appears
to be in the education of children: the fact that
it occurs with children does not necessarily mean
that it is either the most efficient or human way of
facilitating their learning either! However, it is
clear that the teachers of adults, besides having
either the relevant knowledge or experience, require certain other characteristics in order to
help adults learn,including: knowledge of the educational process, appropriate philosophy and attitudes and teaching and personal skills. Hence, it
is rather surprising that the preparation of educators of adults has occupied such an insignificant
place in teacher education, but, since this is the
topic of a subsequent chapter, no further reference
will be made to it here.

Table 5.1 has not stipulated how the teacher
should perform his teaching role with adults but it
does imply that certain styles of teaching may be
more appropriate than others. Perhaps the most significant piece of research that has affected
thought about teaching styles is that developed by
Lippett and White (1958) in a project directed by
Kurt Lewin in the 1930s. They examined leadership
styles of youth leaders in youth clubs with ten
year old boys in the United States. Basically they
noticed three styles of leadership: authoritarian,
democratic and laissez-faire and discovered that
group behaviour tended to be consistent with leadership style. They found that: the authoritarian
leaders create a sense of group dependence on the
leader, that his presence held the group together
and that in his absence there was no work undertaken
and the group disintegrates; the laissez-faire
leadership results in little being done irrespective
of whether the leader was present or absent; the
democratic leader achieves group cohesion and harm-
onious working relationship whether, or not, he is
actually present. (Rogers 1977:84-6 contains a
summary of this research). However, there are a
number of problems in applying these findings to
adult groups or indeed, to any other teaching and
learning interactions: the subjects were children;
the location was a youth club; the task undertakne
by the groups was a specific type of craft work.
Even so, it may not be without significance that the
democratic style of leadership achieved the types of
results that it did.

In more recent years, and perhaps more significantly for educators of adults, McGregor's (1960) work has assumed greater importance. This stems from the field of management studies. According to McGregor, there are basically two approaches to managing people which he terms Theory X and Theory Y: the former assumes that the average human being dislikes work, needs to be controlled, directed or coerced in order to do what is required and that he prefers to be directed; the latter commences with the conception of the self-motivated adult who seeks to fulfil his own human potential. Hence, if the teacher starts with the perspective of Theory X he will seek to manipulate the students either by a hard approach of threats or a soft approach of rewards and permissiveness, but the teacher who adopts a perspective that derives from Theory Y will be more concerned about the potentiality and growth of the students even though he may vary his approach and teaching method to suit the situation.

Hence, it is evident that the democratic approach in the research of Lippett and White and the Theory Y perspective in McGregor's work are most consistent with the philosophy of this study and with the emerging picture of the educator of adults as one who seeks to aid adult learning and to develop the full potential of the learner. However, it must be borne in mind that neither of these approaches actually prescribe the manner in which a teacher should perform his role, although it does circumscribe the number of approaches that might be utilised. Perhaps, Kidd (1973:306-7) summarised this perspective most clearly when he, recognising that there are differences, pronounced his own decalogue for teachers of adults:

1. Thou shalt never try to make another human being exactly like thyself; one is enough
2. Thou shalt never judge a person's need, or refuse your consideration, soley because of the trouble he causes
3. Thou shalt not blame heredity nor the environment in general; people can surmount their environment (or perhaps some of their heredity) author's addition
4. Thou shalt never give a person up as hopeless or cast him out
5. Thou shalt try to help everyone become, on the one hand, sensitive and compassionate and also tough minded
6. Thou shalt not steal from any person his rightful responsibilities for determining

119

his own conduct and the consequences
thereof
7. Thou shalt honour anyone engaged in the
pursuit of learning and serve well and
extend the discipline of knowledge and
skill about learning which is our
common heritage
8. Thou shalt have no universal remedies nor
expect miracles
9. Thou shalt cherish a sense of humour which
may save you from becoming shocked,
depressed or complacent
10. Thou shalt remember the sacredness and
dignity of thy calling and, at the same
time, "thou shalt not take thyself too
damned seriously"

(Reprinted from *How Adults Learn* © 1973 J Roby Kidd
with the permission of the publishers, Cambridge
Book Company).

Roby Kidd's creed summarises much of the humanistic
philosophy explicit in this discussion. Having examined some of the approaches to teaching, it is now
necessary to explore the teaching process

THE PROCESS OF TEACHING
In contrast to initial education, adult education
has tended to emphasize the learner and learning
more than the teacher and teaching. Traditionally,
in initial education the teacher and his skills have
constituted a subject for discussion but rarely has
that discussion sought to elaborate upon the process
of teaching. Adult education has tended to regard
the teacher as an adjunct to learning, often necessary and frequently important, but never as
essential to it. Consequently, the process of adult
learning has been explored but rarely that of adult
teaching. Hence the focus of this section is upon
the teaching process in adult and continuing education. Three types of teaching were mentioned earlier, didactic, socratic and facilitative, and it is
necessary to recognise that they do have totally
different approaches. Initially, therefore, an
over-simplified model of didactic teaching is discussed. Thereafter, the socratic approach is mentioned and then the teacher-centred teaching process
is combined with the learning cycle. Finally, the
facilitative approach to teaching is discussed.

Didactic Teaching: Teaching has traditionally been regarded as the process of making a selection of

120

knowledge, skills etc. from the cultural milieu,
those aspects which 'it is intended that pupils should
learn' (Hirst and Peters 1970:80), and transmitting
it to them by the use of some skilled technique. It
has been assumed that such rewards as the teacher's
approval, good grades in assignments and success in
examinations (all forms of conditioning) would ensure that the pupil learned and was, therefore, able
to reproduce that selection of culture thereafter.

Figure 5.1:   A Stereotypical Picture
of Teaching

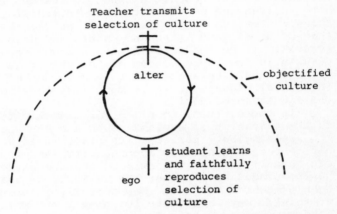

Figure 5.1, which is very similar to Figure 3.1,
locates the teaching process in the wider socio-
cultural milieu and it may be seen that the teacher
is the agency of transmission of a selection of
culture (a curriculum). That selection may have
been made by an examination board, an education
committee of a profession, or an acknowledged expert
in the field. The student is expected to learn that
which is transmitted to him and to be able to reproduce it, which may equate with the lower order of
Gagné's (1977) hierarchy of learning but it is
certainly no higher than the middle. In terms of
Bloom's (1956) taxonomy of educational objectives,
the student may be expected to have understood what
was transmitted to him and, perhaps, be able to
apply it but not necessarily to be able to analyse,
synthesize or evaluate it. In university education,
however, it might be argued that expectations are
higher than this, but Hegarty (1976.81) suggests
that legal education may 'easily degenerate into
mindless book learning ... any student of university

calibre could obtain a comfortable honours degree by doing little more than memorising the set text book in each subject and doing the occasional problem'. The extent to which Hegarty's assessment is applicable to all undergraduate courses is another matter, but it is doubtful if that assessment of legal education would be unique.

Not only does the level of learning not necessarily scale the heights of the learning hierarchies but the selection of what is to be learned is made by agencies other than the learner, so that the relevance to the learner of what is learned may often be reduced to the rather instrumental end of being successful in the assessment procedures, rather than being able to learn and understand something relevant to the learner. This approach frequently results in the reproduction of the status quo and while it could be argued that this is no bad thing in initial education, it is much less convincing in the education of adults.

Is there, then, no place for didactic teaching in the education of adults? Such a claim would be too sweeping but, perhaps, its place is less significant than generally accorded it. An exposition can actually transmit knowledge and the students may be encouraged to consider the validity of what has been presented to them; may actually provoke them to think; may facilitate learning; may motivate them to continue their learning, especially if it is superbly presented. Hence, a didactic approach may prove very useful, especially if the students are encouraged to analyse what is transmitted to them, rather than merely to reproduce it.

A variation on this theme is for the teacher to encourage the learners to ask questions, so that they actually initiate the learning process but the teacher still provides the answers. By adopting this approach the teacher had overcome one of the initial problems of didactic teaching, that it may not start from a diagnostic basis. Yet it is the teacher still who transmits knowledge and expects that his transmission will be received are learned by the students who are still the receptacles of knowledge, rather than the 'creators' of it. Frequently during the education of adults, students ask questions that the teacher is unable to answer, so that the teacher has to discover that he can confess his ignorance to them without losing his credibility with them. Indeed, it is possible to argue that a display of fallibility may help to establish the teacher's position in the group, both as

122

a teacher and as a human being. After all, why
should the teacher know everything? No other profession expects its members to be omniscient! Many
conscientious teachers, having admitted that they
are unable to respond to the question, ask the class
if anybody in it is able to answer. Here the experience and expertise of the group can be put to
good use and the teacher can learn from the class as
well as contribute to the group's learning. However,
many very conscientious teachers when confronted
with a question that they cannot answer tell the
group that they will go and find out the answer.
This they do, and they inform the students on a
future occasion. A certain irony emerges in this
situation: the student's question has revealed a
teacher's ignorance. The teacher is made aware of a
learning need and goes and learns, so that he can
provide the students with an answer. Examine closely what has occurred. The students asked a question
which the teacher could not answer, so he went and
discovered an answer for the students. In short, the
student's question facilitated the teacher's learning! But what did the teacher do for the student's
learning? The teacher merely made the students more
dependent upon him, but the teacher actually became
a more independent learner. Two points emerge from
this: firstly, perhaps the teacher should encourage
the students to seek an answer as well as doing it
for himself; secondly, it is the questionning process that facilitates independent learning and so,
perhaps, a good teacher leads his students from
question to question rather than from answer to answer. After all, that is how the learning need becomes apparent in children, as it has been argued in
earlier chapters, and it is also a way that effective learning may be facilitated with adults.

Socratic Teaching: This method incorporates questioning into the teaching and learning process; it consists of the teacher directing a logical sequence of
questions at the learners, so that they are enabled
to respond and to express the knowledge that they
have, albeit implicitly, but which they have never
crystallized in their own mind. However, unless the
teacher is actually skilful in his use of questions
and also perceptive in his response to the students,
this approach is still likely to result in an expression of knowledge reflecting the accepted body of
cultural knowledge and, therefore, a type of conformity. The reason for this is that the method assumes
that the learners have internalized a great deal of

123

cultural knowledge during their socialization, which itself is a conformity producing process. The questioner then utilises questions in order to help the learner to respond and express ideas and knowledge which he may have implicitly but which he may never have articulated; it is, therefore, partly a formalization of the externalization process, depicted in Figure 1.2. However, conformity to and expression of the established body of knowledge is by no means wrong, so that it is a useful method to empoly, especially in teaching adults since it utilises both their store of knowledge and their experience of life, which are quite essential learning resources in the education of adults. However, it must also be noted that if this method is used with great skill it can and does help the learners "create" rather than reproduce knowledge. Another advantage to its use is that the learners are always actively involved in the learning process.

A Learning and Teaching Cycle: The above discussion indicates that the teacher often plays the role of an agent in the transmission of the culture of a society in the formal educational process, even in the education of adults. However, it is clear that Figure 5.1 does not really discuss the actual process of teaching and learning, so that it is now important to draw together some of the conclusions about adult learning and these observations on teacher-centred teaching: Figure 5.2 suggests a learning and teaching cycle in which these are combined.

Figure 5.2:   A Learning and
Teaching Cycle

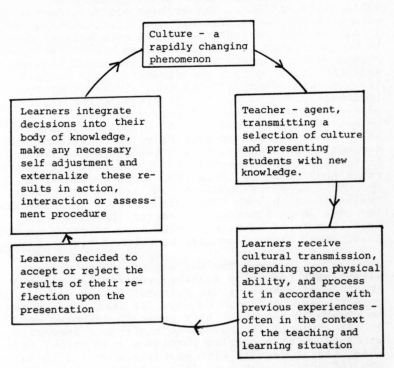

It may be seen in the above diagram that the teacher
is an agent transmitting a selection of culture to
the learner(s) and, at the same time, the teacher
may have devised   methods whereby the student may
have opportunity to reflect upon it through discussion group, tutorial or written assignment, etc.
Thus the process of reflection may be regarded as an
integral part of the learning and teaching cycle.
However, it must be borne in mind that unless the
opportunity for reflection on the knowledge and
ideas that are presented by the teacher occurs individually, the decision that a person may be influenced by the dynamics of the learning group and considerable research exists to show that group pressure results in conformity in many situations. (eg.
Krech, Crutchfield and Ballachey 1962: 507-515).

However, the process of selecting that aspect
of culture to be transmitted is itself an important
one, but it is sometimes omitted as a phase in these
considerations. Some teachers merely take for

granted that they will seek to transmit all the knowledge, etc. that the examination board or syllabus, specifies. Yet if teachers see themselves as agents for the transmission of cultural knowledge, it may be that they should become more active agents in deciding what they should transmit and that this should also be determined by the amount of knowledge and understanding that the student brings to the teaching and learning situation. It is, therefore, incumbent upon the teacher to diagnose the student's level of knowledge and, thereby, his learning needs, before he actually endeavours to teach anything at all. Diagnosis is, consequently, an intrinsic element in the selection of knowledge to be transmitted and this is especially significant with adults since they bring to their learning a considerable amount of previous knowledge and skill, etc. That adults do bring such resources to their learning has led some adult educators to regard themselves as facilitators of learning rather than teachers in the traditional sense discussed here.

Facilitative Teaching: The teacher of adults may not always want to employ teacher - centred techniques in the performance of his role but he may wish to be more student-centred. He may, for instance: seek to create an awareness of a specific learning need in the student; endeavour to confront a student, or students, with a problem requiring a solution; provide the student(s) with an experience and encourage reflection upon it. In all of these instances the outcome of the activity should be that learning has occurred, but the teacher has performed his role differently: he has facilitated learning. Hence, it is possible to reconstruct the experiential learning cycle discussed in the third chapter in order to incorporate the teacher's role in the process.

Figure 5.3 : A Facilitative Learning
and Teaching Cycle

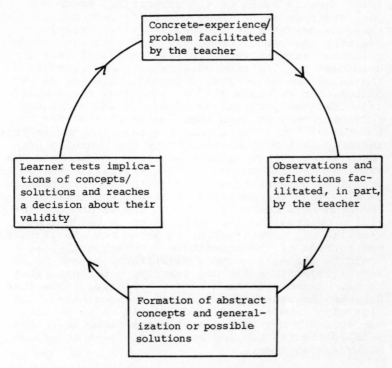

It may be seen from the above diagram that the
teacher can create the situation in which the learning cycle is activated and, additionally, he may
help in the process of observing or reflecting. But
should he actually influence the process in this way?
Dewey (1938:71), suggests that, with children, the
teacher should be involved:

> Sometimes teachers seem to be afraid even to
> make suggestions to members of the group as
> to what they should do. I have heard of cases
> in which children are surrounded with objects
> and materials and then left entirely to them-
> selves, the teacher being loath to suggest
> even what might be done with the materials
> lest freedom be impinged upon.

Dewey goes on to warn of the opposite extreme: of
the teacher who abuses his office and who channels
children's work along the paths that suit the

127

teacher's purposes rather than those of the children themselves. He maintains that teachers should be intelligently aware of the capacities, needs and past experiences of those under instruction, so that they may assist them in creating a co-operative learning exercise. Obviously Dewey was writing about children learning in a progressive educational environment but the same observations are relevant to the education of adults. Indeed, it might be recalled that McKenzie (1979) recognised the similarities between progressive education and andragogy.

Thus it may be seen that the teacher's role may be that of facilitator and/or guide, but not in this instance that of the director of the learning process, since that would detract from the adult's own autonomy and independence. (See Williams, 1980 for a practical outworking of some of the ideas presented here). Thus the facilitator is one who assists in the student's learning, even to the extent of providing or creating the environment in which that learning may occur, but he is never one who dictates the outcome of the experience. Consequently, it would be impossible for a facilitator to set behavioural objectives for any learning experience that he may create, although he may have expressive ones. Because the learning experience is open-ended, facilitation is often a difficult role to play since the learners may reach conclusions other than those held by the teacher and he must not seek to impose his views on them.

It should be noted in the two diagrams constructed in this section that the teacher has a role in the early stages of the teaching and learning cycle but that, since the teacher cannot make any individual learn and since one of the aims of adult education is the creation of the autonomous learner, the teacher plays little part in the final stages. Even in distance learning, where adults meet with a tutor for an occasional tutorial after having learned from the teaching material, the teaching and learning cycle is only recreated with the students bringing more of their own learning from the initial stages. However, it might be objected that even in these two diagrams the teacher's involvement in the learning process, even as facilitator, inhibits the student's freedom to learn. But, it may be asked, what is freedom in this context? Boud and Bridge (1974:6), for instance, distinguish four types of freedom: pace, choice, method and content. By this they mean that students should be free to work at their own speed, choose to study particular aspects of a course, adopt whatever learning style that suits them best and be free to choose what to learn. More recently, Boud, Bridge and Willoughby (1975:18) modified this slightly and they suggest that the four types of freedom are: pace, method, content and assessment.

Clearly the traditional teaching role does not seem to fit easily into the teaching and learning process for adults if these freedoms are considered an important element in it and class teaching seems to recede into the background. Indeed, one of the outcomes appears to be an individualised or small group approach in which the participants are engaged in the pursuit of knowledge that is relevant to their own problems or experiences. Certainly, the class as a whole is perhaps a little less significant in this approach, small group learning is frequently undertaken in adult education and individualised learning has been developed in both adult basic education and in higher education. Considerable research has been conducted into individualised learning and although it appears to have an idealistic perspective, Crane (1982:33) notes that:

> Unexpectedly perhaps, in view of the persuasive role played by committed Romantics in decrying the old and urging a renewed concern for the individual and individual differences, it was largely men with behaviourist training and outlook who actually produced innovations of value.

Certainly the group/class versus the individual is one of the problems that emerges logically from any analysis of this type of teaching and learning. Each student's learning must be regarded as his own, so that the teaching and learning cycle must ultimately relate to the individual, although this does not preclude the teacher interacting with the learner(s) during the learning.

The focus of this section has been upon the teaching process and three types of teaching has been discussed: didactic, socratic and facilitative. These may be seen as being either teacher-centred or student-centred and it has been suggested that those approaches that are extremely teacher-centred may be inappropriate for some education of adults. However, the actual teaching methods remain undiscussed, so that they are now examined.

TEACHING METHODS

It is impossible in the space available in this section to elaborate adequately upon every aspect of each teaching method that can be employed in the education of adults, so that it is intended only to highlight the variety of approaches that can be used. Since there are such a wide range of different methods it is initially necessary to classify them for the purposes of discussion. Chadwick (personal communication) has suggested that one approach would be to consider the three modes of search, interactive, and presentational. While this is a very attractive form of classification, it might be more consistent here if the division between tutor-centred and student-centred approaches is maintained. However, it must be borne in mind that a variety of methods might be employed in any single teaching and learning process and that it might be more stimulating to the learner if such an approach were to be adopted.

Teacher-Centred Methods: Before individual methods are itemised, it is necessary to recognise that the tutor may lead a session and still adopt two basically different approaches: he might be didactic and teach the subject in the traditional method of providing the information or he might be socratic and seek to elicit the information from the students by careful questioning. The art of questioning is a technique that teachers should acquire, so that they are aware of how to gain the most effective response from the learners but, frequently, it appears to be assumed that this is a skill that teachers have either naturally or as a result of their socialization process. However, this assumption may be false and it may be a skill that needs to be taught.

Six frequently employed teacher-centred methods are discussed in this sub-section: demonstration, guided discussion, controlled discussion, lecture-discussion, lecture/talk/speech and the tutorial.

The Demonstration: This is one of the most frequent approaches to skills teaching. The teacher shows the student(s) how a specific procedure is undertaken and then they are expected to emulate the teacher. However, the demonstrator is usually very skilled so that his performance appears easy and effortless. But if the students are unable to repeat the same skill with the same fluency they may become discouraged. Perhaps this is because the

teacher may not have analysed his own techniques
sufficiently in order to be aware of all the minut-
iae of correct procedures that combine to produce
effortless action. Belbin and Belbin (1972:44-5),
suggest that if a skill is broken down into a number
of discrete stages and that in both the demonstration and in the subsequent practice sessions, each
sequence is initially performed slowly it is possible for learners to acquire new skills fairly
rapidly. They (1972:44) recognise that 'it takes
time for someone who hitherto has been pressed to-
ward greater speed, to accept that a really slow
performance is .... required'.

Additionally, it needs to be recognised that a
possible danger in the teacher acting as a role
model is that he may transmit any imperfections in his
performance to his students and that they may not
have the opportunity to be exposed to an even more
accurate performance of the skill that they are en-
deavouring to acquire.

Guided Discussion: This approach has been separated
from the more general discussion techniques because
it is one of the approaches that epitomises the
socratic method: it is sometimes called step-by-
step discussion. In this approach the teacher has a
carefully prepared sequence of questions that are
directed towards the end of drawing from the learners the knowledge that they have implicitly but
which they may not have articulated, crystallised or
related to a wider theoretical perspective. It is a
method that can be employed to elicit from students their
own understanding of experiences that they have undergone. For instance, a teacher of theory may endeavour to draw from the students their understanding
of some elements of a practical work experience in
which they have already participated as part of their
vocational education. However, the teacher should
be careful not to artificialise the approach by being
inflexible, since the student's responses may actually direct the discussion along paths other than
those planned by the teacher. If this is so, it
might be wise for the teacher to follow the students'
lead and redirect his questions, although it must be
borne in mind that there are times when the teacher
has to ensure that the steps he has prepared should
be followed. While this method sometimes appears
simple and easy to prepare, it is one that requires
confidence in the teacher as well as a great deal of
knowledge and preparation.

Controlled Discussion: By contrast to guided discussion, controlled discussion is quite didactic and
much closer to the next method to be examined. In
this approach the teacher sets the theme for the
class and begins to talk about it but the students
are encouraged to contribute to the learning process
or to elicit information. However, the teacher is
still at the centre of the scene and most of the
questions or comments are directed at him rather
than at other members of the class and one of the
problems in this approach is that there is a tendency for only the dominant or the confident to in-
terject so that the learning needs of the silent
members of the group may not be met. If the teacher
wants the learners to address each other he has to
ensure that the environment is arranged so that he
has no dominant seat etc. and that the learners
have eye-contact with each other. Hence, he must
arrange the seating in a circular formation (with or
without desks). It is difficult sometimes for a
teacher to change the seating arrangements of a room
especially if he arrives after many of the students,
so that it is often wise to arrange with a caretaker
to have the room arranged in the required manner in
advance. If this is impossible, it is useful to
explain to adult students why the room should be re-
arranged and, in the majority of instances, they will
undertake the task themselves.

Lecture-Discussion: The lecture-discussion is very
similar to the previous method mentioned but it may
assume a different form: a short lecture/address
followed by discussion. Once again, however, it is
self-evident that the teacher controls both the
learning process and its content. By contrast to
the previous method, the teacher has a larger initial input rather than merely focusing on the topic
to be discussed, so that the discussion may tend to
develop or to endeavour to demonstrate the weaknesses in the position taken in the lecture. It is
worth remembering that unless the content of the
lecture is controversial or provocative then the
discussion may not be particularly valuable since it
may merely rehearse the arguments previously presented.

     All forms of discussion require careful prep-
aration on the part of the teacher and a willingness
to endure silence by the class especially during the
early part of the discussion. It is a common fail-
ing to try to prompt the class to talk by too much
early tutor intervention. Confident and talkative

132

adults are, consequently useful allies during early
phases of a discussion session but then it may be
necessary for the teacher to draw other people into
the debate and help the talkative members of the
group to contribute a little less. It is, however,
part of the human process that the teacher should
facilitate both of these aspects without injuring the
self-esteem of any of the class members, so that it
is often unwise even to ask individuals directly
either to participate or to contribute a little less
to the discussion. Hence, the social skills of the
teacher are as important to the teaching and learning process as are his knowledge and his teaching
techniques. (Legge 1971a).

Lecture: Lecturing is perhaps the most frequently employed teaching technique despite all the
criticisms that have been levelled against it at
various times. Bergevin et al (1963:157) define the
speech, or lecture, as 'a carefully prepared oral
presentation of a subject by a qualified person'.
However, many students know to their cost that lectures are not necessarily carefully prepared on all
occasions prior to delivery, nor is the presentation
always given by a qualified person. Hence, this is
more of a description of an ideal type rather than a
definition of the lecture, so that it may be more
accurately defined as 'an oral presentation of a
subject', although this still leaves the definition
of 'subject' open to question. Thus far the distinction between lecture, speech and talk has not been
raised but it is significant to note that Beard
(1976) discusses the lecture in her work on higher
education but neither Bergevin et al (1963) nor
Legge (1971a) concentrate upon it a great deal, preferring to use the other terms, and they are more
concerned with teaching adults. This reflects a
little of the conceptual problems of the second
chapter but higher education has traditionally been
discussed separately to the education of adults,
despite the fact that students in higher education
are adults. It is maintained here that this sep-
aration has been to the detriment of higher education. Bergevin et al clearly regard the speech as a
rather formal presentation while Legge's orientation
towards non-examinable liberal adult education enables him to focus upon the less formal concept of
the 'talk'.
      Many criticisms have been levelled at this
particular approach to teaching but, despite these,
nearly all teachers continue to use the lecture

133

method. Perhaps it is important to put the lecture in perspective and Bligh (1971:4) summarises the research on this topic when he argues that:

> (1) with the exception of programmed learning, the lecture is as effective as any other method of transmitting information, but not more effective; (2) most lectures are not as effective as more active methods for the promotion of thought; and (3) changing student attitudes should not normally be the major objective of the lecture.

Thus it may be seen that only in the transmission of information is the lecture as effective as other methods of teaching and then it must be borne in mind that most of this research was not conducted with adult students. However, Davies (1971:163) claims that the lecture is a useful teaching method with less able adult students. Yet adult basic education has tended not to employ the lecture approach in teaching, so that this raises questions about his claim. Hence, it is necessary to pursue this point because if the lecture is no more effective than a variety of other teaching techniques, why is it so frequently employed? This question certainly requires consideration at this point in the discussion.

It might be argued that since many educators of adults are not actually trained to perform the teaching role they do not have evidence of the effectiveness of other approaches, or that they do not know how to teach apart from the lecture, or that they do not have the confidence to attempt other approaches. This may be an argument for introducing more teacher training into the education of adults, a point that will be developed in a subsequent chapter. Additionally, it is clear that because students are familiar with this approach to teaching, or because, it means that some of them may be passive learners, they prefer this approach. But these may be quite superficial and even wrong reasons: students may put pressure on a teacher to give a lecture because they may not want to reveal their level of knowledge or understanding of a topic and they may feel threatened if they think that their lack of comprehension will become apparent for others to see. Teachers, or at least some tutors, may also obtain satisfaction from having given a "good" performance, as they may simply like it because it enables them to control the content of the session in such a way as to ensure that any gaps in their own knowledge may not become apparent, which might occur if the students directed the session. The maxim 'if you don't know a subject well lecture it' is perhaps a reflection of a teacher's sense of insecurity, especially before a class of adults. Programme planners also like the lecture method because of the ease of timetabling and room planning.

In addition, it might be argued that the lecture can be an instrument of motivation and it may be true that the superb lecture may actually produce this result but, perhaps, few teachers actually possess such oratorial skills, so that Legge's (1971:57) ironic comment that 'the really hopeless teacher, ie. the one who fails to communicate at all, drives the good student to the library to do the work for himself' may be closer to the real situation! Lectures, it has been claimed (eg. Beard 1976:101; Legge 1971a), may be economical in teaching many students at the same time and ensuring that the whole syllabus is covered. While there may be some truth in these claims, it must be recognised that covering the syllabus without ensuring that the students learn it is far from efficient (Bligh 1971: 3) and, since there is evidence to show that the level of concentration varies at different phases of the lecture (Legge, 1971a), it is difficult to ensure that learning actually occurs during the presentation. Additionally, individual learning needs may not be catered for and unless the learners have opportunity to question the lecturer they may never actually interact with him. Even if they are provided with the time to raise queries, individual students may not do so because they may not wish to reveal their ignorance nor wish to hinder the remainder of the group. If a student does interrupt the speaker with questions, the rest of the class may become frustrated while these are answered. This is a dilemma that is intrinsic to the lecture method and it appears to have no resolution that would result in effective learning from every participant. The lecturer may seek to resolve the problems by not taking any questions but this may result in reduced learning efficiency. But even if questions occur they may interrupt the thought processes of other learners, who may then lose the flow of ideas with which they were grappling. Thus it may be seen that many unresolved problems surround this approach.

Where the lecture method is employed there are a number of errors in techniques that should be avoided: the conscientious lecturer may prepare too

135

much material for the time he has available but still
endeavour to complete his self-appointed task by
speeding up his presentation, so that he actually
delivers it all but to the detriment of the learner.
Hence, out of the best intentions the lecturer may
hinder rather than help learning. Additionally, the
lecturer may be bound to his notes, even to reading
them, so that he achieves little eye-contact with
the class which results in his being unable to detect and respond to any of the students' manifest
learning needs. Hence, it may be wise for the
teacher to reduce his volume of notes, even to head-
ings, sub-headings and references in order to ensure
that he has both contact and fluency of delivery.
In a similar manner a teacher may wish to illustrate
a point by writing on the blackboard, but if he continues to speak whilst he has his back to the class
some adult learners, especially those with deficient
hearing may be unable to follow every word. This
is also true when a lecturer, who is not bound to
his notes, wonders around the room while he is
speaking. Since the lecture has to be prepared before its presentation, it may not always be sufficiently appropriate or relevant to the learning needs
of all the students and it may prove difficult for
the lecturer to adjust the content of the presentation to the needs of the learners during the actual
lecture. Finally, the lecture may not provide
sufficient opportunity for the adult students to remember and internalise all the ideas presented,
neither may they always have the opportunity to reflect upon the knowledge transmitted after the presentation. Hence, it is useful to provide the opportunity for group discussion or question and
answer during the session, or for a handout to be
distributed at the end of the session, in order to
help adult students memorize ideas, etc. Finally,
other forms of audio-visual stimuli may also be useful in helping students recall the information and
ideas with which they have been presented.
     Having raised a number of critical points
about the lecture, it must still be recognised that
it is a useful teaching tool, especially when it is
well used, but only for the transmission of knowledge. However, it should perhaps be employed a
little less frequently than it is at present and
used only by those trained in its use rather than
its being the basic technique used by those who are
employed to transmit ideas to others.

The Tutorial: This teaching method is more likely

to occur within the formal system of education
rather than in liberal adult education. However, it
might be possible to classify some small classes in
the latter as group tutorials. In addition, it must
be remembered that in the university extension tradition a three year course is referred to as a tutorial. But the normal use of the word refers to a
teaching and learning method and, according to
Davies (1971:167-8), there are three basic types:
supervision, group and practical. The first type
involves a student and a tutor and the former is
often expected to read a prepared piece of work to
the latter and then to defend the argument in the
ensuing discussion. This is quite normal practice
at Oxford and Cambridge universities, but since it
is labour-intensive it is not so widely practised
elsewhere. Another similar use of this type of
tutorial is for the student and tutor to meet after
the latter has marked an assignment by the student
and then the student may seek to clarify his argument or challenge the tutor's assessment grade,
while the tutor may seek to explain his comments,
point out ways in which the work might have been
improved and, even, to defend the grade that he has
awarded. By contrast, group tutorials employ one
tutor to a number of students. Davies (1971:134-5),
argues that the optimum number in the group depends
on the ability of the tutor rather than a figure
beyond which the group cannot function. Nevertheless, he suggests that six or seven is probably
sufficient because of the number of possible relationships that can exist between the students.
Practical tutorials may be either individual or
group and are often based in a laboratory, gym-
nasium, workplace, etc. In all of these tutorials,
the tutor's role may be either didactic or socratic,
although it may result in a more effective tutorial
if the latter approach is adopted. Apart from
teaching style, it must also be stressed that the
tutorial requires a tutor who is trained and sensitive in the processes of human relations, and in
the group tutorial, the tutor should have some understanding of the group dynamics, or else the
tutorial may fail as a teaching method.

Thus far all the teaching methods examined have been
tutor-centred, but in the education of adults the
tutor should play a less dominant role than that
generally assumed by the teacher, so that is is now
necessary to discuss these teaching methods in which
the tutor also acts as facilitator.

Student-Centred Group Methods: In this section student-centred teaching methods are considered, demonstrating throughout the discussion that since the students referred to here are adults each brings to the teaching and learning situation a vast and unique experience of life. This is a major resource as was shown previously, since they have knowledge, reflections upon their experiences and an interpretation of meaning and purpose of life for them. Peer teaching is not, therefore, necessarily 'the blind leading the blind' as some people have claimed since it can be an approach that capitilises on the resources of the learners themselves, although it has to be borne in mind that there may be technical knowledge, etc. that none of the members of a group possess and then the teacher may have a more didactic role. Generally, however, in student-centred teaching the teacher is a facilitator of the learning rather than a source of knowledge and while he is responsible for creating the learning situation he does not control the learning outcomes. Indeed, if he ever does this, he may actually be involved in indoctrination rather than education.

There are many different methods of teaching that might have been incorporated in this section but to discuss them all in detail would require a whole book, so that fourteen different approaches have been selected here because they are frequently used, or have the potential for future use. Even so, the list does not purport to be exhaustive, but it is: brainstorming; buzz-groups; debate; discussion groups, interview, listenting and observing; panel; projects and case studies; role play, simulation and games; seminar; snowballing; therapy groups; visits and study tours; workshops.

Brainstorming: Bergevin et al (1963:195-6) call this an 'idea inventory'. It is an intensive discussion situation in which the quantity of ideas produced, or potential solutions are offered to a problem, is more important than the quality. All the points made by the participants are recorded over the period of time mutually agreed by the group for the brainstorming to operate. No group member may criticise any idea or suggested solution during this period, irrespective of how strange or ludicrous it might appear, since this might create inhibitions in the learners contributing to the inventory. At the close of the agreed period, the group is free to analyse the points raised and to arrive at a consensus, if possible, about potential courses of action or solutions to the problem under scrutiny. Clearly this approach is an aid to creative thinking in decision making or problem solving but Davies (1971:170) reports one study that raises questions about the effectiveness of this method since, it is claimed, that the notion of expressing 'all ideas may have a deleterious effect on the group members'. By contrast, he reports another in which many good quality ideas were produced, suggesting that some of the claims made for it are valid. The construction of a list of ideas, or possible solutions, may be seen as the initial stage in the facilitative learning and teaching cycle (Figure 5.3) and the next phase in the process is that of observing and reflecting upon the outcome of the first one. Since this is true of many of the methods discussed in this section no further reference is made to the theoretical perspectives outlined initially.

Buzz-Groups: In many ways these are similar to the previous method, but in this approach smaller groups, usually between two and six members, are used for a short period of time during the process of a lesson in order to discuss a particular item or topic. Small groups encourage participation by all members of the class, and may help in the process of reflection. It is often a useful technique to use in conjunction with a lecture, especially to help divide the session and retain student concentration.

Debate: This is a more formal approach to teaching and learning and one that is not used so frequently in adult education although it is often regarded by students in higher education as an enjoyable leisure time pursuit. Nevertheless, Legge (1971b:87) claims that the debate is a useful method of presenting students with sharply contrasting viewpoints and demonstrating how these different opinions can be analysed and assessed. In addition, he points out that because the debate is a staged performance it provides certain protection for the point of view expressed by the participants, even though there may be quite fierce denunciation of it. Even so, Legge suggests that opinions may be modified as a result of reflecting upon the arguments presented during the performance.

Group Discussion: Discussion re-occurs on the list because it is one of the most frequently employed teaching methods in the education of adults. Many

aspects of group discussion exist, all of which
could have been covered separately. Bligh (1971:126)
mentions *free-group discussion*, which he defines as 'a
learning situation in which the topic and direction
are controlled by the student-group' and which the
teacher may, or may not, observe. He suggests that
this is a useful method in which attitude change may
be produced in the participants. It may also enhance human relations, self-awareness and create a
willingness to consider new ideas. But if the group
fails to function smoothly these positive gains may
not be achieved and problems of human relations etc.
may arise, which the teacher should not ignore. In
contrast to this, there is *problem centred discussion*,
in which the group has a task to perform which may
have been set by the tutor. The outcome of this
approach may be enhanced analytical thinking, ability
to make decisions and to evaluate them.

Bergevin et al (1963:95) claim that a good discussion topic should meet four criteria, it must:
interest all group members; be possible for participants to acquire sufficient information to discuss it meaningfully; be clearly worded and understood; suggest alternative points of view. These
criteria are a useful guide since adult students
may opt out of the discussion if it is not of interest or relevance to them, or if they do not think
that they have anything to contribute to or learn
from the discussion. Hence, it is important for the
teacher to pick discussion topics with care and to
do so in conjunction with the students. Although
discussion groups are frequently organized in adult
teaching there are a number of weaknesses in the
approach: the topic may not be suitable or relevant;
the end-product may not be regarded as useful; the
technique relies heavily on the ability of the participants to articulate and to listen to each other;
dominant personalities tend to come to the fore and
quiet people remain passive. By contrast, there are
a number of strengths in this method: it encourages
learners to accept responsibility for their own
learning; it facilitates group sharing; it assists
individuals to develop a sense of teamwork; it helps
people develop a sense of self-confidence. Legge
(1971:78) claims that many 'of the weaknesses of
discussion as an aid to learning .... result from
the failure of the teacher to use the method with
skill and the failure of the students to take the
role of good discussion group members'. Hence, it
is incumbent upon the teacher to insure that he
understands the technique and is aware of group

dynamics, so that he is able to help students prepare both for the role that they play and the reasons
why this method is used in adult teaching. Perhaps
teachers are less prone to inform students about why
specific teaching methods are being used than they
ought to be, especially since the students are
adults.

Interview: The interview, sometimes called a witness session, is not employed quite so frequently
within the education of adults as it might be but
it is a technique with considerable potentiality. In
this instance, the resource person is the subject to
be interviewed, so that both the topic and often
some of the questions are prepared in advance. However, it is not a scripted exercise since this would
result in an artificial situation. The aim of the
technique is for the interviewer to elicit information from the resource person by means of the questions that the learners want answered. Hence, the
students often prepare the questions for, and
submit them to the interviewer in advance, so that
the session is relevant to their interests and learning needs. This approach may help clarify issues,
provide information, explore and analyse problems
and even to stimulate an interest in a topic.
Advantages of the use of this method include: helping the resource person to communicate his knowledge
without having to present a lecture; helping him to
articulate his idea in response to direct and relevant questions; it is relatively easy to employ; it
helps the less dominant members of the group because
they are enabled to submit their questions before
the session. It is a technique that might be used
more often when visiting specialists are not trained
educators, but it must be borne in mind that the resource person need not be a visitor and it might
even be one of the members of the class who has
specific specialist knowledge that the remainder of
the group consider relevant or interesting to them.
However, the interview does not allow for detailed
presentation of an argument and much of the success
of the session depends upon the skill of the interviewer. If the latter talks too much, is unable to
modify his approach or cannot stimulate the learners
then the interview may fail through no fault of the
resource person.

Listening and Observing: This is a group technique
which is designed to promote active listening and
observing during a lecture, speech or film, etc.

Each group, or each person in a group, is given a
specific task to undertake, eg. one group may be
given the job of listening for bias during a lecture
while another is expected to assess the relevance of
the presentation for a specific category of learners.
Once the presentation is complete the group members
confer amongst themselves and reach decisions that
are then reported back to a *plenary session*. Plenary
sessions are themselves teaching and learning
periods and, in some instances, they are similar to
what Bergevin et al (1963:83) call a *forum*. Listening and observing has the advantages of encouraging
active listening or active observation and then of
helping students crystallise their ideas about the
presentation, but it may have the disadvantage of
the students missing other elements of the presentation because they have concentrated upon the task
that they undertook to the exclusion of all else.

Panel: Like the interview the panel can utilise
both the experience and expertise of visitors to the
group or it may use the class members themselves.
The panel may be established with a number of
slightly different approaches: each member can de-
liver a short address to the whole group and at the
end of three or four talks there can be a period of
questions and answers; the panel members can discuss
aloud a specific topic for a specified length of
time while the class listens to their deliberations
and then the class may be invited to raise questions;
the discussion between panel members might occupy
the whole time; a panel might be set up merely to
respond to the questions of the class, without an
initial input or stimulus but, in this instance, a
considerable amount of preparation is necessary beforehand in order to ensure that the questions are
forthcoming. The panel technique may be utilised in
order to present opposing views on a topic and to
create a wider understanding of the subject. As a
method, it is useful in stimulating interest and
demonstrating to a class the validity of opposing
perspectives. By contrast, it has a number of
difficulties: the chairman needs to be proficient
in the arts of chairmanship if the session is to be
successful; the class might have to undertake considerable preparation beforehand in order to familiarise themselves with the complexities of some of
the arguments; class members should have sufficient confidence to pose questions, since there is a
tendency to consider that students' queries are not
worthy of an expert's consideration. However, if

these problems can be surmounted successfully the
panel session can be both a stimulating and relevant
teaching and learning method.

Projects and Case Studies: While these approaches
are frequently employed in the education
of adults, it is widely recognised that they are
difficult techniques to use in courses which are
assessed, since grades are generally awarded to individuals. Yet they do incorporate the highest
level in Gagné's hierarchy of learning, so that they
are techniques that should be encouraged. There are
some notable examples in liberal adult education of
group projects. Coates and Silburn (1967) conducted,
with their class, a sociological study of a deprived
area of Nottingham and after three years of research
they had gathered enough data to write a book that
was subsequently published. During the course of the
project the students gained considerable knowledge
of the discipline, of the area of Nottingham in
which the research was conducted, of the social and
political processes of society and of research
methods. Such approaches do not have to be restricted to the social sciences for it would be just as
possible to undertake such work with the environ-
mental, health and natural sciences. Fletcher (1980)
regards community studies, such as that conducted by
Coates and Silburn, as a form of practical adult
education, but it must be recognised that if a class
makes discoveries about a community it might want to
use the results in an active manner thereafter.
Tutors mounting such project type courses should be
aware before they commence, that this is a possible
outcome of studies of this nature. Case studies are
very similar to group projects but the group may
seek to focus upon a specific phenomenon and in this
instance it may incorporate a multi-discipline perspective. Group projects and case studies can,
therefore, assume an exciting and innovative ethos,
in which the class learn by doing and then use the
results in a practical manner. However, the
attrition rate from such classes may be greater than
average, especially if the activity becomes politically orientated in the community but more research
into this is necessary.

Role Play, Simulation and Gaming: These are other
approaches to teaching in which the student group
activly participates and they are included together
in this section because of their similarities but
discussed separately for the sake of convenience.

Role play is similar to psychodrama and socio-drama but it has educational rather than therapeutic aims. It can be employed when a tutor wishes students to experience something about which they are cognitively aware. However, it must be recog-nised at the outset that it is an approach that has difficulties, so that it should not be used care-lessly or thoughtlessly. It should be used natur-ally and students should feel that what they are doing fits logically into a planned learning sequence. Rogers and Lovell (Rogers 1973:78), state that it 'often makes for a smooth, easy introduction to the techniques if at first role playing is done by the teacher,' so that the students see the sig-nificance of what they are undertaking. Usually role playing is a brief episode acted from someone else's life or from the role for which an individual is being prepared. Hence, in vocational education it is possible to devise many learning situations in which role play would be a most natural method to employ and when this has been done with adult stud-ents they are often most positive about the use of the techniques. Stock (1971:93) suggests that role play encourages active participation, enables prob-lems of human behaviour and relationships to be pre-sented and extends the cognitive into the emotional. Rogers and Lovell (Rogers 1973:77-8), also indicate that students of any ability can be involved, that this approach helps to break down social barriers in the class, motivates students to learn more, tele-scopes time so that a longer procedure may be enact-ed in a brief period and that it may be therapeutic. Hence, it is clear that the approach has much to commend it, especially in the education of people who are socially mature enough to participate ser-iously and then willing to reflect and to learn from their experiences. However, it is widely recognised that some students may feel reluctant to participate and it is wise for the teacher to leave them to re-spond to the situation in whatever way they wish, so that they will not feel over-embarassed by it. Additionally, the technique has other disadvantages: there are difficulties relating role play to reality in some instances; role-play cannot be predicted precisely, so that the learning outcomes will vary with the role players; it may be time-consuming in preparation: it is hard to evaluate its effective-ness; it may create crises in individuals to which the teacher, if he is not a trained counsellor, may be unable to respond competently. However, in order to help overcome this last potential problem, there should always be a period of debriefing afterwards, during which students can re-adjust to their normal situation and, obviously, the more the emotional involvement demanded by the role play the greater the need for a debriefing period. Indeed, if teachers do not provide it they may discover that adult students request it. Such a period also provides opportunity to reflect upon the experience, a stage in the facilitative teaching and learning cycle. Stock (1971:93) also claims that role playing should not be used when the educational objectives are complex, where there is any danger that they may be obscured by the involvement and he notes that bad casting may destroy the learning situation.

Role play is often a constituent element of simulation, when the teacher may involve the students in a much more complex problem and even to relate it to a future occupational role in vocational education. For instance, it is possible for trainee lecturers to simulate a complete board of examiners meeting, so that each member of the group learns something about the process before actually having to attend a meeting in a professional capacity. However, the preparation of a simulation is extremely time consuming and unless the simulated situation relates closely to reality the point of the exercise might be lost. Since role playing is also expected in these types of learning exercises most of the problems noted above are significant here also. In addition, since simulations involve a specific number of actors it may be difficult to involve all the students in any one exercise, so that the learning experiences of participant and observer will vary. Simulation should also be followed by a period of debriefing, during which time the learning experience may be reflected upon and ideas be allowed to crystallise in the minds of the participants.

Unlike the previous two techniques, gaming may not involve role play in quite the same way, so that there might be a greater cognitive element to the initial learning experience. Since there are pattens of behaviour in human interaction and regulation in social living it is possible to design games which highlight these pattens and regulations. Because the same is true of the physical universe it is possible to learn about aspects of that through gaming techniques. Rogers and Lovell (Rogers 1973: 78),note that they are aware of a Marxist economics lecturer who gets his students to play 'Monopoly' in order to demonstrate the working of the capitalist system. Other games are appearing on the market in a variety of topics but one of the problems with educational games is that their potential sale may not be large enough to attract the volume games producers and thereby keep the price low, so that, while lecturers should be aware of the games that have been commercially produced in their own area of expertise, they might also consider producing their own. Davies (1971:169) also points out that some business games have been produced that involve role play as well. He also notes an important fact that evaluation on the use of the gaming is scarce and such a conclusion is also more true in the education of adults than it is in the education of children.

Seminar: The seminar is in complete contrast to the methods discussed above since there is usually an introductory statement or paper by one, or more, students or a visiting specialist and this forms the basis for a group discussion. The thesis of the paper should be sufficient to ensure, or provoke discussion so that it may be controversial, provocative topical and relevant. The method has all the advantages and disadvantages of lecture-discussion but it also results in active learning by the presenter(s) of the topic as well as passive learning by the remainder of the group who are recipients of the presentation. However, the seminar may prove to be a daunting method to students if they are to teach their peers and this may prove too off-putting to ensure success. This highlights the significant fact that this method is dependent upon the ability of the presenter to provoke discussion or else the tutor may have to intervene to ensure that the session is a useful learning experience.

'Snowballing': This is an approach that starts with each individual learner but then becomes a group process. Initially, individuals are asked to reflect upon a task, proposition, etc. and to reach some conclusions about it. Thereafter, they are asked to work in pairs and to reflect upon their original conclusions and reach a joint conclusion. Thus each individual has the opportunity to share his thoughts and ideas with another member of the class. When this process is complete, the pairs are asked to form groups of four and to repeat the process. There is a likelihood that all will join in the discussion, knowing that they have the support of their partner from the previous stage. Each group should then elect a rapporteur to report upon the group's collective findings in a plenary session.

Gibbs (1981) advocates this approach since, initially, the individual's own experiences are utilised and
all members of the class actually participate in the
process. Since this method actually assists in dem-
olishing the barriers of interaction it is a useful
method to be employed early in a course, as an ice-
breaking exercise. However, there is an important
point to note in this method: the timing is very
significant and it is very easy to over-run, so that
the plenary session is cut short. Tutors have also
to beware in this type of teaching and learning
session, especially when the time is restricted,
that they do not seek to provide a summary of the
group's reports in which they superimpose their own
ideas upon them. Even so, this is a useful method
which can be employed with large numbers of students
and which encourages full participation by all of
them.

Therapy (T) Groups: This is 'a method of teaching
self-awareness and interpersonal relations based
upon therapeutic group techniques in whch individual
group members discuss their relationship with each
other'. (Bligh 1971:128). This approach may be employed in sensitivity training and in developing individual self-awareness, so that it can be useful in
certain forms of professional education where the
trainees have to learn to work closely with other
people in order to practise their profession effectively. However, this approach can result in situations in which the outcome is social disharmony within the learning group that may continue for long
after the learning session has been completed. Indeed it is an approach that can, unless used with
professional care, be damaging to an individual's
self-esteem, so that is is unwise to use it unless
all the participants have consented to participate
and unless there is easy access to a trained counsellor.

Visits,Tours and Field Trips: Adult education has a
long history of arranging study tours both at home
and abroad and also of arranging field trips. The
purpose of these has always been to provide personal
experience for the learner; but it should be noted
that it can also provide a common learning experience for a group and that this may become a resource for further learning activities. Not only
does a visit provide a learning experience, it may
also help integrate a group, so that it may be a
useful technique to use early in a course - although

it is also recognised that it might constitute the whole of the course. It is often necessary to have some form of debriefing session, or group discussion, in order to ensure that the learning experiences are reflected upon and shared. However, there are limitations to this approach: trips take a lot of time to organize and may be relatively expensive; they may preclude some people from participating in them, especially the handicapped or those who are extremely busy with many different activities; they may have to be organized in conjunction with another party, so that the tutor may not be totally responsible for the arrangements of the learning activity. More recently, study tours have been organized in continuing professional education (Jarvis - forthcoming) but the problems of organization are exaccerbated when the applicants for the course have to gain study leave, paid or unpaid, in order to participate.

Workshops: The final method to be examined in this section is the workshop, which has similarities to the project and case study method. Here a group of students are encouraged to apply theory to practice in some area of their interest or occupation. Students may actually design their own working programme or else they may participate in one devised a tutor. In the workshop situation, students are enabled to undertake a piece of work, either individually or in groups, and the product of the exercise may be subjected to the critical scrutiny of the class for discussion and appraisal. The end-product of such a workshop may be improved skills, a product useful to professional practice or, merely, additional learning. This approach can be employed in liberal adult education and recently one branch of the Workers Educational Association offered a workshop on Robert Tressell. No tutor was present although the local tutor-organizer acted as convenor. The group which was convened not only studied his work *The Ragged Trousered Philanthropists* but went on to write about it and then proceeded to publish a book on the subject entitled *The Robert Tressell Papers* , (WEA 1982). The group actually undertook all the production of the book, so that the end-result of the workshop was a total learning experience. Hence, the workshop may be seen to provide a wide range of learning experiences and is a method that is attractive to adults, especially those who have some previous experience of a topic.

Whilst a considerable number of student-centred

group methods have been examined in this section, no attempt has been made to ensure that the list is exhaustive. The main purpose has been to demonstrate that a variety of approaches exist, so that adult teaching should not always follow the same format. Additionally, Bligh (1971) suggests that a number of different methods may be employed in a single teaching session. Hence, it is necessary for the teacher to be proficient in the use of a variety of methods in order to provide stimuli to the students and to enable them to learn in ways to which they are best suited. Yet, thus far, the discussion has focused only upon student—centred group methods, so that it is now necessary to examine some individual student-centred methods.

Individual Student-Centred Methods: In contrast to the previous section, the focus in this one is the individual student and the methods that might be employed to facilitate his learning. There are a variety of approaches that can be employed ranging from self-selected learning to tutor-set projects. It is proposed to discuss six methods only in this section, chosen because of their significance to the education of adults: the assignment, computer assisted learning, distance learning, personalised systems of instruction, the practical and the personal tutorial. Each is elaborated upon briefly, in the order listed above.

Assignments: Assignments are a common feature of most courses of teaching and learning and may involve, for instance, writing: an essay, a case study, or a research project. In addition, assignments may have a more practical application, so that students can be asked to produce a teaching aid, or some other piece of equipment relevant to their course or occupation. If more practical assignments are produced it is necessary to ensure that expert assistance is available for consultation. An advantage of encouraging students to work in media other than the written word is that adults bring to their learning their own interests and skills and these may be utilised to the benefit of the learning process. Additionally, it has to be borne in mind that the written word is only one method of communicating knowledge and it may be one which some adults have not used extensively since their initial education. At the same time, writing an assignment is perhaps the most common method by which results of research undertakings are communicated, so that adult

149

students should seek to be proficient in the use of this medium. But the proficient use of the written word may be a skill that adults have never been taught, so that it may be necessary to diagnose adults' learning needs in the arts of writing, prior to setting such assignments and if there is a learning need tutors should help students acquire the necessary skills to undertake the task.

Once the tutor is sure that students are able to use the written form, assignments of this nature may be set. The title of any assignment may be tutor-set, student-set, or a choice of either may be given to the group. Advantages of tutor-set assignments include: ensuring that the whole syllabus is covered and producing a standardization of grading at the end of the process. Yet grading is a subjective process, affected by many variables, including handwriting, length and style, that it is dubious whether the latter advantage could actually be substantiated. Encouraging a student to select his own topic may mean that he is more likely to choose an area relevant to either his learning needs, or his interests, or both. However, there is also a tendency to choose subjects that are already known, especially if the assignment is to be graded, and this may partially defeat the object of allowing students to select their own assignment topic. Even if this disadvantage can be overcome, it is not always easy for students to select a subject which they can handle in the time or space available, so that the tutor may have to offer help to the students to get sufficient precision into their titles to enable them to do justice to their topic, within the limitations imposed upon them. Essays are perhaps the most frequently employed method, which may be because the tutors themselves were expected to write them, although projects and case studies to appear to be assuming a more important place in adult learning and teaching than they did previously. The use of these methods is significant because they enable students to follow the sequence of the learning cycle; engaging them in an analytical approach to the problem; discussing the title and its implications; collecting data to construct an argument in response to the analysis; planning a structure in which they can reveal the results of their reflections and evaluations of the data collected; showing something of the process of reflection during the sequence of the argument; reaching conclusions and testing them against the wider reality. Hence, the preparation of the written

150

assignment is a method of learning, and setting
assignments is a technique of facilitating that
learning

Usually written assignments are submitted to the
tutor who marks and returns them to the student.
Little training is given to tutors in marking
written assignments since it is generally assumed
that because the tutor,as an expert in a subject,is
able to assess and grade a piece of work. There are
a number of problems about this assumption: that the
tutor is competent to assess both the structure and
content; that the completed assignment is the end-
product of the learning process; that there is some
objective standard against which the work is judged.
Clearly some tutors do not assess the structure,
only the content of the argument, even though the
structure may constitute as important an element in
the learning process and reveal the way in which the
learner has been able to organize his thoughts and
manage his data. This suggests that tutors might
need to be trained in the arts of marking assignments, which may be even more true when the students
are adults. However, it is perhaps a totally false
assumption that the completed assignment is the end-
product of the learning process and it reflects the
behaviourist psychology that has dominated education
for so long. Many adult students do continue to reflect upon what they have written and tutors are
often asked for feedback about work that they have
marked. The written assignment, therefore, actually
constitutes another medium through which teachers
and learners engage in dialogue. Since marking may
be regarded as part of that dialogue,and it is a
delicate part,as the tutor may be seeking to correct
misunderstandings that the adult students have acquired, it is often useful to adopt a socratic technique. Hence the tutor highlights strengths and
weaknesses by means of questions, so that students
are enabled to reflect upon what they have written
and reach conclusions of their own, which maybe more
beneficial to their self-image and self-esteem than
being corrected. In addition, the questions facilitate a continuing process of learning, whereas didactic comments might inhibit the learners from continuing to pursue ideas in the assignments that they
have written. This is not to deny that there is a
place for didactic comment, but only to claim that
too much information may not be helpful, so that
didacticism should play a less significant role in
marking than it frequently does. (Jarvis 1978).

However, if grading is to be regarded as part of the teaching and learning process, perhaps the tick or the cross is the least helpful of all comments since it merely provides reinforcement, positive or negative, for what is written and, unless it is used in response to empirical fact, it suggests nothing necessarily about correctness, or otherwise - only agreement or disagreement on the part of the tutor.

Computer Assisted Learning: This technique may not be quite so common at present as it will almost certainly become in the future. With the growth in popularity of the personalized micro-computer, it will probably not be many years before the majority of the population are familiar with its use. However, those adults who have not been familiar with the computer in their youth and who are not scientifically orientated tend to be a little over-anxious   about using one, so that tutors may have to introduce adult students to it gently. As the computer becomes more commonplace, so more learning packages will become available and it will be easier for educators of adults to employ this approach. Even so, the popularity of the computer might well result in more privatised learning projects, such as those discussed by Tough (1979), being undertaken: no doubt there are already a multitude of such learning activities being undertaken in Western Europe and America. Yet not all educational institutions have the facilities for adult teaching to be assisted by computer programmes, so that this approach is still in its infancy. Yet its potentiality for responding to the learning needs of students is great. Nevertheless, the lack of personalised contact with tutors may not always prove satisfying to learners, so that it does not necessarily mean that there will become a time when human teaching is redundant.

Distance Teaching: Distance learning has been popularised in the United Kingdom with the establishment of the Open University, although correspondence tuition has existed far longer. Many variations on the Open University exist throughout the world (Rumble and Harry, 1982), and some of the more conventional teaching institutions are also adopting this mode of teaching for some of their courses. Certainly in continuing education in the professsions there is considerable scope for this mode of teaching, so that in both liberal adult education and in vocational education this approach is being

employed more frequently. It is also more convenient
Much has already been written about the topic, which
Holmberg (1981:30) defines 'as a method of guided
didactic discussion'. While the emphasis on discussion in this definition is commendable, the didactic element may be limiting. While much material
prepared for distance learning is didactic it need
not necessarily be so and it has been argued elsewhere that it is possible to assume a more andragogic approach. (Jarvis 1981). Hence, distance
learning need not assume a didactic perspective, so
that it must be emphasised that teaching at a distance contains a totally different set of techniques
from those of conventional teaching and, therefore,
it is not really a single teaching method. Realization that there are a variety of methods that can be
employed in distance teaching might result in the
new developments innovating beyond the approach introduced by the Open University over a decade ago.

Distance teaching is particularly conducive to
adult learning because it enables the adult to feel
more independent, to undertake his study at a time
convenient to himself and to study at his own pace.
In many ways it enables the adult to retain his own
autonomy whilst adopting the role of the student, so
that it is essential that the materials produced for
adult learning and the way in which the tutors respond to the students should also ensure that the
student continues to retain his autonomy, as an independent learner. Since a great deal has already
been written about distance learning it would be unwise to elaborate upon it in great detail here but
four elements are noted: writing course material,
tutoring at a distance, preparing students to study
at a distance and student support. Some academics
appear to regard the preparation of course material
as an opportunity to write a learned discourse on a
topic and to present it in printed form for the
students to digest, rather like a lecture, instead
of considering the learning needs of the students
and trying to prepare teaching and learning material
that responds to their needs. In the same way that
the lecture has a number of weaknesses, so the
printed learned discourse has similar ones although
they are fewer in number. Secondly, the relationship between tutor and student is essential for many
students, so that tutors should always provide adult
students with the opportunity to contact them in
order to discuss their studies. However, tutors
should always endeavour to make students independent
of them, so that this should affect the manner in

which they play their role. This may mean that tutors involved in distance learning require special preparation for their role. Similarly, students may require preparation for their role and already many colleges do organize preparation courses for study with the Open University, and some other educational institutions using this approach also mount an orientation programme for their students. Finally, the students may need support during their studies and it is possible for students to turn to their academic tutor for this, but it may be that a personal tutor system is also necessary: the Open University calls the personal tutor a counsellor, a term that sometimes gets confused with therapeutic counselling. In addition, it was pointed out earlier that tutor-less learning groups do exist and it is useful in distance education for teachers to try to establish learning networks among students, so that they do not feel too isolated as 'the loneliness of the long distance student' is a widely recognised phenomenon. Clearly distance teaching is an important development in the education of adults and it is an aspect of teaching adults with which adult educators should be familiar.

Personalised System of Instruction: The personalised system of instruction refers to the Keller Plan (Keller, 1968; Boud and Bridge, 1974), which is perhaps the most well known, but not the only programmed learning system to emerge. Crane (1982), for instance, refers to: Postlethwait's audio-tutorial system; individually prescribed instruction; programme for learning in accordance with needs; the personalised system of instruction. The Keller Plan consists of units of work which the student studies at his own pace and in his own time without a teacher. Each unit must be passed successfully before the student proceeds to the next one, which is referred to as mastery learning. Lectures and other learning activities are provided but attendance is not compulsory since they are regarded as an additional and occasional stimulus. Keller (1968:83) summarises his plan in the following five points:

1. The go-at-your-own-pace feature, which permits the student to move through the course at a speed commensurate with his ability and other demands upon his time;

2. The unit-perfection requirement for advance, which lets the student go ahead

to new material only after demonstrating
mastery of that which preceded;

3. The use of lectures and demonstrations as
vehicles of motivation rather than
sources of critical information;

4. The related stress upon the written word
in teacher-student communication; and,
finally:

5. The use of proctors, which permits respected
testing, immediate scoring, almost un-
available tutoring, and a marked enhance-
ment of the personal-social aspect of the
educational process.

This method has been acclaimed by Taveggiaas'proven
superior to conventional teaching methods with which
it has been compared' (cited by Holmberg, 1981:127).
Rogers (1977) discusses British counterparts to this
approach in her chapter on discovery learning but it
was Leytham (1971:140) who elaborated a set of
principles for programmed learning, when he suggested that:

- aims and objectives should be clearly specified
- materials selected for learning should relate
to aims and objectives
- each new stage should only introduce sufficient new material to ensure that it is
not too difficult so that the student makes
few, or no, mistakes
- the level of difficulty of new material should
be commensurate with the student's previous
experience
- the student should work at his own pace
- the student should be an active learner
- the student should receive feedback
- no new stage should be inserted before the
previous one is mastered

Clearly Leytham's principles are in accord with the
points stressed by Keller, with the exception of the
latter's use of proctors who undertake the administration of the tests and provide the feedback.
While this approach to teaching can be instituted
within the educational organization, it is also
clear that many of the principles of distance learning are encapsulated within these formulations. However, one of the drawbacks of this approach is that
all the material that is taught and learned is
selected by the teacher and while the learner is

left to learn it, it remains the teacher's choice
and the learner's need is not necessarily a determining factor in the selection of content. Perhaps
this is one reason why it has found a niche in adult
basic education (see Crane 1982 for an example) and
in higher education but, as yet, it has only established a place in liberal adult education through
distance learning. Yet this approach appears to
offer considerable potential as disciplines become
even more specialized and interests even more
diverse.

Practicals: In many professions the teaching of
practical skills has been left to the learner to
copy the demonstrator and stress has been laid on
learning through experience. Yet, as Beard (1976:
147) points out 'there is some evidence that this
method is unnecessarily slow since students have insufficient practice and feedback'. Hence, there has
been a gradual movement in some areas of education
to teach practical skills in a simulated situation,
so that students can practise the skills until they
are mastered. Belbin and Belbin (1972) emphasize
that most adult students, left to learn at their own
pace, can master skills especially if each skill is
sub-divided into separate elements and each element
mastered separately. It is immediately noticeable
that there are considerable similarities between
skill teaching and the programmed learning discussed
above: much of the learning being tutorless, the
student being left to work at his own pace and in
his own time and that each phase is mastered before
progression to the following one. However, in some
other forms of education for adults there is another
aspect of the practical and that is the work undertaken in the laboratory. In this instance, it is
necessary for the tutor to decide whether the purpose of the exercise is merely to learn facts by doing the experiments or to learn the use of experimentation by repeating other people's experiments.
Naturally, these are not mutually exclusive but if
one of the aims is to help students understand the
process of experimentation it is necessary to combine the practical with some other learning technique, such as a discussion or a tutorial, so that
reflection upon the process can be stimulated and
additional learning occur.

Personal Tutorial: The tutorial has already been
discussed from the perspective of the tutor but it
can be used in order to respond entirely to the

student's learning needs. In this instance, the
tutor plays the role of respondent to the questions
and problems raised by the adult student about the
content and method of what the latter is studying.
Hence the tutor is merely answering questions and
the student is effectively guiding the progress of
the tutorial, but when this occurs it is perhaps
wise to agree beforehand upon the length of time to
be allocated to the session.

Thus far in this chapter there has been a division
between tutor-centred and learner-centred and this
has been done for ease of discussion. Clearly, however, in any teaching and learning session it is
possible to combine a number of approaches and, it
is often a useful technique in teaching adults to
negotiate with them about aspects of both content
and method. This is not relinquishing professional
responsibility but rather exercising it in a mature
manner with adult learners who may contribute greatly to the teaching and learning process. Finally,
in this chapter, it is now necessary to move from
methods of teaching to aids for teaching and this
constitutes the next section of this chapter.

TEACHING AIDS

In the same way that the teacher of adults should be
aware of and able to employ a variety of teaching
methods, he should also be aware of and able to use
a variety of teaching aids. A multitude of different ones exist and, with the continuing growth of
technology, there is an increasing sophistication of
equipment. Table 5.2 lists many of the teaching
aids and much of the equipment about which the
teacher of adults should be aware, some of which
he should also be competent to use in the classroom.

Table 5.2: Teaching and Learning
Aids and Equipment

AIDS			
Audio	Audio-Visual	Visual	Learning Aids
Audio cassettes	Films	Artefacts/Models	Articles/Journals
Audio recordings	Tape-slides	Charts	Books
Radio	Tele-vision programmes	Diagrams	Computer programmes
Records	Video-recordings	Drawings	Handouts
		Graphs	Home experiment kits
		Illustrations	Games
		Photographs	Media programmes
		Slides	Role play
			Simulation exercises
			Study visits
			Work books/sheets

EQUIPMENT	
Basic	Technical
Chalkboard	Camera/cine camera
Flannelgraph/Feltboard	Cassette recorder
Flipchart	Closed circuit television
Magnetic board	Computer
Plasticgraph	Epidiascope
Whiteboard	Episcope
	Projectors - cine
	- mico
	- overhead
	- slide
	Radio

Table 5.2 (continued)

EQUIPMENT	
Basic	Technical
	Record player Television Video recorder

Many of the above aids are now in daily use so that they require little comment here, although there are many publications that deal with the technological aspects of teaching (eg. Stephens and Roderick 1971) which may be referred to as appropriate. Therefore, it is intended to raise only a few points here.

Initially, it is important for the teacher of adults to know that such a variety of aids exist and that it is useful to have some expertise in their use. Many teaching and learning aids are produced commercially and can be purchased either by the individual teacher or by the educational institution in which he is employed. At the same time, if the teacher works in an educational institution with an audio-visual aids department it is always worth his while discovering precisely what services it offers, so that his lessons may be enhanced by the technical help that such a department can render. Additionally, if the library facilities in the college/institution are limited, many of the public libraries are prepared to cooperate with teachers of adults in order to ensure that they have sufficient stocks of books on a specific subject to enable class members to borrow them. Local museums also are often prepared to loan boxes of teaching materials, eg. relevant artefacts, on specific topics if they are approached. They are, of course, also pleased to receive class visits when it is appropriate.

When a teacher of adults either prepares his own aids, or uses the services of the audio-visual aids department, it is wise to be aware of the laws of copyright, since infringement of these may occur out of ignorance. Many companies and organizations are prepared to grant permission for the reproduction of their materials, given acknowledgement, so that it is often advisable to seek permission from them. Moreover, some companies and organizations will also provide teaching resources to teachers who approach them.

159

Such a variety of teaching aids and equipment ensures that students may be able to learn in accordance with their preferred learning style. Indeed, the greater the variety of appropriate aids employed the more likely it is that students' learning will be helped; but teachers should not employ too many aids in a single session for the sake of their performance because this artificialises the learning environment and interferes with the learning process. Considerable research has already been conducted into the relationship between learning and audio-visual communications and it is necessary for the teacher to be aware of some of this. Recently, for instance, Sless (1981) has examined the relationship between learning and visual communications and, while he admits that his own coverage is incomplete, he (1981:77) maintains that students are not trained in the use of visual stimuli, so that if teachers use them they must 'also show how people can learn from these forms'. This may be an element that educators of adults take for granted merely because adults have been recipients of visual stimuli for a long time.

Thus it may be seen that a wide variety of aids and equipment are available and the teacher is able to enrich the learning experience if some of the techniques are employed in the teaching and learning situation. It is, therefore, the responsibility of the teacher of adults to be aware of what provision is made by his own educational institution and by other institutions in the locality, so that he is able to perform his role effectively

SUMMARY

This chapter has reviewed a great deal of material about teaching adults. It began by seeking to draw relationships between learning and different approaches to teaching, in which it was recognised that the humanity of the adult students and of the teacher are paramount in the process. It was clearly seen that the adult teacher's role is rather different from that of the traditional lecturer, since while he may perform in a didactic manner, there are also socratic and facilitative styles that are often more appropriate. Different teaching styles were then discussed, and it was once more apparent that these contain within them implicit philosophies, with the humanistic one being more consistent with adult education.

In the next section of the chapter the process of learning and teaching was discussed, in which the differences between teacher-centred and learner-centred approaches were highlighted. Teacher-centred methods can be didactic or socratic whereas learner-centred methods are more facilitative. Yet it was recognised that there is a place for the former in the education of adults, but perhaps, it is not quite such a dominant one as it is usually maintained. Having examined the process of learning and teaching a wide variety of teaching methods were reviewed; some were teacher-centred and others learner-centred. Since there is such a variety of methods available it should mean that teachers of adults are able to use techniques that are appropriate to the aims and content of their teaching and that they may wish to include a variety of teaching methods in any one session. In order to enrich the teaching and learning experience teachers may also wish to utilise the wide variety of aids and equipment that have been produced and the chapter concluded by examining briefly some of these.

Thus far few theorists of teaching have been examined, so that in the next rather brief chapter a number of theorists are analysed and, in the following chapter the preparation of teachers of adults constitutes the focus of the discussion.

SELECTED FURTHER READING

Teaching and Learning in Higher Education   R Beard 1976- *(3rd edition)*

This book covers many of the methods used in teaching and learning and reviews the research in considerable detail but it is focused upon higher education so that the scope of its review is limited.

Adult Education Procedures   P Bergevin et al 1963

A most useful handbook, practically orientated, listing a variety of methods appropriate to the teaching of adults. It reviews the advantages and disadvantages of each method, gives examples about the use of the techniques and guidance about how to practise them.

Whats the Use of Lectures?   D A Bligh   *1971*

While this book is not orientated to the education of adults it reviews a variety of teaching methods, highlighting some of the strengths and weaknesses of some of them, especially the use and deficiencies in the lecture method

The Management of Learning   I K Davies *1971*

A very thorough book, useful to all who teach in post-compulsory education whether their main concerns are cognitive or skills. This is a guide through the literature and at the same time it is a useful handbook for those who teach. There is one chapter on teaching older people but many chapters are useful, although the book has a behavioural bias. This book is more useful for those who teach adults within an institutional setting.

Helping Others Learn   P A McLagan   *1978*   *revised edition)*

A handbook, not mentioned in the chapter, in which the author guides readers through the techniques of teaching adults - a simple but useful little book.

Teaching Techniques in Adult Education   *(eds)*
M D Stephens and
G Roderick 1971

A symposium containing some very useful chapters on a variety of methods. While the book is a little dated in some aspects, there are other parts of it that will not date. Its orientation is towards teaching adults in a variety of settings.

Chapter Six

THEORETICAL PERSPECTIVES ON TEACHING ADULTS

In the previous chapter the process of learning and
teaching was discussed and it will have become
apparent from the numerous methods mentioned that
there are a diversity of approaches to teaching and
many theoretical perspectives about it, so that it
is now necessary to examine some of the latter in
this chapter. Before undertaking this, however, it
is essential to highlight the fact that since teaching and learning is a process of human interaction
in which both sets of participants should be affected, it cannot be a neutral process. Indeed, it is a
moral one! In this study it has been consistently
maintained that education itself is humanistic and
some teaching and learning processes may fall short
of these ideals. Hence, in the first instance, it
may be necessary to consider not only the appropriateness of the teaching methods for the aims and
content of a particular session but the morality of
the approach in relation to the participants in the
process. Thereafter, it is necessary to consider
the effectiveness of the methods employed, so that
while there may be no single correct method there
are some techniques that should not be utilised
since they fail to incorporate the morality of the
educational process within them.
    Three major approaches to teaching were recog-
nised: didactic, socratic and facilitative. It was
also pointed out that while didactic teaching has a
place in teaching adults, it is perhaps less significant than generally assumed, and that both the
socratic and the facilitative styles are important
in the education of adults. However, it must be
recognised that teacher-centred approaches do ensure
that the teacher has control of the learning process,
whereas learner-centred methods surrender some of
that power to the students. This is a significant

distinction since it has political overtones, to which reference is made in this chapter and which it is most important to realise. It will be recalled that Rogers (1969:103) claims that for him teaching is 'a relatively unimportant and vastly overrated activity' since he believes in the natural propensity of human beings to learn. But if the powerful in any society, profession or occupation wish to control what human beings learn, it is necessary to ensure that there are mechanisms for ensuring that learners only learn what they wish them to, so that the curriculum, a selection from culture, has to be carefully managed. Hence, for the elite, it might be claimed, it is quite necessary that teacher-centred teaching initiates the learners into acceptable cultural knowledge. Teaching is, therefore, not relatively unimportant socially nor is it neutral. It may, thus, be seen that some theories of teaching may have a political bias but, by contrast, learning is a psychological activity, and also other theories of teaching focus upon the individual rather than the social process. The idealistic, political and psychological are all present in the theories of teaching explored here. Not all the writers actually concentrate upon teaching adults but yet in their different ways they are all significant in developing theoretical perspectives on teaching adults. Five theorists are examined: Bruner, Dewey, Freire, Illich and Knowles.

JEROME S BRUNER

Bruner in his classic study *Towards a Theory of Instruction* (1968),recognises that the human being is a natural learner and he (1968:127), claims that schools often fail to 'enlist the natural energies that sustain spontaneous learning'. This might appear to be an indictment upon modern schools but it is also a recognition that they perform a socializing and moulding function to equip children to take their place in society as much as an educational one. Bruner (1968:53) therefore, recognises that any instruction that is given in school should be regarded as having an intermediate as well as a long-term aim, the latter being that the learner should become a self-sufficient problem-solver. However, it might be claimed that any didactic process, such as formalised instruction, is actually helping to create a sense of dependency in the learner rather than one of independency, especially if the

164

school teacher is unable to detach himself from the
process and encourage independent learning in children. Consequently, by the time that children grow
into adults they will have learned to expect that
teachers will instruct them. Indeed adult students
do exert considerable pressure upon educators of
adults to conform to their expectations of teachers
playing a didactic and, often, an authoritative role.

It is against this discussion that Bruner's
theory of instruction may be viewed. He (1968:40-1)
claims that a theory of instruction should have four
main features, and these are that it:

- should specify the experiences which most
  effectively implant in an individual a
  predisposition towards learning
- must specify the ways in which the body of
  knowledge should be structured so that it
  can be readily grasped by the learner
- should specify the most effective sequences
  in which to present the materials to be
  learned
- should specify the nature and pacing of rewards and punishments in the process of
  learning and teaching

Clearly Bruner has posited his theory against the
background of initial education, so that some of the
above points appear to be diametrically opposed to
some of those already mentioned in the education of
adults. Yet the first of these four points is quite
significant since Bruner maintains that instruction
should facilitate and regulate the exploration of
alternatives and a major condition for undertaking
this is curiosity. It will be recalled that curiosity is aroused in adults, as well as in children,
when their interpretation of their socio-cultural
environment no longer provides them with relevant
knowledge to cope with their present experiences.
Hence, in teaching adults it is possible for the
teacher to provide experiences that arouse this
questioning process, so that the adult students'
questioning is orientated in a specific direction.
Clearly the structure and form of knowledge are significant in teaching adults and Bruner (1968:44)
recognises that the mode of representation, the
economy of presentation and the effective power of
the representation varies, 'in relation to different
ages, to different "styles" among learners, and to
different subject matters'. Hence, this second
point may be seen as relevant to adult teaching. The

relevance of his third point is also clear since he (1968:49) claims that instruction 'consists of leading the learner through a sequence of statements and are statements of a problem or body of knowledge that increase the learner's ability to grasp, transform, and transfer what he is learning'. Finally, all learners need some re-inforcement, so that the relevance of this is very evident in the education of adults. However, it must be recognised that Bruner is only discussing one type of educational method, instruction, or a didactic presentation of knowledge and the relevance of his theory must be seen in relation to this.

There are also considerable similarities in Bruner's formulation and those in the personalised system of instruction discussed in the previous chapter, so that it may be seen that Bruner has highlighted many of the points that underlay a theory of instruction. Instruction is obviously didactic and there is a sense in which, as a teaching method, it controls the amount of knowledge to be learned by the students, so that it is open to the accusations that some of the analysts discussed later in this chapter would make about it. Nevertheless, many of more informal methods of teaching also include some teacher direction and guidance, so that they may not be quite so free of control as might appear on the surface. However, it might be true to claim that all teaching methods may be located on a continuum between student-centred and teacher-centred and, perhaps, more are located towards the latter end of the continuum than adult educators might like.

While Bruner is clearly concerned about the humanity of the participants in the teaching and learning process, there is no explicit place within his principles for a humanisitc perspective, although he does recognise the importance of the relationship between teacher and learner. Nevertheless, Bruner has outlined a set of principles that educators of adults should be aware because they form part of the theoretical perspective of teaching.

JOHN DEWEY

Perhaps Dewey is the most significant of all educationalists to the development of adult education, so that it is hardly surprising that he should be considered within this context. Many of his ideas have already been discussed in earlier chapters of this study, so that it is not intended to repeat them at length here. However, Dewey was one of the major exponents of progressive education and his earlier books were clear expositions of this position and among his basic principles were that the concept of education had to be reconceived, so that it related to the whole of life rather than to its early years. For Dewey, the human being is born with unlimited potential for growth and development, and education is one of the agencies that facilitates growth. Another tenet of progressivism that is significant to comprehension of Dewey's thought is the recognition that prominence is given to the scientific method; so that the individual needs to start with a problem, develop hypotheses about it and test them out by examination of the empirical evidence. Hence, the problem-solving method, discussed in relation to Gagné's hierarchy of learning was significant in the work of Dewey. Dewey recognised that this resulted in a changed relationship between teacher and taught, so that the teacher might facilitate and guide the learning but he should not interfere with nor control the process in the way that a didactic teacher would.

Some of the above ideas appear in *Education and Democracy* (1916) but in many ways the book that he wrote on *Experience and Education* (1938), reflects some of his more developed thinking on teaching. He was concerned to contrast his approach to education to that of the more traditional schools of thought and he considered freedom and experience to be significant. Additionally, he maintained that continuity of experience and interaction between young and old are both important to learning. Hence, it is clear that Dewey was actually writing about initial education, especially after his own experiences of running a progressive, experimental school for a number of years. But it may be recognised that some significant ideas for the education of adults evolved from children's education, so that it is important for the former to be aware of theoretical approaches to children's education.

Dewey considered that since experience is at the heart of human living and because continuity of experience leads to growth and maturity, then genuine education must come through experience. Hence, the teacher's role is to provide the right type experience through which the leaner may acquire knowledge and understanding and this would facilitate the process of growth and development. The learner would mature without having a structure of knowledge

167

and the body of social rules imposed upon him. However, it might be argued that if the teacher's main task is to provide the conditions in which the student learns, and if he may actually be involved in directing the process when the students require help (Dewey 1938:71), then the teacher is involved in a much more subtle process of control than that which occurs in traditional, didactic teaching. However, Dewey does recognise that this possibility exists and he (1938:71) condemns those who 'abuse the office, and ... force the activity of the young into channels which express the teacher's purpose rather than that of the pupils'. According to Dewey the teacher's leadership responsibilities include:

- being intelligently aware of the capacity, needs and past experiences of those under instruction
- making suggestions for learning but being prepared for the class to make further suggestions so that learning is seen to be a cooperative rather than a dictatorial enterprise
- using the environment and experiences and extracting from them all the lessons that may be learned
- selecting activities that encourage the learners to organize the knowledge that they gain from their experiences in subject matter
- looking ahead to see the direction in which the learning experiences are leading to ensure that they are conducive to continued growth

These points are collected from different pages of Dewey's work but they reflect some of his major points about teaching. It is clear from the above that Dewey's work on teaching may be related to the facilitative learning and teaching cycle (Figure 5.3) in the previous chapter and that many of his ideas are similar to those expounded in earlier chapters of this work. It was Lindeman (1926) who, influenced by Dewey, incorporated many of these ideas into adult education, so that it is necessary to recognise that many elements in the theories of teaching in adult education do reflect a progressive education perspective which can be traced directly back to Dewey.

PAULO FREIRE

Freire's work was discussed in a previous chapter in
terms of the theory of learning implicit in his
writing but the theory of teaching is much more explicitly. Three elements are discussed here and these
are summarised by Goulet (Freire 1973a: viii), who
suggests that the basic components of Freire's
literacy method are:

- participant observation of educators 'tuning
  in' to the vernacular universe of the
  people
- an arduous search for generative words
- an initial codification of these words into
  visual images which stimulate people
  'submerged' in the culture of silence to
  'emerge' as conscious makers of their own
  'culture'
- the decodification by a 'culture circle'
  under the self-effacing stimulus of a co-
  ordinator who is no 'teacher' in the conventional sense, but who has become an
  educator-educatee in dialogue with educatee,
  educators too often treated by formal educators as passive recipients of knowledge
- a creative new codification, this one ex-
  plicitely critical and aimed at action,
  wherein those who were formally illiterate
  now begin to reject their role as mere
  'objects' in nature and social history and
  undertake to become 'subjects' of their own
  destiny

Without raising issues of literacy education, the
first significant point that emerges from this
summary is that Freire advocates, and practises,
going to those who have a learning need and listening to them, so that the educator can become the
learner. While this serves a diagnostic function,
it has more purposes than this: it enables the
educator to learn the language of the potential
learners and also to identify with them. At the
outset of the teaching and learning the teacher
bridges the gulf between him and the learners in
order to create a genuine dialogue, without which
humanistic education cannot occur.
   The second significant point about this process
is that the learners are encouraged to participate
in dialogue and to problematise the reality in which
they are immersed. This is a deliberate attempt to

169

make the learners question what they had previously
taken for granted, so that they can become aware
that they have been socialised into the culture of
the colonizers and that their construction of reality may be false within the context of their indigenous heritage. This occurs through the analysis
and use language, since language is a significant
carrier of the universe of meaning, and through becoming aware of what has happened to them the learners are enabled to reconstruct their universe of
meaning. In this process the learners are not objects of a social process but they are creative
subjects within it.

Finally, Freire does not regard the educator
and the learner as having mutually distinct roles
but that in a genuine dialogue the teacher teaches
the learners but they learn and teach the teacher as
well. Hence, in the dialogue there is also a mutual
planning of the teaching and learning, so that it is
relevant to the needs of the participants. It is in
this dialogue that the humanistic nature of Freire's
teaching method is apparent since he (1972b:61-5)
claims that it is essential to the educational process and that it requires an intense love for and
faith in man. Perhaps Freire's philosophy of teaching is summed up by a Chinese poem:

> Go to people, live among them,
> Learn from them, love them,
> Serve them, plan with them,
> Start with what they have,
>   build on what they have.

(Author unknown)

Perhaps more than in most theories of teaching,
Freire emphasizes that the teacher has to reach out
to the learners and learn from them in order to be
able to contribute effectively to the teaching and
learning process. Like other theories of teaching
adults the humanity of the learners is respected and
emphasized.

Two significant points need to be made at this
stage in the discussion. Clearly Freire presents a
radical approach to teaching and he regards it as a
method by which learners can act upon their socio-
political environment in order to change it. Hence,
he regards the educator as the facilitator of learning and education as a process of change. The educator is not the 'fount of all wisdom' trying to
fill the empty buckets: education is not a process

of banking received knowledge. Rather education is
an active process in which the teacher neither controls the knowledge learned nor the learning outcomes. Because of the politically radical elements
in Freire, there is a danger that other aspects of
his philosophy of teaching may be lost.

Freire offers a humanistic teaching method that
may actually be divorced from the political radicalism, although to do so would fail to do justice to
Freire's philosophy. However, he highlights the
fact that the teacher: has to break down the barriers between teacher and taught; should speak the
same language as the learners; should be aware of
how they construct their universe of meaning and
what they see as their learning needs; should start
where the learners are and encourage them to explore
and learn from their experiences.

From Freire's unique synthesis of Christanity,
Marxism and existentialism he has produced a theoretical approach to teaching that is both inspiring
and challenging. That he is regarded as a political
radical should not detract educators of adults from
seeking to emulate elements of his method, since it
epitomises the high ideals of humanistic education.

IVAN ILLICH

Like Freire, Illich is a radical Christian who
presents an alternative approach to education. He is
included here, however, not because of his radicalism but because one of his major ideas is already
finding expression in adult education in America and,
to some extent, it is being incorporated into the
Universtity of the Third Age that is being established in the United Kingdom and because his approach presents a warning to those adult educators who
seek to professionalize their occupation.

In order to understand Illich thoroughly it
must be understood that he offers a radical critique
of some of established institutions in Western
society, including medicine, the Church and teaching,
so that it is necessary to summarise his concerns
before they are applied to education. Illich (1977)
claims that the professions dominate ordinary people,
that they prescribe what the people need and in-
stitutionalise it within the professional's own
territory. Hence, doctors determine when a person is
ill, prescribe an acceptable remedy to the need and
ensure that health cure takes place in 'hygienic
appartments where one cannot be born, cannot be sick

and cannot die decently' (Illich 1977a:27). Similarly teachers determine what children need to learn,
prescribe the educational remedy in a building which
artificialises the real experiences of living.
Professionals dominate people's lives, prescribing
what they regard as right and proper and the general
populace are no more than the recipients of the
process. This is the crux of Illich's position.

Since education has fallen into the trap of
institutionalization, Illich (1973a) proposed that
it was necessary to deschool society. He considered
this essential because not only education but social
reality itself has become schooled. Accepted knowledge and credentials for occupational advancement
have become incarcerated within the institution of
the school but there is no equality of access to it,
so that expenditure on education is unequally distributed in favour of the wealthy. Every time some
other area of social living is incorporated into a
school curriculum a new class of poor is generated
so that, for instance, with the introduction of new
training initiatives for young adults in the United
Kingdom a new class of poor who are unable to attend
the courses and gain the advantages is generated.

In precisely the same way, Illich and Verne
(1976) offer a critique of lifelong education.
Continuing education specialists will generate the
need for more learning, prescribe how and where it
should be learned and perpetuate the school system
throughout the whole of the lifespan. They (1976:
13) claim that in 'permanent education we are no
doubt witnessing a further reduction of the idea of
education, this time for the exclusive benefit of
the capitalists of knowledge and the professionals
licensed to distribute! Clearly, Illich is offering
a valid criticism of the process of institutionalisation in western society, and indeed in other societies as well, even though he has over-stated his
argument to make his point. What then does he pre-
pose as a remedy for the malady that he has diagnosed?

Illich (1973a) proposes that learning networks
should be established and that resources are required
to establish a web-like structure throughout a society. He (1973a:81) proposes four different approaches which enable the student to gain access to
any educational resource which may help him to define and achieve his own goals: reference services
to educational objects; skill exchanges; peer
matching; reference services to educators at large.
This clearly requires organization and some of the

172

resources spent on the school system could be used for this purpose and the professional teacher, liberated from the bureaucratic control of the school, would be free to provide a service to these learners who require it. Such a scheme is idealistic and revolutionary, so that there is no likelihood of a society reforming its educational institution in this manner but the free university system in America appears to be fulfilling these criteria. A free university, according to Draves (1979:5), is "an organization which offers non-credit classes to the general public in which 'anyone can teach and anyone can learn'." Some of the free universities are sponsored by traditional colleges while others are sponsored by libraries and some others are independent. They exist to coordinate learning and teaching opportunities, to introduce potential students to potential teachers. There is a national conference of free universities each year and in 1979 there were over 180 free universities established in America, with over 300,000 participants. A similar approach is envisaged for the University of the Third Age as it is being established in the United Kingdom at present.

Illich, then, offers a radical critique of contemporary society and of the dominant position occupied by the professionals. While his radical alternative to schooling does not appear to have gained a great deal of support in initial education, there is evidence that some adult educators are seeking to respond to the learning need in people and to create networks where teaching and learning can occur outside of the institutional framework. Nevertheless, such free institutions must run the danger of ossifying and becoming established, so that it remains to be seen whether learning networks will survive and multiply in the coming decade.

MALCOLM KNOWLES

Like Freire, Knowles was discussed in the chapter on learning theorists but, unlike Freire, he is included again because he has actually produced a text-book in which he specifically discusses the two processes. It was pointed out in the previous chapter that he actually produced a table similar to Table 5.1, in which he specifies sixteen principles of teaching in response to conditions of learning. He demonstrates that he regards teaching as the process of designing and managing learning activities.

173

His (1980:57-8) principles indicate the process of teaching, so that they are summarised below: the teacher
- exposes learners to new possibilities for self-fulfilment
- helps learners clarify their own aspirations
- helps learners diagnose
- helps learners identify life-problems resulting from their learning needs
- provides physical conditions conducive to adult learning
- accepts and treats learners as persons
- seeks to build relationships of trust and cooperation between learners
- becomes a co-learner in the spirit of mutual enquiry
- involves learners in a mutual process of formulating learning objectives
- shares with learners potential methods to achieve these objectives
- helps learners to organize themselves to undertake their tasks
- helps learners exploit their own experiences on learning resources
- gears presentation of his own resources to the levels of learners' experiences
- helps learners integrate new learning to their own experience
- involves learners in devising criteria and methods to measure progress
- helps learners develop and apply self-evaluation procedures

This list of principles clearly demonstrate the facilitative teaching style of a humanistic educator of adults. Knowles sees andragogy as embracing the process of teaching and learning rather than merely learning or teaching and, within this context, it is perhaps important to understand that these principles embrace progressive education for adults, so that they are rather different in perspective from the other approaches that have been examined in this chapter.

Elsewhere in the same work, Knowles (1980:222-247) applies these principles to the process of teaching, which he regards as having seven stages: setting a climate for learning, establishing a structure for mutual planning, diagnosing learning needs, formulating directions for learning, designing a pattern of learning experiences, managing the execution of the learning experiences and evaluating results and rediagnosing learning needs. Each of these phases is discussed briefly.

The climate of learning is perhaps more significant than many educators actually assume:
Knowles includes both the physical setting of learning and the psychological ethos. He recognises that
the learning climate is also affected by the way in
which the teacher and the adult students interact.
This is especially true in the early sessions, a
point that many adult educators focus upon, so that
it is significant that the teacher endeavours to
establish good relationships between him and the
class and between the learners themselves, from the
outset of a course. Only within this climate can
diagnosis occur within which he recognises three
stages: developing a model of the desired end-state
of the teaching and learning, assessing the present
level of knowledge and the gap between the two.
Thereafter, learning objectives can be formulated by
the teacher and the learners together. Having reached this stage, Knowles advocates including the adult
learners in designing the pattern of learning experiences, which should contain continuity, sequence
and integration between different learning episodes.
It is the teacher's role to manage the learning experience and Knowles (1980:239) maintains that the
teacher should 'serve both as a strong procedural
technician - suggesting the most effective ways that
the students can help in executing the decisions -
and as a resource person, or coach, who provides
substantive information regarding the subject matter
of the unit, possible techniques, and available materials, where needed'. Finally, the teacher should
join with the students in both an evaluation of the
process and a rediagnosis of future learning needs.

Thus it may be seen from the above sequence
that Knowles clearly regards the learners as active
explorers in the learning process, participating in
every stage and the teachers as resource persons for
both content and process. He is obviously in accord
with many of the ideas that Dewey expounded so that,
unlike McKenzie (1979), it is maintained here that
Knowles has applied progressive education to the
education of adults. Therefore, it may be seen that
the ideology of andragogy is humanistic.

SUMMARY

Five different teaching theorists have been discussed briefly in this chapter: Dewey and Knowles
clearly have similar humanistic, idealistic approaches

to education, seeing the learner as one who is
motivated to learn, so that the tutor's role is
mostly facilitative; Illich and Freire both place
their analyses in a wider context, Illich as a critique of professional institutions and Freire of the
power of the elite; Bruner's analysis is much more
specifically in relation to instruction. No doubt
Freire and Illich would not want to dispute the
humanistic perspective of Dewey and Knowles although
the former may consider the latter as having a restricted analysis but, indeed, all four might well
agree with Bourdieu and Passeron when they (1977-
5-11) assert that all pedagogic action 'is objectiv-
ly, symbolic violence insofar as it is the imposition of a cultural arbitrary by an arbitrary
power'. Bruner may not wish to disagree too violent-
ly with this claim either, since he focuses upon
man's curiosity as an activator in the process of
learning. Nevertheless, Bourdieu and Passeron do
raise issues that are important to the role of the
teacher which need to be considered briefly at this
point.
     If education is regarded as the process of
learning that knowledge which society considers
worthwhile, then it might be argued that skilled
techniques that transmit that knowledge is 'good'
education. But if education is regarded as the
process of learning and understanding, then the content is less significant, and the ways in which the
students are encouraged, or enabled, to learn becomes more significant. In this instance, it could
be maintained that 'good' education is concerned
with the process of learning, irrespective of what
is learned, and that adult learners should become
sufficiently critically aware to reject that which
incorrect or irrelevant to them. Hence, to transmit
to learners accepted or received knowledge and expect them to learn it uncritically may be regarded
as 'bad' education and, therefore,'bad'teaching. If
techniques are used to ensure that the students are
persuaded to accept such knowledge, then it may be
symbolic violence, in the way that Bourdieu and
Passeron claim. However, it would not be maintained
here that all pedagogic action is symbolic violence,
although some of it most certainly is. Clearly
there is a place for pedagogy in the education of
adults, but it has been argued that it is not such
a significant one as it is generally assumed to be
and that the teaching method employed has to relate
both to the learners and also to the nature of the
topic and the knowledge being learned.

Hence, the issues raised by the more radical theorists do relate to the perspectives adopted by those educators assuming a more humanistic perspective. It is clear that there are moral and social policy issues involved in the process of teaching and while it has been one of the purposes to highlight them, it is not the intention of this chapter to resolve them. Yet the manner by which teachers resolve these issues for themselves may well affect the way that they perform their own role and, indeed, it is an issue with which they should be confronted during their own training.

SELECTED FURTHER READING

Towards a Theory of Instruction   *J S Bruner 1968*

This is a well known study of teaching which, while it is especially appropriate for teaching school children, has a number of points that adult educators might wish to consider. This is especially true in the way that Bruner sees instruction within his wider philosophical perspective.

Experience and Education   *J Dewey 1938*

This is a short book, written after Dewey's experiences with progressive education. It is orientated towards initial education, but both the philosophy and many of the ideas are most appropriate to the education of adults.

Deschooling Society   *J Illich 1973a*

This is one of Illich's many books on a variety of subjects, which focus upon his concerns about professionalization and institutionalization. He has clearly a part to play in making educators critically aware of the process in which they are engaged and some of the solutions that he poses are significant for branches of adult education such as

community education. It is wise to see Illich's
work as a whole rather than merely regarding him as
a idealistic critic of schooling.

Please note that two of Freire's and two of Knowles'
books have already been included in selected reading
for earlier chapters.

Chapter Seven

TEACHERS OF ADULTS AND THEIR PREPARATION

The concept of 'teacher of adults' appears on the
surface to be a relatively straightforward one and,
therefore, easy to discuss but once analysed it is
soon apparent that initial conceptions can be misleading and ill-conceived. Earlier in this study it
was pointed out that during human interaction everybody is an agent in the transmission of culture, in
fact everyone is an educator of adults. However,
the topic under consideration here refers specifically to the occupation of teaching adults, so that
it is possible to restrict the analysis accordingly.
But even then the adult education or education of
adults question becomes an issue once again: if
adult education refers specifically to a part of the
education of adults, then it would be necessary to
restrict the discussion to those employed part-time
and full-time in that branch of the service but, on
the other hand, if the teacher of adults refers to
anybody employed to teach adults in whatever capacity
in education, the professions etc. then the problem
is much more complex. This problem is compounded
because in the second report of the Advisory Committee in the Supply and Training of Teachers
(Haycocks 1978) adult education teachers were included within the further education, and it is stated
that in the academic year 1974-5 there were: 66,500
full-time staff, 57,000 staff teaching vocational
subjects part-time and another 108,000 part-time
staff teaching non-vocational education. But further
and adult education teachers were not specified separately. Clearly these statistics refer only to
those educators employed in the educational service
and not those in the professions and yet the confusion between further and adult education here does
not help clarify the concept: indeed,it points only
to the fact that administratively the adult education

service is regarded as a branch of further education.
Nevertheless, the Russell Report (1973:131) indicated that there were about 1,300 full-time and
100,000 part-time staff employed in the adult education sector. Since many of the professions and
other organizations employ their own teaching staff,
about which it is much more difficult to obtain precise statistics, it is an extremely difficult undertaking to discover how many people are actually employed full-time and part-time in any one year to
teach adults.

Mee and Wiltshire (1978:20-1) claim that there
are three main categories of adult educators employed within the Local Educational Authority adult education service: the full-timer, the part-timer and
the spare-timer. While their distinction is perfectly valid, it is a pity that they employ the term
'spare-timer' with all of its connotations to refer
to the category of adult education employment that
is often referred to as part-time. Indeed, these
implicit values may not actually be substantiated by
their own findings, so that the term 'spare-timer'is
not employed here. However, it is essential to
clarify what they meant by part-time adult educator:
he is the teacher who has joint responsibility,
'part of his time being given to adult education and
part to the youth service, school teaching or vocational Further Education'. (Mee and Wiltshire 1978:
20). While there clearly are many people in this
category it is not proposed to use the term part-
time to refer to them here. Another three-fold division of adult educators was made many years
earlier by Houle (cited Verner 1964:35-8) who distinguished between those who teach adults on a voluntary basis, those who perform this and other educational roles on a part-time basis for renumeration
and full-time professional adult educators. Houle's
category of volunteer adult educators is quite a
significant one, which Elsey (1980) investigated in
the United Kingdom, but one which should not be
classified as a branch of the occupation of 'adult
educator'.

Without exploring this any further, it may be
seen that the teacher of adults, or the adult educator, may not be quite such a straightforward concept
or occupation to describe and that the majority of
people who appear to be classified as adult educators undertake the role on a part-time basis only.
Description of the role may, therefore, be an easier
undertaking than actually conceptualizing the occupation, but even this assumption may be doubtful.

Houle, for instance, distinguishes between the administrative and instructional roles of the full-time professionals, suggesting that they may perform both. While this may have been true two decades ago, it is less likely to be true today. Many full-time adult educators who regard their role as tutor-organizer may be organizers of tutors more than teachers who organize as well. Additionally, principals of adult education institutes may be managers rather than teachers and Mee and Wiltshire (1978:64) record one principal of an adult education institute who maintained that the 'next group of principals should be accountants not educationalists'. As some adult education institutes expand in size it is inevitable that the managerial role will continue to develop. It is not only the full-time staff whose role is moving in this direction since many part-time staff have in recent years been employed as part-time heads of an adult-education centre and their responsibility has been managerial rather than professional. In some Local Education Authorities, however, adult education has been located within colleges of further education, community colleges etc. and, in this instance, the role of the adult educatorsmay be both professional and administrative, since they may be expected to teach in the college, etc. and organize adult education classes in either their discipline or locality. Hence, it may not be quite so simple to describe the role of the adult educator!

Thus full-time adult educators may be employed in a variety of institutions, with or without a teaching role, while part-time and voluntary adult educators are more likely to be teachers of adults. Hence, two questions may be raised: what is the job of an educator of adults and is it even an occupation at all? Hall (1969:5-6) defines occupation as 'a social role performed by adult members of society that directly and/or indirectly yields social and financial consequences and that constitutes a major focus in the life of an adult'. Hall's definition contains four basic components: a social role, social consequences, remuneration and a major life focus. While it would be possible to dispute the validity of this definition, it does reflect considerable research findings in occupations and professions and so it is proposed to adopt it here. Once the definition is adopted it does raise some interesting conceptual issues about the teacher of adults. The social role of many full-time adult educators may be that of a manager rather than that

181

of a teacher but others are employed and perform
the role of teacher of adults. Some may spend all
their employed time in administration while others
may be teachers. Yet some who are actually teachers
of adults, may not regard themselves as such since
they see themselves as engineers, university teachers, etc. Hence, a university teacher employed in
a school of dentistry, for example, may teach adults
all the time, without having a major administrative
responsibility. But he may regard himself as a
dentist, or a university teacher, rather than as an
educator of adults. A similar argument may be made
for adult educators in University Departments of
Adult Education. Hence, the differential status of
the occupation may be reflected in the role-player's
own perception of his occupation, which relates to
the second and fourth of Hall's criteria. Thus an
individual may objectly be a teacher of adults but
neither regard himself as an adult educator nor be
employed in adult education. By contrast, many who
see themselves as adult educators and employed in
the education of adults may not actually teach
adults. Additionally, some part-time adult educators may be employed full-time in another occupation
and define their occupational role in terms of the
latter occupation, while other part-time adult educators may have no other employment and regard their
occupation as educators of adults. Thus the idea
that adult education is an occupation is open to
certain questions. That those employed in it full-
time are in an occupation is not open to conjecture,
but it is difficult to specify precisely what the
role entails.and to delineate its boundaries is even
more problematic. This confusion clearly reflects
some of the problems surrounding adult education itself, but it is quite fundamental to an understanding of its marginality. Whether adult education
is either a separate occupation or a separate discipline remain questions to be discussed further
elsewhere in this study.

Having expanded this initial problem, it is now
necessary to outline the other concerns of this
chapter. The first continues the exploration of the
adult educator and his role and this is followed by
an examination of the training and qualifications
that adult educators have. Recent developments in
training, especially the aftermath of the Advisory
Committee's report, are examined and some possible
criteria for the basis of training are then discussed. Finally, the topic of adult education as an
occupation is returned to and its professionalization

is discussed.

THE ADULT EDUCATOR AND HIS ROLE

From the above discussion it is clear that the occupation of adult education, if it actually is an occupation, is a very diverse one. This becomes even more apparent when examining the varying roles performed by different adult educators. Teachers of adults in the professions, working in the field of higher education, are expected to research and publish in their professional field, prepare students for the appropriate qualifying examinations, and undertake whatever administrative tasks appertaining to the work that arise within their university or polytechnic. By contrast, a lecturer in a university department of extra-mural studies is expected to perform all the above roles of a teacher of higher education, but also to organize university extension classes in his discipline(s), liaise with the adult education service outside the university, interview part-time staff, train them in the art and science of teaching adults and to offer them support, help and advice as appropriate. A similar role is performed by Open University staff tutors. Part-time tutors in both university extension classes and in Open University tutorial work have similar class contact responsibility but the major difference in their work is that the former actually prepare their own courses whereas the latter teach a course prepared by a central course team and mark the students' work. Kirk (1976) records the sense of loneliness that some Open University part-time tutors experience because they are at the periphery of the University's tutorial activities but similar research among university extension class tutors remains to be undertaken. A similar division of responsibility between full-time and part-time staff in the university extra-mural departments exists in the Workers Educational Association, so that the full-time staff have largely an administrative role although most undertake some teaching.

Similarly, part-time staff in local education authority adult education institutes tend to have a predominantly teaching role, although there are a minority who are employed in an administrative capacity. By contrast, the full-time staff perform a multifarious role which Newman (1979) characterised as: entrepreneurs - they have to establish courses and then ensure that there are sufficient students to make them viable; wheeler-dealers -

they have to overcome all the problems of enter-
preneurs employed in a bureaucratic education
service; administrators - they are responsible for
planning programmes and employing staff; managers -
their job is to manage the part-time staff and the
educational premises; animateurs - they have to
make things happen; trouble-shooters - having to
deal with the multitude of problems that complex
organizations like adult education institutes
create; experts on method - they might be called
upon to provide guidance and assistance to part-time
adult education staff; campaigners - since adult
education, as a marginal branch of education, is
always under threat. It is quite significant that
Newman does not include teaching amongst these roles.
Hence, it may be concluded that for some full-time
staff in local education authority adult education
teaching plays a fairly insignificant part of their
work. Thus, the full-time adult educator may be regarded as a manager and an administrator as much as,
if not more than, a teacher, which raises quite
significant questions about the notion that adult education is an occupation undergoing professionalization, which is discussed later in this chapter.

According to Mee and Wiltshire (1978:61-2) this
diversity of role that the full-time staff play provides them with a sense of autonomy and independence
that they enjoy. Certainly autonomy and independence are significant factors in many studies of job
satisfaction in work, so that the extent to which
this sense of independence will survive where adult
education is located in community schools and
colleges of further education, where there are constraints of organization, will be significant to
observe in the coming decade. Another factor that
might contribute to full-time adult educators having satisfaction in their work might be because they
regard it as both important to respond to people's
needs and to provide another chance for the most needy
(Mee and Wiltshire 1978:95). In contrast to this,
part-time adult educators tend to acknowledge that
adult education is recreational, according to Mee
and Wiltshire, and this was confirmed by Graham et
al (1982:57) who suggested that enjoyment was the
part-timers main reward for teaching in adult education. Elsey (1980:136), however, notes that for
volunteer adult literacy tutors there is an
altruistic motive to their work.

Newman (1979) also depicted the part-time tutors
in the same rather journalistic manner as he did
the full-timers. In this instance, he categorised

them by motive and type rather than by the role they
perform. He described four types: the professionals - who spend their leisure time teaching about
their full-time johs; the horses' mouth - who teach
about their experiences rather than any academic
discipline that they have studied; the passionate
amateurs - who teach their hobbies; the school-
teachers - who teach the discipline that they teach
at school or college or that they studied when they
were at college. Like Newman, Graham et al (1982:
59-63) also classify the part-time adult educators
in a four fold manner: qualified school teachers,
subject specialists, professionals and apprentices.
While their first three types are self-explanatory
the last one does require some explanation: the
apprentice in the adult educator who began by attending adult classes in the subject that they now teach
and who have worked their way from student to teacher.
      Despite this diversity,adult education still
conforms to other occupations in a number of ways.
For instance, Verner (1964:47) states that in
America 64% of paid adult educators were male but
men only constituted 44% of the volunteer force.
Mee and Wiltshire (1978:59) note that 'there are
probably some nine male organizers to every female'
in the United Kingdom. Similarly, in the higher
status adult teaching, 87% of responsible body
(university extension work) tutors were male, but in
local authority adult education provision 57% were
women (Hutchinson 1970). Similar findings are recorded from other research in local education authority adult education; Graham et al (1982:51) report 64%
of their sample were women; Handley (1981:82) noted
73% of her respondents were women; Jarvis (1982b)
recorded 79% of tutors in a small village adult education centre prospectus were women; Martin's
(1981:122) research revealed about two thirds of the
respondents were women. While this evidence is
piecemeal and circumstantial these studies all indicate that while many women are employed in adult
education they are scarcer in the higher eschalons
of the work.
      Unlike other occupations, however, adult educa-
tion has not yet developed a career route directly
from initial training into the work of an adult educator, since there has been no full-time initial
training! This has had certain repercussions on the
age structure of the occupational group. Verner
(1964:45), citing a study by Brunner et al (1959),
states that:

      Individuals enter the field of adult education

relatively late in their careers. Brunner
found the medium age to be 35.5 years. Furthermore, 23 per cent did not enter the field until
they were forty-two or older, although some 34
per cent of the membership of AEA (Adult
Education Association) were employed in the
field by the age of thirty one. Thus, adult
education tends to recruit its leadership from
other fields at the midpoint in the individual's
career rather than gaining its membership
directly out of college.

It would be interesting to compare Brunner's findings with statistics for adult education in America
in the 1980's to see if the age of entry has lowered. Since there is also little provision for initial training on the education of adults in the
United Kingdom, a similar picture probably exists,
although there is little published evidence to
support this assumption. It is certainly true that
the professions generally expect candidates entering
into teaching to have practised for a number of
years prior to entering, so that many educators of
adults in these occupations tend not to commence
their teaching career until they are relatively old.
Mee and Wiltshire (1978:59), however, fail to con-
firm this assumption for local education authority
staff when they discovered that the mean age for
centre organizers was 43 years, which is about the
point of mid-career.
    Statistics for part-time staff are also in-
conclusive since the National Institute of Adult
Education discovered that 49% of local education
authority adult educators were between 35 years and
54 years, whereas 61% of university extension tutors
were in the same age range (Hutchinson 1970:173).
Graham et al (1982:51) recorded that their sample of
part-time tutors were spread across the whole age
range: 13% between 20 and 29 years; 36% between
30 and 39 years; 25% between 40 and 49 years; 17%
between 50 and 59 years; 8% over 60 years. By contrast, Handley (1981) recorded a much less even
distribution from her sample which was, however,
very small: 18.5% of her male respondents, but only
2.7% female respondents, were under 30 years of age
and, at the other end of the age range, 11.1% of the
male respondents were over 60 years. (This may
suggest that, for some, teaching in adult education
is regarded as a retirement occupation for a few
years). In common with Graham et al, Martin (1981:
122) discovered a more even distribution of tutors
by age, with a slightly greater proportion being in

the 31-40 years age group.

It would not be surprising if individuals did
not want to teach adults until they had achieved a
degree of maturity themselves, since it requires considerable confidence in the teacher if the majority of
his students are older than he is.. Nevertheless,
adult learners do not appear to mind having a young
teacher so long as he is seen to be competent in his
subject. This acceptance by the older ones of the
younger persons as teachers may itself be an indi-
cation of the speed of aspects of cultural change
and the latter's realization of how difficult it is
to keep abreast with developments. However, it
would be most interesting to discover if more younger people would enter this field at an earlier age
if there were more full-time training provision.

The main route into full-time local education
authority adult teaching appears to be through
school teaching or college lecturing (Mee and
Wiltshire 1978:60) and it will be interesting to see
if more teachers enter the field at a younger age in
those local education authorities which are locating
their adult education provision in community schools
and colleges of further education. It will also be
recalled that about a third of part-time adult educators
are school teachers, eg. Newman's (1979) typology above.
The National Institute of Adult Education's survey
in 1967-8 confirmed this since 116 of the 309 respondents to a questionnaire were school teachers, of
whom 79% were male. A further 75 were in business,
of whom 69% were men and the remaining 102 were
housewives. In Handley's small study, she (1981:63)
records that 'fifteen subjects were full-time
teachers, fifty four were housewives, eighteen were
employed other than in teaching (and) six had part-
time employment'. There were also four miscellan-
eous respondents. Thus school teaching appears to
be a major full-time occupation for part-time educators of adults and this raises some quite significant questions about the extent to which teacher
training equips people to teach adults, a point to
which further reference will be made elsewhere in
this chapter.

That so many of the part-time adult educators
are housewives does call into question the assertion
by Mee and Wiltshire (1978:93) that since 'the
spare-timer's career is committed elsewhere ... he
is, therefore, much less affected by the feelings of
insecurity which conditions the attitudes of his
full-time colleagues'. Such a claim may be true for
many of the male part-time adult educators who have

full-time careers but it may be much less true of
the housewives whose part-time adult education
teaching is their only occupation outside of the
home, especially those who fall into the category of
full-time part-time adult educator. Graham et al
(1982) discovered, for instance, that 8% of their
respondents taught more than four classes per week,
that is at least eight hours classroom contact, and
Jarvis (1982b) found two part-time staff in a small
village adult education centre who had at least the
same amount of teaching. Yet these tutors have no
more job security than those who only teach one
class per week. Indeed, it is the very conditions
of insecurity among part-time teachers, claimed
Hetherington (1980),that prevented many of them
from wishing to professionalize, an assumption that
itself requires further examination.

Insecurity may be one reason for the apparently
rapid turn-over of part-time tutors in adult education. The Advisory Committee's report suggests that
between 20% and 25% per annum untrained staff per
annum leave the service and the average length of
time spent in the form of part-time employment is
about four years. Graham et al (1982:82) confirmed
this statistic, having discovered 18% of their
sample had taught for less than one year. A quarter
of the respondents in a recent study in Lingfield
(Jarvis 1982b:84) were new to the centre in the year
of the research but since no questions were asked
about their previous teaching experience it would be
false to conclude that this research also confirms
the figure. Tutor mobility between centres is
clearly a possibility and the extent to which it
occurs is still to be investigated. The system of
annual contracts certainly encourages mobility,
especially if a tutor's class has not run successfully in a centre in any year, then there is no
reason why he should not seek employment elsewhere
on another occasion. Such mobility might result in
tutors becoming committed to adult education but not
to the local adult education institution.

Having examined the adult educator and his role
it is now necessary to see the orientation towards
training and to examine the assumption that
Hetherington made.

THE ADULT EDUCATOR'S TRAINING AND QUALIFICATIONS

Adult education, like most other branches of education in the United Kingdom, except initial education,

has been slow to produce a national pre-service teacher training scheme. While it was hoped that this would develop from recent developments in the United Kingdom, which are discussed below, it does appear to be rather idealistic although in-service training is beginning to occur nationally. Campbell (1977) and Caldwell (1981) both indicate that a similar situation prevails in North America. Indeed, many who enter adult education on a full-time basis, let alone those who are part-time teachers, have no qualification in the education of adults at all; their teaching qualifications being in the education of children. Hence, it is possible to see that the discussion about the differences between andragogy and pedagogy has practical implications since, while there are common elements, there may be enough significant differences to raise questions about the appropriateness of a pedagogic qualification for teaching adults and, also, it is fundamental to the consideration about the extent to which adult education can professionalize.

Training for adult education teachers was raised in the 1919 Report when it was suggested that more opportunities should be provided for training (para. 261) and that such teachers 'should have adequate remuneration and a reasonable degree of financial security' (para. 271). Thereafter, tutor training occupied the minds of adult educators on a number of occasions: Peers (1972:217) noted that:

> The matter was raised again by the Adult Education Committee of the Board of Education in a report published in 1922 (The Recruitment, Training and Remuneration of Teachers). In a report published by the Carnegie United Kingdom Trust in 1928, the result of an enquiry undertaken jointly by the British Institute of Adult Education and the Tutor's Association, the problem of training was discussed more fully and an account was given of existing experiments. Finally, after some years of discussion by a sub-committee of the Universities Council for Adult Education, the whole ground was surveyed again with some thoroughness in a report published in 1954. (Tutors and their Training).

Peers (1972:223) claims that training for adult education should be a major activity for all extramural departments but this suggestion has been slow to be adopted and, for a while after the 1954 report tutor training ceased to occupy a significant place in the concerns of adult education. Martin (1981:124) for instance, notes her disappointment that Mee and Wiltshire, whose work was published in 1978, 'dealt so little with training'. Indeed, when Legge (1968) wrote about the topic in the late 1960s there were few other adult educators expressing the same interest. This is very evident from the relatively little space devoted to tutor training in the National Institute of Adult Education's national survey (Hutchinson 1970:177) but which stated that the 'proportion of Local Education Authority tutors claiming some kind of training was markedly higher than among their Responsible Body colleagues (34%: 8%) and (that) a higher proportion was in favour of the provision of training facilities (74%:57%).' However, there were movements at this time to initiate training schemes and the East Midlands Regional Advisory Council for Further Education introduced one in 1969 which had three stages (Elsdon 1970): an introduction, a more advanced course and, finally, a certificate course which was to be validated by the University of Nottingham. This scheme was introduced, and a description of this is given by Bestwick and Chadwick (1977); it has subsequently assumed greater significance since it was the model upon which the Advisory Council for the Supply and Training of Teachers used for its recommendation a decade later. However, before these recommendations are discussed it is necessary to review the research that puts these developments into perspective.

As Martin noted, little empirical research was actually published during this period either to demonstrate the expressed or felt needs of part-time or full-time staff for training or the extent to which provision was being made for their training, although the Russell Report (1973) suggested that part-time staff might be prepared to be trained and argued that appropriate training should be introduced. By the time that such research was published the Russell Report's recommendation had been acted upon and the Advisory Committee Report published. Even so, Martin (1981:122) noted that while 41% of her sample of 3,313 part time tutors in the East Anglian Regional Advisory Council area were qualified day school teachers, 37% of her respondents had no qualifications or had undertaken only an induction course mounted by the local adult education institute to familiarise new recruits with the institute, its procedures and adult education generally. The remainder of her sample had a variety of teaching qualifications ranging from the City and Guilds of London Institute, course 730, and teachers

certificates of the Royal Society of Arts to
specialist sports coaching qualifications. In addition, a few actually held an ACSET Stage I award.
Handley discovered a similar picture in her smaller
sample and she (1981:72) records that from:

the total sample 49% had attended training
courses for primary education, 11.8% for
secondary school teaching, 11.8% for further
education and 24.5% for adult teaching.
Another 7.8% had attended combined further
education/adult education teacher training
courses, 2% had attended both primary and
adult training courses and 1% secondary and
adult courses. Of significance is the 23.5%
who had not attended any type of training
course, and the further 12.7% who were non-
respondents.

Graham et al (1982:54) discovered a similar picture
from their sample: 30% (462) had some qualification
in adult education, 34% had school teaching qualifications, 12% had subject qualifications only but
23% had received no training at all. They noted that
women were more likely than men to have undertaken
training in adult education which may indicate that
women who might otherwise have been restricted to
the role of housewife regard this training as important to their future careers. Of the 30% who had
received adult education training about half had a
Stage I qualification from the East Midlands and a
quarter had started the second level, or City and
Guilds 730, course. Only 3%, however, had acquired
a Stage III qualification, from either the Universities of Leicester or Nottingham, which indicates
that the length of time and amount of study required
to complete this course may deter some part-time
staff. Bestwick and Chadwick (1977) also record
that out of the twenty eight part-timers who originally expressed interest in the East Midlands Stage
III scheme, only eight actually completed it.
Clearly if part-time staff are not going to spend
longer than four or five years teaching in adult
education, as was noted previously, then there is
little incentive to study part-time for two of those
years. However, possession of Stage III certificate
may, in itself, be an incentive for part-time staff
not to depart after a short time in the service.

The variety of courses attended by and qualifications held by part-time adult educators is considerable: Handley (1981) notes that the sixty
eight tutors in her sample who had attended courses
in adult and further education held fourteen

191

different qualifications between them. Graham et al
(1982:37-46) actually list the variety of different
teaching and coaching qualifications awarded by nine-
teen organizations whose teachers may be employed in
part-time adult education and yet they did not exhaust the list by any means. In addition, it has to
be recognised that professions, such as nursing,
award their own variety of teaching qualifications, so that before a national scheme for the
training of educators of adults can be introduced
it will be necessary to work out equivalences in
these qualifications. This is already occurring to
some extent since nurse tutors are already being
allowed to enrol as registered nurse tutors if they
held specific teaching qualifications, such as the
Post Graduate Certificate in the Education of Adults
from the University of Surrey and the Certificate of
Education (Further Education) awarded by the Council
of National Academic Awards in specified colleges.

In nursing, unqualified tutor status is regarded as temporary, so that all nurses appointed as
unqualified tutors are expected to seek a course of
study as soon as they are able. This is not the
case in some other professions and neither is it in
adult education. Both Handley and Martin, however,
record some statistics that indicate that a number
of part-time adult education staff experience the
need to undertake training: Handley (1981:76) discovered that 50% of her sample would be prepared to
take advantage of any training provision whereas
38.2% were unsure and 11.8% were unwilling to do so;
Martin (1981:12) records that 240 of her sample had
actually attended the Regional Advisory Council's
Stage I course during their first year of teaching
adults.

It is apparent from these research findings
that training educators of adults had become a significant issue by the late 1970s and that the East
Midlands scheme had played an important part in the
process. Yet an adult education qualification is
not mandatory for practice and no qualified teacher
status actually exists. Indeed, qualified teacher
status, ie. having been trained to teach children,
is still regarded as valid educational qualification
for adult education and Elsdon (1975:29) noted that
while some school teachers undertook training in
adult education they 'would have been theoretically
exempted'. Elsdon's own publication on training
part-time staff may be regarded as another significant landmark in the development of training educators of adults, appearing as it did at about the time

that the Advisory Committee on the Supply and Training of Teachers was giving serious consideration to this topic.

RECENT DEVELOPMENTS IN TRAINING EDUCATORS OF ADULTS

The Advisory Committee on the Supply and Training of Teachers, under the chairmanship of Prof. N Haycocks, published three reports on the training of teachers in further and adult education. The first, in late 1977, concerned itself with the training of full-time further education staff and recommended a two year part-time Certificate of Education (Further Education) course, with a qualification to be awarded at the end of the first year for those who did not wish to progress to the second year. The first year, it was suggested should be more practical but should be planned in conjunction with the second year centre in order to ensure continuity. This report was published at the time that school teacher education was just recovering from the re-organization forced upon it by the James Committee, during which a number of colleges of education were amalgamated with polytechnics and had either become, or expanded, their departments of education. Hence, they, and some of the colleges of education that had retained their independence, were in a position to develop certificate courses in further education and, therefore, they became centres of training for further education teachers.

These colleges, once they had been approved by their Regional Advisory Council, submitted their courses to the Council for National Academic Awards for validation. Initially, the Further Education Board received mainly submissions that led to a certificate of education but, during the first four or five years courses were developed and submitted leading to first degrees, post-graduate certificates and higher degrees. All of these courses concentrated on full-time staff, or at least upon those that had at least ten hours teaching per week, a few demanded only five hours class contact but this tended to be the exception. Hence, the courses were devoted almost exclusively to further education, the majority of adult educators being excluded by the teaching requirement.

In March 1978, the Haycocks Committee made its second report, the subject of which was the training of part-time staff in further and adult education and the training of full-time staff in adult

education. This report commenced by reviewing the
then current provision for training for adult educators and noted that the College of Perceptors and
the City and Guilds of London Institute courses
provided a considerable amount of training at that
time. This was especially true of the City and
Guilds of London Institute Further Education
teachers course (CGLI 730) which attracted some
3000 candidates in 1975 and 1976. About half of
those were tutors in branches of education outside
of further and adult education, notably the health
service professions, Her Majesty's Forces and industry. Nursing has certainly taken advantage of
the existence of this course for many years although, recently, the Panel of Assessors for
District Nursing has withdrawn recognition of it as
a qualifying route for practical work teachers since
it tends to be further education orientated rather
than specifically orientated towards the professional clinical situation. Nevertheless, this course
did attract 700 from the ranks of the part-time
staff of further and adult education, but it was
recognised that it is predominately a further
education course and the City and Guilds of London
Institute has subsequently devised a new course
(CGLI 942) which was piloted in London in 1982.

The Advisory Committee's second report focused
upon the East Midlands Regional scheme and noted
that this was already being regarded as a model upon
which the North West Region was considering constructing its own training programme. Finally, the
Committee recommended that there should be a coherent
scheme of initial training for all teachers working
at post-school level which should lead to the award
of Certificate of Education (Further Education) and
to qualified teacher status, although this was more
fully developed in a subsequent report.

The Haycocks Committee then went on to outline
its proposal for this scheme, which was a three
stage scheme similar to the East Midlands scheme.
The first stage, it was recommended, should be widely available, as an induction, should preferably be
undertaken prior to employment although it was recognised that this was perhaps idealistic, so that it
was suggested that this initial stage might be offered during the first two terms of teaching. While
this proposal appears more realistic it must also be
recognised that new teachers do find preparation
time consuming, so that it might not be as realistic
as it appears at the outset. Caldwell (1981:8) notes
that pre-service training in adult education is also

something of a rarity in the United States. Table
7.1, below, records the suggested content of the
course, which should involve thirty-six hours of
attendance.

Table 7.1:   The Recommended Content
             for Stage I Courses

Motives and expectations of
teachers and students
Setting aims and objectives
Introduction to learning theory
Planning learning situations
Introduction to teaching aids
Introduction to lesson
Evaluation

In addition to learning about the above, it was
suggested that new part-time teachers should have a
mentor who would work closely with them. More
recently, Holt (1982) has argued that there are more
cost-effective ways of preparing teachers in the
classroom, such as micro-teaching. While this is a
useful simulated exercise there is a great deal of
artificiality about it, perhaps even more than there
is about a supervised lesson in a classroom. Even
so, micro-teaching is a very useful tool in training
teachers.
    The second stage of the recommended course was
to be more advanced and involved sixty hours in the
classroom and thirty-six hours of supervised teaching practice. This amount of supervised teaching
practice certainly places the emphasis of the course
on practical teaching but there is little doubt that
this was both an expensive and time-consuming recommendation. Table 7.2 specifies the subjects to be
studied at this level.

Table 7.2:   The Recommended Content
for Stage II Courses

Setting objectives for teaching
Psychology of learning in post-
adolescent stages of life
Teaching methods with post·
school students
Audio-visual aids
Teaching specialist subjects
Context of Further and Adult
Education

It was noted that each of these modules should involve between eight and twelve hours of attendance.
Initially it was considered that some of this might
actually be reduced by the utilisation of resource
based packages which is clearly an interesting suggestion,although the final report did not make such a
recommendation. Little distance learning material at
this level has been produced,except the Open
University's course, which is produced in conjunction with the Council of Europe. The draft scheme
of this course was published in 1982 and its content
includes three booklets:
   - adult learners: needs, motivations and
          expectations
   - adult learners: responding to need
   - further reference booklet, containing fif-
          teen short papers on different but relevant
          topics
Ventures of this nature are important for the development of adult education, since they highlight
specific elements of the emerging discipline of
adult education. However, it is difficult for skills
based courses to be provided by distance education
and while resource based packages can reduce contact
time, the skills elements still involve some form of
supervision.
     Stage II courses are pitched at about the same
level as the City and Guilds of the London Institute
Further Education Teachers' Certificate, course 730.
The revised course (City and Guilds 1978) includes
the following topic areas:

Table 7.3: The Recommended Content
of the City and Guilds
Course 730

Principles of learning
Principles of teaching strategy
Learning resources
Course organization and
curriculum development
Assessment
Communication
The teacher's role in relation
to students in further
education

This course also has supervised teaching practice,
so that it approximates even more closely to the
Stage II courses. Recently, the City and Guilds
have actually piloted a course (CGLI 942) which is
specifically orientated to Stage II of training for
adult education.

The third stage of this training, the Advisory
Committee recommended, should lead to full certifi-
cation and should be provided by institutions in
which 'there is a substantial nucleus of experienced
staff who have themselves completed courses in advanced study in education and whose major commitment
is the professional education and development of
teachers at the post-school stage'. No other
specific location was suggested for these courses
nor was the content of the curriculum specified.
However, it was stipulated that the course should
take one year full-time or two years part-time study.

In addition, the Advisory Committee recognised
the diversity of adult education, so that it made
the following recommendations for the training of
full-time staff:
- new, untrained teachers entering full-time
  teaching in adult education should embark
  upon the first stage of the full-time
  Further Education Certificate recommended
  in the first Haycocks Report
- for those trained as teachers, in sectors
  other than further education, a six week
  part-time, conversion course
- for part-time adult educators who have
  taken Stages I and II, a Stage III course

> leading to a Certificate in Education (FE)
- a one year full-time, or eqivalent part-time,
for those who possess the Certificate in
Education (FE) for those who wish to work
as organizers and administrators in adult
education - leading to an advanced diploma
in adult education or higher degree

Thus, it may be seen that no division between further
education and adult education existed in the recommendations for initial training at all three levels
and that it was only at post-certificate level that
adult education was regarded as a specialism. Hence,
there is a conceptual confusion in the report that
is also evident in its recommendations. This was
one of the criticisms made by the Advisory Council
for Adult and Continuing Education (1978) in its
formal response to the recommendations. In addition,
it criticised them for being too narrow, for trying
to combine forms of training that ought to be separated and for omitting any consideration of using
the university departments of adult education in initial training. These are all valid criticisms of
an important but conceptually confused report, so
that it is not surprising that the training of education staff has developed less rapidly than that of
further education staff. By mid-1981, Graham et al
(1982:1) report that there was considerable variation in provision both between and within Regional
Advisory Council areas. They also noted that while
areas had introduced Stage I schemes, fewer Councils
had approved guidelines for Stage II. Stage III
schemes appeared to be assuming one of two forms:
either the Certificate of Education (Further Education), as recommended by the Advisory Committee on
the Supply and Training of Teachers,but in other
regions consideration was being given for special
arrangements with universities in which Certificate
of Education (Adult Education) would be awarded.
This is a confusion that, in retrospect, the
Advisory Committee might have prevented had its
recommendations been a little clearer, but it must
be borne in mind that in the United Kingdom adult
education is usually coupled with further education
for administrative purposes. However, one university (Surrey) has already introduced a post-graduate
certificate in the education of adults, in which the
process of teaching and learning among adults is
paramount, irrespective of what professional background the trainee teacher comes, although the
specific sphere of intended teaching does constitute
an option within the study and is also the area in

which the teaching practical experience is gained.
Thus the term 'education of adults' rather than
'adult education' does overcome some of the conceptual difficulties raised by the Advisory Committee's
report and the scheme at Surrey allows for teachers
of adults to be trained together irrespective of
whether they come from adult, further or higher education or from the professions. More recently (1983),
there has also been a proposal by the new Advisory
Committee for the Supply and Education of Teachers
for a Certificate in Education course for all
teachers, irrespective of their background.

Higher education has rarely been mentioned in
the above discussion since it is usually regarded as
distinct from further and adult education. Even so,
this division has been blurred recently with a
number of colleges being called 'colleges of further
and higher education'. Indeed, some of the early
proposals for certificate in education courses made
to the Council for National Academic Awards specified that they were in further and higher education.
The Council, however, did not recommend acceptance
of many titles incorporating the term and yet most
students in higher education are adults, so that
teachers in higher education are actually teachers
of adults. Some initial training of teachers is
occurring in some universities and polytechnics, but
few have moved in the direction of awarding qualifications, such as Stage I etc. in higher education.
Nevertheless, the London Region of the Workers
Educational Association, which offers a variety of
part-time courses for adults including university
extension classes, has introduced a training scheme
for its own part-time staff, which is based on the
Advisory Committee's recommendations and which is
recognised as a Stage I course. This may prove a
precedent for other organizations to introduce
similar schemes for their part-time tutors, if not
for their full-time staff.

Planning schemes for the first two stages of
training has become the responsibility of the institutions offering the courses and validation rests
with the Regionsl Advisory Councils. However, the
Advisory Committee on the Supply and Training of
Teachers recommended that there should be some type
of national forum established in order to ensure
comparability and transferability. At the time of
writing, it is clear that the training schemes have
not been established long enough for such a forum to
emerge. However, the Council for National Academic
Awards may perform this role for the Stage III

199

courses that it validates but since some universities also offer these courses, there would still be no single national forum.

Having examined the education of adult education in some detail it is now necessary to discuss the qualities of the adult educator and possible criteria for curricula of training.

THE QUALITIES OF THE ADULT EDUCATOR AND CRITERIA FOR CURRICULA OF TRAINING

While the Advisory Committee made certain recommendations for the curriculum for the first two stages of training in the education of adults, no recommendations were made about the third one. However, even the first two stages reflected the values and philosophies prevalent in the Committee at that time. Clearly, the Committee expected the initial training to be very practical, almost a survival kit for teachers. The fact that 'objectives' occur in both stages suggests that the Committee were concerned with a teacher–centred approach to teaching and, one that might allow for a behavioural objectives approach, which it would be claimed here is contrary to much in the philosophy of the education of adults. Curriculum recommendations can never be free of the values of the designer, but these values do need to be assessed before accepting uncritically the curriculum content suggestions made in the report. It is also necessary to explore the relationship between curriculum recommendations for training and the role of the practitioner. Four such relationships are examined here: the role of the adult educator as the basis for the curriculum for training; the idealized, or theoretical, role of the adult educator as the basis of the training curriculum; the elements of role competency which might form a base; the demands of the emerging descipline. Each of these four possible relationships are now examined.

The Role of the Adult Educator as a Basis for the Curriculum of Training: Earlier to this chapter the diversity of roles of the educator of adults was discussed and the difference between the work of the full-time and part-time staff were clearly noted; the former playing an administrative and managerial role and the latter performing a predominately teaching function. Hence, it might be argued that the full-time adult educators need a diploma in management as much as they need a certificate of education, since the

current situation is one in which they may be performing roles for which they have not been trained
and trained for ones they are not playing! It is
perhaps significant that educational management
formed a part of the final report from the Haycocks
Committee (August 1983).
     Even if the role of the adult educator were to
form the basis of training, a number of problems
exist, such as: the extent to which it is possible
to analyse such a diverse role; the fact that no
analysis has been conducted scientifically and, even
if it had, it would only be valid for the contemporary situation; it includes no predictions about
how the role will change in the future, so that it
does not consitute an adequate basis for training
the next generation of adult educators. Does this
mean that the training curriculum need bear no relationship to the manner in which the role is performed? No, this is certainly not the case - any
role analysis should be taken into consideration
when designing curricula for training adult educators but they should not form its only base.

The Theoretical Role of the Adult Educator as a Basis for a
Curriculum of Training: In contrast to the actual role
of the educators of adults it might be argued that
it is better to train new recruits into the role
that they should play, rather than the one that
current practitioners are actually performing. Yet
the values in this perspective must be recognised
since the varying approaches to the role, radical,
political, social welfare, etc. have been explicit
in the previous discussion. Even so, many attempts
have been made to construct criteria of the ideal-
ised, or theoretical, role of the adult educator and
having reviewed many of them Campbell (1977:58)
wrote:

>   Such lists are well nigh endless, indeed tire-
>   some - but useful to a degree. Out of this
>   formidable, though by no means exhaustive
>   array of analyses it is possible to identify
>   three distinct, significant clusters of com-
>   petencies marking the ideal adult educator
>   which can be taken as generalized goals for
>   training. The first is a conviction within
>   the adult educator of the potentiality for
>   growth of adults, and a strong personal commit-
>   ment to adult education exemplified by the ex-
>   tension of his own education. The willingness
>   to accept others' ideas, the encouragement of
>   freedom of thought and expression is fundamental

as is a dynamic rather than a static view of
the field of adult education. The second is
the possession of certain skills - of writing
and speaking, certainly - but also the capacity
to lead groups effectively, to direct complex
administrative activity, and to exercise a
flair in the development of programs. Finally,
the adult educator must understand the conditions under which adults learn, their motivation for learning, the nature of the community and its structure. Underlying all of these,
and essential, is an understanding of oneself
undergirded by a sustaining personal
philosophy.

Tough (1979:181-3) echoes many of these points in
his discussion of the characteristics of the ideal
helper as: warm and loving; having confidence in
the learner's ability; being prepared always to
enter a genuine dialogue with the learner; having a
strong motivation to help; being an open and growing person. Both Campbell and Tough reflect the
humanistic tradition that is prevalent in adult education, but which may be less strong in other areas
of the education of adults. For instance, Gibbs and
Durbridge (1976) asked Open University full-time
staff tutors what they looked for in effective part-
time tutors. The replies that they received were
reported under the following heading: knowledge of
the subject matter; ability to handle the subject
matter; general teaching skills; classroom skills;
correspondence skills; social competence; academic
suitability; values and work rate; administrative
competence; interesting style; systematic style;
understanding style; informal, flexible style.
Hence, it may be seen that more emphasis was placed
upon the teacher and his teaching skills by Open
University staff, than upon the adult educator as a
human being who facilitates adult learning. More
recently, Mocker and Noble (1981:45-6) have sought
to construct a fairly full list, but even they warn
their readers that it is neither exhaustive nor is
it a blue print for training. Their twenty four
different competencies are that an adult educator
should be able to:

1. communicate effectively with learners
2. develop effective working relationships
   with learners
3. re-inforce positive attitudes towards
   learners
4. develop a climate that will encourage

            learners to participate

5. establish a basis for mutual respect with learners
6. adjust rate of instruction to the learners' rate of progress
7. adjust teaching to accommodate individual and group characteristics
8. differentiate between teaching children and teaching adults
9. devise instructional categories that will develop the learners' confidence
10. maintain the learners' interest in classroom activities
11. adjust a program to respond to the changing needs of learners
12. use classrooms and other settings that provide a comfortable learning environment
13. recognise learners' potentiality for growth
14. place learners at their instructional level
15. summarize and review the main points of a lesson or demonstration
16. participate in a self-evaluation of teaching effectiveness
17. provide continuous feedback to the learners on their educational progress
18. select those components of a subject area that are essential to learners
19. coordinate and supervise classroom activities
20. determine those principles of learning that apply to adults
21. demonstrate belief in innovation and experimentation by willingness to try new approaches in the classroom
22. plan independent study with learners
23. apply knowledge of material and procedures gained from other teachers
24. relate classroom activities to the experience of learners.

At first sight this list appears full and exhaustive and yet on closer scrutiny there are points with which some adult educators may wish to dispute. Indeed, this would be the case with any such list, however long it might be. The values of the person who constructs such an inventory must always be apparent in it, so that no such list could provide an undisputed basis for devising a curriculum of training. If many lists were consulted, it might be possible to distil out the common factors which

might provide something of a foundation but without
an agreed theoretical perspective this approach
fails to provide a problem-free approach.

A Conceptual Framework of Professional Competency: Instead
of attempting to utilize every element in the professional role, Jarvis (1983a:35) has suggested that
it is necessary to analyse the concept of competency
and this might help provide a basis upon which a
curriculum could be constructed. It was suggested
that this could be built upon the triple foundations
of the practitioner's knowledge, skill and attitude:
-   knowledge and understanding of:relevant aca-
       demic discipline(s),psycho-motor elements,
       interpersonal relations, moral values
-   skills to: perform the psycho-motor tech-
       niques, interact with members of the role
       set
-   attitudes that result in: a knowledge and
       commitment to professionalisalism, a
       willingness to play the role in a profess-
       ional manner
From such a basis it should be possible to devise
the content of any training curriculum but, at the
same time, it allows for negotiation between all
interested parties as to what is actually included.
However, it might be objected that attitudes should
not constitute part of the training but, since adult
education is a humanistic enterprise, it is maintained here that attitude education is an important
element in the preparation of educators of adults.

The Demands of the Discipline: The previous approach
outlines only broad guidelines rather than specific
content and the approaches before that have attempted to relate the training to the role performance.
Yet some professions have sought to separate theory
from practice and tend to regard competence in the
academic discipline underlying their practice as
sufficient grounds for entry into the profession.
Turner and Rushton (1976) outline the training programmes of a number of different professions and it
is significant to note the place that the academic
discipline plays and the way by which skills are
underplayed. It is claimed here that new en-
trants to adult education should never be trained in
this manner, and even if adult education had its own
discipline, the theory should never take total precedence over the practical.

Having examined a number of different approaches to

the relationship between training and practice it is
maintained that no single, simple set of guidelines
may be constructed that would enable trainers to
construct a universally accepted training curriculum,
so that it might be appropriate at this point to recall Legge's (1981:64-5) conclusion about training
teachers of adults:

> There are many questions to which we have had
> no firm answers, and whole areas in which re-
> search has been thin. Trainers should, there-
> fore, plan each course as a new venture and not
> allow themselves to fall into the rut of just
> repeating a previous course. It is, of course,
> easier and less time consuming to develop a
> standard pattern, but it is as vitally import-
> ant to keep the experimental nature of training
> as it is to focus sharply on the objective of
> improving the quality of teachers in the real
> world of classes and tutorials.

THE PROFESSIONALIZATION OF ADULT EDUCATION?

The introduction of these new training schemes for
adult education is going to have some effect on the
structure of the occupation over the coming years
and it is suggested here that this may be viewed as
a stage in the process of professionalization. Yet
some writers on adult education, eg. Elsdon (1975),
Mee (1980), Wiltshire (1981), claim that it is
already a profession. However, there has not yet
been a full and detailed analysis of adult education
from the perspective of students of occupations and
professions, so that these claims appear to be little
more than adult educators making claims on behalf
of their own occupation. No attempt is made to analyse these claims here since this is a separate
study. However, it is maintained that the present
structures of adult education conform closely to
those occupations generally regarded as semi-
professions, so that the introduction of training
may be regarded as a stage in its professionalization. Jarvis (1975) suggested that a semi-
profession has the following characteristics: no
firm theoretical base; no monopoly of exclusive
skills nor special area of competence; the existence of rules to guide practice; less specializa-
tion than occupations generally regarded as professions; control exercised by non-professionals;
service ethic. Space forbids and full discussion

of each of these points, although it is essential
to note that the development of a body of knowledge
about the education of adults has received a stimulus from the introduction of these training courses
for adult educators, a movement towards a more firm
theoretical base. However, the area of competence
may be teaching rather than teaching adults, so that
the debate about the differences between andragogy
and pedagogy may be seen in this context too. If
there is no difference, then adult education has no
separate disclipline(s) and the adult educator is
not a member of a separate occupation but a member
of a branch of teaching. Yet if there is a separate
area of competence in teaching adults, how does this
competence differ from that of the craftsman who
instructs the apprentice on the job or the salesman
who teachers his client to use the sophisticated
technical equipment that he has just sold him? There
are no rules to guide practice, at least not codified and enforceable ones, and autonomy was one
aspect that gave job satisfaction, as Mee and
Whiltshire (1978) highlighted. However, it has been
clearly demonstrated that there is little special-
ization in the occupation since teachers of adults
may be qualified in teaching, qualified in some other
occupation or not qualified at all. With few exceptions control over adult education is now exercised
by non adult educators and there is no professional
body of adult educators which can exercise the control over adult education that the British Medical
Association exercises over its members. There is a
strong service ethic in adult education which also
conforms to the semi-professional model.

Even so, it must be recognised that this model
of a semi-profession is characterised by a number of
traits, which is one of its major weaknesses since
there is no theoretical reason why other characteristics should not be added to or subtracted from the
present list. Consequently, this type of analysis
is open to some criticism, but it is also the
approach that Mee (1980:105) employs for his analysis of adult education as a profession. It is a
frequent analytical approach in the study of the
professions but one that is of suspect value.
Another reason why it is not favoured is that it
presents a rather static picture of occupations and
yet they are undergoing rapid change. It is for
this reason that the term 'profession' is regarded
as a conceptual 'ideal type' rather than an actuality and the idea of professionalization, a process
of change in the direction of the ideal type, is

more frequently employed. A number of attempts to describe the process of professionalization have been published, eg. Caplow (1954), Greenwood (1957), but that very widely accepted is the formulation by Wilensky (1964). He suggested that as occupations professionalize they undergo a sequence of structural changes which, while not invarient, form a progression.

1. The occupation becomes full-time
2. It establishes a training school, which it later seeks to associate with universities
3. It forms its own professional association which seeks:
   - to define the core tasks of the occupation
   - to create a cosmopolitan perspective to the practice of the occupation
   - to compete with neighbouring occupations in order to establish an area of exclusive competence
   - to seek legal support for the protection of the job teritory
4. It publishes its own code of ethics to assure the public that it will serve its needs

If this approach is adapted to the analysis of adult education it may be seen immediately that it is still functioning at the first two stages of the process and the recent developments described above merely indicate that adult education has just begun the process. Yet Illich (1977) must serve as a reminder to adult education that while there may be advantages in pursuing this process, there are also many dangers.

Yet it may be asked further whether it is important that adult education should be regarded as a profession? Perhaps it is important because adult education has traditionally been regarded as marginal to education. However, a much more important question may be whether its practitioners are professional? The term 'professional' has at least three meanings: one who receives emoluments for the performance of his occupational tasks; one who practises an occupation generally regarded as a profession; one who is an expert since he is both master of a specific branch of learning and of the skill to practise the occupation based upon it. It is this last meaning to which reference is being made here since it is much more important that adult educators be professional than it is that the occupation should be regarded as a profession. Nevertheless, if its practitioners were generally regarded as experts then it would, perhaps, be easier for the occupation to progress along the pathway of professionalization.

SUMMARY

Teachers of adults and their preparation has formed the basis of this chapter, which began with a consideration of the extent to which adult education is actually an occupation and ended with an analysis of the extent to which it is a profession. The first question was raised because there are comparatively few full-time adult educators and many who teach on a part-time basis. It was also recognised that many who actually teach adults full-time, eg. those in the professions, who would not regard themselves as being members of an educational occupation but who regard themselves as members of their original profession. Thereafter, the roles of the adult educator were discussed and it was recognised that the full-time adult educators may be managers, employers, entrepreneurs, trainers, supervisors but that they may not actually be educators! - except when they supervise their part-time staff or train their new recruits. By contrast, the part-time educator is actually the teacher who facilitates the students' learning. The characteristics of both full-time and part-time staff were examined and it was noted that, in common with most occupational groups, it is male dominated in those areas having higher status and more power.

The qualifications of adult education staff were analysed and their lack of training in adult education noted. This led to a discussion about the introduction of a national training scheme for adult educators, having three stages rather like the East Midlands Regional scheme that was already in operation before the report by the Advisory Committee was published. The confusion between adult education and further education was noted and it was recognised that this might lead to differing schemes in different Regional Advisory Council areas.

The qualities of an effective educator of adults were discussed an it was recognised that any list of qualities would be a subjective assessment which hardly constituted a sufficient basis upon

which to construct a programme of training. Other
criteria for devising training curricula were discussed and it was concluded that every new course
should be regarded as a new venture and that this
would help to keep the training of adult educators
experimental and prevent it from ossifying.

Finally, it was suggested that adult education
may he viewed as a semi-profession in the very early
stages of professionalization rather than as a fully-
fledged professional occupation. Having examined
the concepts surrounding the education of adults,
learning and teaching and the teacher of adults, it
is now necessary to analyse the educational process,
so that the following chapter focuses upon the
relation between curriculum theory and the education
of adults.

SELECTED FURTHER READING

Adult Education as a Field of Study and Practice
    D D Campbell 1977

This is a thorough survey of a great deal of comparative literature in which the whole field of
training is discussed. It contains many insights
and much valuable material.

Training the Educators of Adults   *A Charnley, M Osborn*
                                    and A Withnall 1982

The National Institute of Adult Education has published a number of reviews of existing research in
specific fields of adult education. This is a
thorough review of a great deal of literature. It
provides a comprehensive introduction and some comparative material.

Training for Adult Education   *K T Elsdon 1975*

This book, now a little dated because of the recent
rapid developments in training, remains the only one
published in the United Kingdom that seeks to

explore the rationale for, and provides a number of
models of, training. Therefore, it is an important
book to read for any one concerned to place training
in a broad, theoretical, framework.

Preparing Educators of Adults   *S M Grabowski et al 1981*

One of the series of studies produced by the Adult
Education Association of the United States of
America, containing chapters on different aspects of
training in America. This book is thorough and most
interesting to read.

The Training of Part-Time Teachers of Adults
T B Graham et al 1982

This is a research report conducted by members of
the Department of Adult Education at the University
of Nottingham. The empirical study is thorough and
enlightening but there are few theoretical references and a very limited bibliography. Nevertheless,
this is an important piece of work because it documents the present situation in respect to training
very thoroughly.

The Training of Adult Education and Part-Time Further
Education Teachers   *J N Haycocks (chairman) 1978*

This is a report of the Advisory Committee on the
Supply and Training of Teachers on which many of the
current developments in training are based. It is
important to read since it is widely quoted and because it is very influential. It is short and easy
to read.

Training of Adult Educators in East Europe   *J Kulich (Ed)*
1977

One of a series of monographs published by the
University of British Columbia, providing a description of the training programmes for adult education being organized in Eastern European societies.
It is an interesting study, especially for those
interested in comparative education.

Chapter Eight

CURRICULUM THEORY IN ADULT AND CONTINUING EDUCATION

'Curriculum' is a relatively common word in initial
education but one used rarely in the education of
adults. In the United Kingdom, in adult education
it is more common to refer to a 'programme' while
American writers, use the terms 'design of learning'
(Verner, 1964) or 'design of education (Houle,1972).
The concerns of adult education have tended to be
centred around the topics that have already been
discussed in this study and yet there has always
been an implicit curriculum theory and also some
explicit statements of rationale for adult education. In this chapter some of these elements will be
discussed and, at the same time, the curriculum
theory implicit in the ideas already raised in this
study will also become apparent. At the outset it is
necessary to clarify the concept itself and, thereafter, the reasons why the term has not beem employed in the education of adults will be examined.
Various types of curriculum models will then be discussed and this will be followed by an analysis of
the elements of the curriculum, including a discussion of the concept of 'need' which has been
central to considerations in adult education. The
chapter will then conclude with a brief discussion
on the hidden curriculum in the education of adults.

THE CONCEPT OF CURRICULUM

The word derives from the Latin 'currere' which
means 'to run' and its associated noun which has
been translated 'a course'. Hence, the word has
been used to refer to following a course of study
but, like many other terms, its meaning has been
subtly changed over the years and Lawton (1973:11)
notes that 'in the past definitions ... tended to

emphasize the content of the teaching programme, now writers on the curriculum are much more likely to define it in terms of the whole learning situation'. Similarly Kelly (1977:3) suggests that it is necessary to 'distinguish the use of the word to denote the content of a particular subject or area of study from the use of it to refer to the total programme of an educational institution'. From these two brief quotations it is possible to see that even these writers are referring to slightly different usages of the word. Perhaps Griffin's (1978:5) comment that curriculum refers to 'the entire range of educational practices or learning experiences' summarises the problem. The word can mean the total provision of an educational institution, it can also refer to the subject matter of a particular course of study or even to the learning that is intended. Hence, it relates to both the known and the intended, ie. the educational organization and provision, or to the unknown and unquantifiable, ie. the learning experiences. Perhaps the various usages of the word can be clarified slightly by the following diagram.

Figure 8.1: The Uses of the
Term CURRICULUM

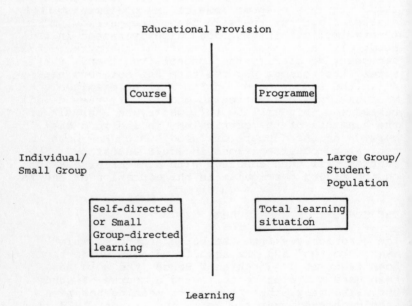

The above diagram illustrates the different ways in which the term has been employed over the past two decades, especially in initial education. However, it is necessary to clarify the terms used and to explain each of the four boxes. Educational provision refers to either what is organised and offered to students by the institutions or to what is organised and offered to the students by the teachers within those institutions. Learning refers to what the students actually acquire from having been the recipients of the educational provision. The large group/student population can refer to the actual or the potential student population of a whole institution eg. a college, or to a large part of the institution, eg. a department within the college. The small group may refer to a single group within the department, eg. the health visitor students in a department of health studies, or to an even smaller group working together within a class.

Hence the programme may be either the prospectus provided by an educational institution, or a section of it, or it may refer to the actual number of courses that are organised after enrolment. The total learning situation refers to all the learning experiences, intended or unintended, provided by the educational institution, or by that part of it to which reference is being made. A course may be the course of study followed by an individual within the institution or it may refer to a single course offered to a specific group of students, eg. the health visitor course. Finally, the self-directed, or the small-group directed, learning refers to the learning experiences gained by individuals working on their own projects. It must be emphasized that these terms are not all mutually exclusive since, for instance, the health visitor course may be advertised in the college prospectus and the health visitor students will experience learning within the total learning situation. By contrast, the self-directed learning need not occur within the context of an educational institution, eg. the adult's learning projects discussed by Tough, so that this is a slightly different understanding of the term.

It is perhaps easy to recognise how the confusion in the use of the term has arisen, since each of these terms has an affinity with the others. It is also important to note that the emphasis on learning is a comparatively recent addition and reflects the ideas of the romantic curriculum and progressive education that were prevalent in the United Kingdom in the 1960s. However, it is now necessary to

consider the concept of curriculum within the framework of the education of adults.

THE CONCEPT OF CURRICULUM AND THE EDUCATION OF ADULTS

It was pointed out at the commencement of this
chapter that the term 'curriculum' has not had a
great deal of currency in adult education in the
United Kingdom, apart from the work of Griffin (1978,
1979, 1982) and a little space in Mee and Wiltshire
(1978) and this is because initial studies in the
curriculum were in the compulsory education sector.
Hence, both the term and the studies in curriculum
may appear to have greater relevance in further,
professional and continuing education than in adult
education. In all of these former terms, there are
implications for the organization and provision of
education that are absent from adult education and,
to some extent, this distinction may be reflected
in the implications of control implicit in the
classical curriculum model, which is discussed later
in this chapter. The content of the educational
provision is selected by either a professional body
or by the teachers rather than by the students,
whereas in some adult education, but by no means all,
the students have some opportunity to select what
they wish to learn. Hence, it may be seen that
Lawton's (1973:21) suggestion that the curriculum
content is a selection from culture is significant
and fits into the theoretical perspective of this
study. In the classical curriculum model that content is selected for the students to learn and transmitted by the teachers, but in the romantic curriculum model the content may be selected by the learners. In this approach the learners' own recognition
of their needs, wants or interests are paramount and
recognition of this within the process of learning
and teaching is important since it demonstrates that
the learners' adulthood is taken into consideration
in the total design of their education.
     It could be argued that since the learners are
ignorant of the content of what is to be learned in
some forms of further and professional initial education it should be the perogative of the professional body or the teachers, who should be experts in
the field, to make that selection. This point would
not be disputed here but the manner by which the
selection is made and the methods by which it is
transmitted do require considerable discussion. By
contrast, in continuing professional education the

learners should be aware of what they think that
they ought to learn, so that the student-centred
approach may be more significant and, therefore,
approximate more closely to the model of adult education. Thus, if the learners are free to choose, it
might be argued that the educational institution
should prepare a programme and advertise its courses
to potential students in the professions and occupations in the same way as adult education institutes have offered their courses to the general
public. Hence, it may be seen that the word
'programme' reflects the content of the prospectus
or the total number of courses that are actually
organized by and taught within the educational institution. It may, therefore, be understood why the
term 'programme' has been used so widely in adult
education and why the term 'curriculum' has received
far less consideration. Nevertheless, discussion
about content or how the content is selected does
not exclude consideration of how the content is
learned or transmitted, so that it would be quite
mistaken to endeavour to omit wider curriculum considerations from the study of any sector of education. However, before these differences in approach
are discussed it is necessary to examine the different types of curriculum that have thus far been
mentioned.

TYPES OF CURRICULUM

A great deal of curriculum theory has been produced
as a result of studies in initial education but it
will only be referred to here where it is specifically relevant to the education of adults. Clearly
the distinction between romantic and classical
curricula is relevant since andragogic approaches
may be no more than an extension of the philosophy
of progressive education into the realm of adult education. However, before this distinction is discussed it is necessary to analyse some of the models
of curriculum that have been formulated within the
context of the education of adults and after it is
discussed it will be useful to examine how it has
been applied to different theoretical approaches in
the education of adults. Consequently, this section
contains three parts: curriculum models formulated
in the study of adult education; classical and
romantic curricula; application of classical and
romantic curricular models to the education of
adults.

Curriculum Models formulated in Adult Education: Earlier in this chapter it was noted that some of the American theorists in adult education have concentrated upon the design of education and two of these writers, Verner (1964) and Houle (1972), are examined here. Finally, in a recent study of an adult education institute in the United Kingdom two models of curriculum were developed and they are modified slightly and discussed here.

A considerable proportion of Verner's (1964) study is devoted to the curriculum and table 8.1 below summarises the main elements of his work.

Table 8.1:   A Diagrammatic Portrayal of Verner's Approach to the Curriculum in the Education of Adults

Programme Planning	Programme Administration	Managing the Learning Experience
Determination of need	Promotion and probability	
Identification of educational goals	Finance Facilities	Selection of: methods techniques devices
Arrangement of learning tasks	Instructor training and selection	
Measurement of achievement	Scheduling Counselling	

Evaluation

It may be seen from the above table that Verner bases his planning on a needs meeting approach, a topic that will be considered in detail later in this chapter. He also distinguishes between planning, administration and the actual teaching, but it will be recalled from the discussion on the role of the educator of adults that the managerial and teaching roles were clearly highlighted, so that Verner's threefold distinction may be a little artificial in relation to role performance. Nevertheless, the distinction that he draws between planning and

administration, on the one hand, and managing the
learning experiences, on the other, does reflect the
earlier discussion. Verner employs the term
'techniques' to refer to the ways in which the
teacher establishes a relationship between the learner and the learning tasks, while 'devices' are the
audio-visual aids that the teacher uses to assist
him in his task. Verner's model is a clear taxonomy
of some of the elements of the curriculum but he did
not seek to build it into a comprehensive curriculum
theory. It is, therefore, necessary to examine the
work of Houle, one of the most well known of writers
on this topic in America, who sought to illustrate
the design of education.

Houle (1972), whilst recognising the complexity
of designing an educational programme, produces two
different types of models. He recognises that there
are a variety of different educational situations
in which a programme may be designed and table 8.2
illustrates the eleven different ones that he (1972:
44) considered significant.

Table 8.2: Houle's Major Categories
            of Educational Design
            Situations

Individual

c1 An individual designs an activity for
    himself
c2 An individual or group design an activity
    for another individual

Group

c3 A group (with or without a continuing
    leader) designs an activity for itself
c4 A teacher, or a group of teachers, designs
    an activity for, and often with, a group
    of students
c5 A committee designs an activity for a
    larger group
c6 Two or more groups design an activity which
    will enhance their combined programs of
    service

Institution

c7 A new institution is designed
c8 An institution designs an activity in a
    new format

Table 8.2 continued

    c9 An institution designs a new activity in
        an established format
    c10 Two or more institutions design an activity
        which will enhance their combined programs
        of service

    Mass

    c11 An individual, group, or institution
        designs an activity for a mass audience

It will be seen that these various situations listed by Houle encapsulates a variety of adult learning
situations, so that it is possible to fit within
this framework self-directed learning, on the one
hand, and planning an informative documentary television programme for a mass audience, on the other.
Houle discusses each of these situations very fully
in his writing, which is a most valuable exercise in
the study of the design of education. Nevertheless,
such a classification records nothing of the actual
process that underlies the production of these educational situations, so that he goes on to produce
a model of curriculum design that includes many of
the points that Verner raises, but Houle (1972:47),
does so within the context of a systems approach.

Figure 8.2:   Houle's Decision Points and
              Components of an Adult
              Educational Framework

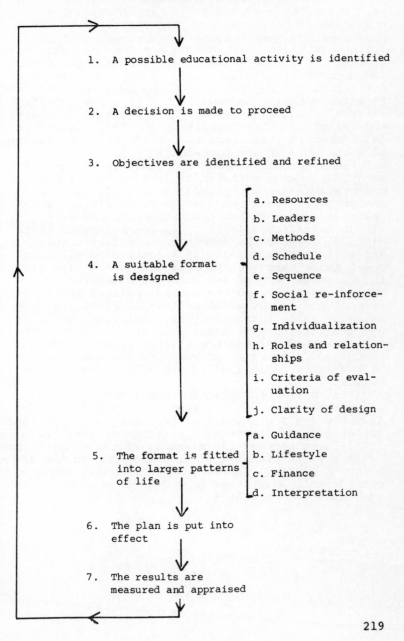

1. A possible educational activity is identified

2. A decision is made to proceed

3. Objectives are identified and refined

4. A suitable format
   is designed

   a. Resources
   b. Leaders
   c. Methods
   d. Schedule
   e. Sequence
   f. Social re-inforce-
      ment
   g. Individualization
   h. Roles and relation-
      ships
   i. Criteria of eval-
      uation
   j. Clarity of design

5. The format is fitted
   into larger patterns
   of life

   a. Guidance
   b. Lifestyle
   c. Finance
   d. Interpretation

6. The plan is put into
   effect

7. The results are
   measured and appraised

219

Houle (1972:46-7) states that in 'applying the
model to a situation, one may begin with any component and proceed to others in any order'. However,
this is not really what the diagram suggests since
it illustrates a sequential cycle which, while
commencement may be made at any point, takes the
programme designer through seven stages with the
fourth and fifth stages having a number of individual
facets. This model is meticulous in its production
and Houle's discussion admirably thorough but it
does adopt the perspective of the adult educator who
is able to design an educational programme free from
external constraint, which may not actually reflect
the reality of what happens during the process. It
is, therefore, necessary to include external factors
as a variable in the process.

In a recent study of one adult education centre
an attempt was undertaken to include the external
factors and also to include the teaching and learning process: this resulted in two different models
being devised - an administrative one and an educational one (Jarvis 1982b). In the following brief
discussion these two models are modified slightly
and their titles amended to a curriculum planning
model and a teaching and learning model. The first
incorporates many of the elements discussed by
Verner and Houle and the second reflects the traditional curriculum model of initial education. The
two models are introduced separately because there
are two distinct processes involved: there is the
the management of the educational process and the
teaching and learning process and there may he many
of the latter contained in one of the former processes.

The curriculum planning model contains a development of some of the elements contained in
Lawton's (1973:21) model of producing a school time-
table and it is important to recognise that there is
an affinity between the planning of the school time-
table and the planning of the programme in the education of adults. However, Lawton's model required
considerable adaptation in order to be relevant to
the education of adults.

Figure 8.3:   A Curriculum Planning Model
for the Education of Adults

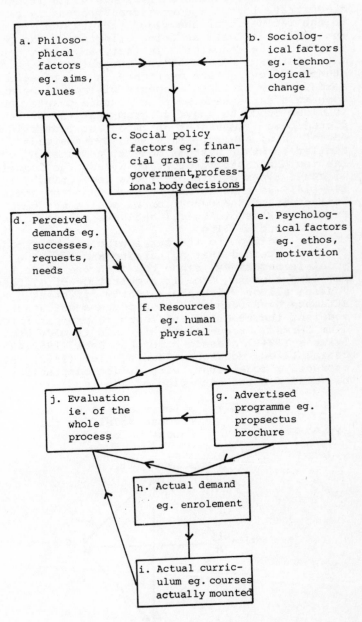

The above diagram represents a much more complicated system than that depicted by Houle since it seeks to demonstrate that the educational process is exposed to the influence of the wider society and its governing bodies, as well as being affected by the philosophy of the educator. In fact, an uneasy tension may exist as a result of the interplay of the forces stemming from factors mentioned in the first three boxes. Each of these elements will be elaborated upon in a subsequent section of this chapter but it is clear from the above diagram that the system depicted here illustrates an important factor in the education of adults. This is a systems model, similar to other systems models, produced by organization theorists in order to assess the functioning of other types of organizations (eg. Child J 1977: 144-178), so that it may be seen how the sociological study of the education of adults may benefit from similar sociological analyses conducted in other areas of social life.

In addition to the curriculum planning model, it is maintained that a learning and teaching process model is necessary, since box 'i' in the above figure may have stemming from it a multitude of different courses all of which are slightly different. Many attempts have been made to produce a satisfactory model of the teaching and learning process in curriculum terms. Frequently, reference is made back to Tyler's (1949) classic study but Taba (1962:425), citing Giles, McCutcheon and Zechiel (1942), has produced a model that, with slight adaptation, may be valid for the education of adults.

Figure 8.4: A Learning and Teaching
Process Model for the
Education of Adults

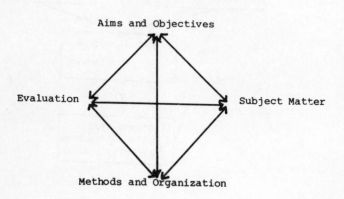

Aims and Objectives

Evaluation

Subject Matter

Methods and Organization

This model is a reasonably familiar one within curriculum theory since it contains the elements that occur in almost every learning and teaching process. Even so, it will be necessary to discuss them later in this chapter in order to relate them specifically to the education of adults.

The distinction between teaching and administration that was manifest in the discussion of the roles of the adult educator is also apparent in the above discussion. It would be totally false to present a picture of the education of adults that does not include both. Together these two models contain a framework within which it is possible to analyse the education of adults both in the United Kingdom and elsewhere. However, before discussing these in any more detail it is essential to highlight another issue in curriculum theory that has particular reference to many of the ideas raised throughout this study.

Classical and Romantic Curricula: The concepts of classical and romantic curricula reflect contrasting educational ideologies, the latter coming to prominence in initial education in the 1960s, which has been regarded as a period of romanticism. These positions have been summarised by Lawton (1973:22-23) in two different tables and his argument is summarised in table 8.3 below.

Table 8.3: The Classical and Romantic
           Curricula - according to
           Lawton

Elements of the Classical Curriculum	Elements of the Romantic Curriculum
subject centred skills instruction information obedience conformity discipline	child centred creativity experience discovery awareness originality freedom
objectives - acquiring knowledge content - subjects	processes - 'living' attitudes and values experiences - real life

Table 8.3 continued

Elements of the Classical Curriculum		Elements of the Romantic Curriculum	
			topics and proposals
method	- didactic instruction - competition	method	- involvement - co-operation
evaluation	- by tasks (teacher set)	evaluation	
	- by examinations (public and competitive)		- self assessment (in terms of self improvement)

Most models must necessarily over-emphasize their salient points, so that the above table presents a polarization of the two curricula models. Yet the fact that the major features are highlighted means that it is possible to see immediately the significance of these formulations for a deeper understanding of the education of adults. Clearly the romantic curriculum, as formulated above, approximates to Knowles' interpretation of andragogy. It will be recalled that Knowles (1980:44-5) suggested that andragogy has four premises that are different from pedagogy: the learner is self-directed; the learner's experiences are a rich resource for learning; the learner's readiness to learn is increasingly orientated to the developmental tasks of his social roles; the learner's time perspective assumes an immediacy, so that learning is problem and performance rather than subject centred. Clearly Knowles did not formulate andragogy in curricular terminology and perhaps his failure to do so has been a major reason why the debate about it has been so wide ranging. Can andragogy be equated with the romantic curriculum? In many ways the response to this must be in the affirmative, although to label it as a formulation of the romantic curriculum and to dismiss it would do it a disservice. Embodied within it is a philosophy that is significant to adult education - the humanistic perspective - and this, it is maintained here is a criterion of education itself.

Without a humanistic student-centred approach it is maintained here that learning and human development may be impaired and this is the crux of Macfarlane's (1978:156) analysis of literacy education in terms of these two types of curricula, as table 8.4 demonstrates:

Table 8.4: Macfarlane's Analysis of Adult Literacy Education in terms of two curricula models

	Curricular attitudes among advocates of the traditional curriculum	Curricular attitudes among advocates of a student-centred curriculum
Role of the student	Passive recipient of externally formulated process	Active participant in defining own goals and needs,
The literacy process	Hierarchies, centred upon skills and stages of progress	Holistic, task centred
Tutor's view of student	One who is deprived and handicapped (and hence inferior)	An equal who is not to blame for failure
Impact on student's self image	Relatively unimportant, a by-product of progress in skills	Purposefully enhanced
Student's view of tutor	'The expert who will cure me'	'The friend who helps me sort things out'
Dangers	Maintains dependency and lack of confidence. Transfer of skills to real world usage very doubtful	Threatens student and tutor with lack of structure and lack of perception of progress

Once again, this type of approach over-emphasizes some of the differences but it may be seen how he suggests that the student-centred approach aids the learner's development and growth. Macfarlane notes that for either approach to be successful in any

way demands quite different methods and organization.
He also maintains that these different approaches
have ramifications for policy, staff-recruitment,
training and resource development. Yet it is clear
from his own analysis that the student-centred
approach is closer to the humanistic ideals mentioned earlier in this study, which is at the heart of
adult education. Even so, this does not mean that
all teaching need be of a facilitative style and in
the following section this will be developed within
the context of an anlysis of some of the writings of
Colin Griffin.

The Application of Classical and Romantic Curricula Models
to the Education of Adults: In the second chapter it
was pointed out that continuing and recurrent education are two philosophies of lifelong education and
that Griffin (1978) has examined these from the perspective of a curriculum theorist. Taking as his
basis the teaching and learning process model; aims,
content and method; he examines both continuing and
recurrent education. His basic premise is that continuing education is related to the classical curriculum while recurrent education has a romantic
curriculum basis. It will be recognised that this
equation is not one that is maintained here but
Griffin's analysis is important because it is a
genuine attempt to apply curriculum theory to the
education of adults. Griffin (1978:7), himself,
recognises that the task he undertook was 'a tentative curriculum analysis' and herein lies its value.
His study may be summarised in tabular form and
table 8.5 contains many of his major points.

Table 8.5: A Curriculum Analysis of
Continuing and Recurrent
Education - according to
Griffin

	Continuing Education	Recurrent Education
Aims	Professional standards of provision Flexible and accessible structures of provision Unity of response to diversity of need Institutionalised stand-ards of achievement and excellence	Autonomous learning Personal authenticity Diversity of learning experiences De-institutionalised criteria of perform-ance

Table 8.5 continued

	Continuing Education	Recurrent Education
	Means/ends rationality model of institutional response. Access to common culture	Assimilation of education to life-experience of individual learners Promotion of cultural diversity in the context of meaning and goals
Content	Public criteria of learning performances Subject structures reflecting forms of knowledge Mutual evaluation of subject demand Mastery of, or initiation into, forms of knowledge and skill Knowledge for rational control and social mobility Culturally appropriate institutional systems	Expressive criteria of learning performances Structures of knowledge contingent upon learning experience Problem-solving response to conditions of alienation Standards of learning performance relative to learning experience Understanding for transformation through social solidarity Relevance for maintenance of sub-cultural identity
Methods	Effectiveness and evaluation Professional criteria of relevance Professional standards based on adult learning theory Standards of teaching methods as a function of institutional provision Methods reflecting the rationality of provision Teaching roles distinguish educational from social authority	Methods stressing individual expression Learners decide learning methods Methods reflecting diverse characteristics of learning situation Standards as a function of a personal authenticity Methods for transforming life-experience Methods reflecting culturally significant aspects of learning

Griffin's work needs to be read in detail in order

to follow his arguments but it is clear from the above table that he sees a clear distinction in curricular terms between the two philosophies in the education of adults. That a practitioner may mix the two approaches is not denied but it is perhaps significant that as the 1960s were left behind, so the concept of romantic curriculum lost some of its appeal and more recently the term recurrent education has lost favour. Even so, many of the curricular aspects that Griffin discusses within this context do find their place within the wider sphere of adult education because, as it has been argued throughout this study, any form of education should have a humanistic basis if it is to achieve the high ideals of education itself.

More recently, Griffin (1982) has turned his attention to lifelong education and he notes that integration between initial education and education for the remainder of the lifespan is a significant issue that has resulted in an unbalanced policy debate, emphasizing access above all other factors. Overall, he (1982:119) recognises that curriculum development in the context of lifelong education is 'by no means as straight—forward as the needs/ objectives/evaluation model might suggest. The co-existence of various curriculum models makes it a much more complicated affair'. This complexity was evident in Macfarlane's (1978) analysis and it is also clear in the distinctions drawn between initial and post-initial education curricula models. Griffin, in this latter paper, highlights that policy factors of social control are fundamental to education and most apparent in the provision of lifelong education.

Implicit in the debate about continuing and recurrent education and in the distinction between classical and romantic curricula is the matter of control: who should control the learning activities? who should control the learning outcomes? etc. Clearly these are matters that educators of adults need to consider and they are highlighted in Griffin's analysis. Nevertheless, it is argued here that it is quite fundamental to education that the learner should develop a critical awareness and that his humanity is respected, so that any form of control that inhibits these is contrary to the high ideals of education itself.

Having examined a variety of approaches to the curriculum, it is now necessary to focus upon specific elements within it and to discuss them in some detail.

ELEMENTS OF THE CURRICULUM

It has become apparent that there are many elements
in the curriculum, each of which requires elabora-
tion but it would be impossible in the space available to take each model and develop it item by
item: it is, therefore, proposed to consider the
fourteen elements in the curriculum planning and
teaching and learning models that were discussed in
the first section of this chapter. These two models
are considered together because they combine the
macro-factors of curriculum planning with the
specific factors of the teaching and learning
process.

A Curriculum Planning Model for the Education of Adults:
Figure 8.3 illustrates this model in which there are
ten separate elements and these are elaborated upon
in order to highlight their implications and to
relate them to the discussion in the previous
section.

Philosophical Factors: Underlying every programme
of education there is a philosophy, whether it is
explicit or implicit, considered or rarely thought
about, consistent or inconsistent; it may be a
philosophy constrained by other factors, such as
social policy, but it remains a philosophy. At the
outset of this study a rationale for the education
of adults was produced which argues that every
human being has a basic need to learn and that in a
rapidly changing society each individual may need to
make many adjustments in order to be in harmony with
his socio-cultural milieu. Most individuals will
develop as a result of their experiences although it
was recognised that growth is not inevitable. This
approach, however, reflects Dewey's (1916) assertion
that education is a means to human growth and that
growth continues throughout the whole of life.
Therefore, it is maintained here that underlying
every curriculum should be a concern about the development of the learners as persons. This is a
humanistic, progressive perspective and one that is
prevalent in adult education.
    It was also recognised at the outset that
society is changing rapidly and that some types of
knowledge change so rapidly that they appear artificial. Hence, it is essential that some people
keep abreast with contemporary developments, so that
it could be argued that society has the need to
produce a specific type of person who will be a

229

lifelong learner. Education is frequently accused
of being a process that moulds and controls people
so that they fit into a niche in society without
disrupting it very greatly. The lifelong learner
may be flexible, adaptable and totally commendable
but that education should thus mould a person is a
more questionable process. If the educator sees his
role in terms of responding to the needs of the
wider society primarily, he clearly has a different
philosophical perspective upon education than the
one being argued in this study. This does not mean
that the humanistic, progressive approach to education has no concern about the needs of society,
only that it sees the development of the learners
as persons as they acquire a critical awareness,
knowledge and understanding as more significant in
educational terms.

Other philosophical perspectives may also un-
derpin the whole of an educational programme. Elias
and Merriam (1980) point out that both liberal and
radical philosophies are also significant in
curriculum design. Hence, it is possible to see
that the literacy programme devised by Freire was
considerably influenced by his own philosophy and
that of his co-workers, so that this approach was
totally different from literacy education in
societies, such as the United Kingdom, in which this
philosophical perspective is not prevalent. Even
so, Freire's own programme was not free to operate
without influences upon it, such as the forces op-
erating in the wider society.

Sociological Factors: It was recognised in the
opening chapter that the curriculum itself may be
regarded as a selection from culture, so that the
social forces that operate upon the educational process are quite profound. Culture is changing
rapidly and various aspects of knowledge are changing rapidly. Yet knowledge itself is not value-
free: some has high status without being very
practical whilst other knowledge has low status but
is most useful (Young 1971). The relevance of
knowledge is also significant in its inclusion in
any curriculum (Jarvis 1978b). If curricula contain
socially organised knowledge selected from culture,
then it is significant to know where, why and by
whom such a selection of knowledge is made. Clearly
in self-directed learning and in some forms of adult
education it is the learners who make the selection
but Griffin suggests that this may not occur in
continuing education. However, Westwood (1980:43),

has indicated that perhaps the selection in adult
education may not be from a wide range of knowledge
and she claims that since adult education is a predominantly middle-class pursuit it 'has a re-
inforcing role .... maintaining the status quo, en-
gendering a state of consensus and contributing
positively to the mechanisms whereby hegemony is
maintained.' If her analysis is correct, then adult
education curricula have reflected the middle class
attitudes and biases that maintain a 'bourgeois
hegemony', so that it then needs to be asked whether
this is a true reflection of its aims or whether it
is a consequence of its existence.

No curriculum in the education of adults can
escape the social pressures exerted upon it, so that
it is necessary that more sociological analysis of
the educational processes undertaken by adults should
be conducted.

Social Policy Factors: Education is rarely free
from the decisions of national and local government,
so that policy factors also affect the curriculum in
any educational establishment. In recent years,
legislation in various countries of the world has
resulted in different countries becoming committed
to various forms of paid educational leave etc. All
forms of continuing education are influenced by such
policy decisions. The Manpower Service Commission
in the United Kingdom has contributed considerable
funds to continuing education so that pre-vocational
and vocational courses have been sponsored throughout the country. However, the Manpower Services
Commission has not only aided the implementation of
such programmes as the Training Opportunities
Scheme, Youth Opportunities Programme and the New
Training Initiatives it has also sought to control
the content by issuing a directive which ensures
that 'inclusion in the course of political or related activities "could be regarded as a breach of ...
.... agreement with the MSC and could result in
the immediate closure of the course"'. (Harper 1982)
From this example it may be seen that even in a
relatively democratic country, like the United
Kingdom, government policy can and does exercise
considerable control over the curriculum content.

Perceived Demands: Newman (1979:35) writes that:

Adult education is designed in the simplest
possible way to respond to demand. It is the
other side of the numbers game. If classes

231

can be closed on the basis of attendance,
then they can also be set up. That is to
say, if you have a group of people eager to
pursue some activity, or if you have evidence
of sufficient community interest you can
approach your local adult education agency
or centre and ask that a course be arranged,
a room and basic facilities provided, and a
tutor paid

This is a different approach to running courses than
that often discussed by adult educators who have
frequently regarded their programmes as being based
upon needs. This term should be distinguished from
the idea of a basic need to learn which was discussed in the opening chapter but since it has played such a significant part in adult education thinking it should be analysed and related to 'wants',
'interests' and 'demands'.

The concept of 'need' has been regarded as one
of the bases of the adult education curriculum and
the moral overtones of the term have provided adult
education with an apparently deep and unquestionable
rationale for its existence. That the adult educator could provide an educational programme that responded to the needs of individuals and communities
has been an ideologically important factor to those
whose occupation is at the margins of the educational service. The Russell Report (1971:5) was unable
to provide a consistant analysis of the term but
used it to provide legitimation to the activities
undertaken by adult education. Mee and Wiltshire
(1978) showed clearly how full-time adult education
staff regarded their work as compensatory,while part-
time staff viewed it as recreational. Hence, for
the full-time staff 'needs' was a more significant
term. The Advisory Council for Adult and Continuing
Education has also adopted the term (ACACE 1982b)
but the term is clearly confused and, on occasions,
'wants' or 'interests' could be substituted for
'needs' without any change in meaning, although the
moral overtones would be lost in the process.

That such a substitution is possible suggests
that the term requires considerably more analysis
before it could be regarded as a basis for a
curriculum theory. Indeed, once such an analysis is
undertaken, it is not difficult to concur with Hirst
and Peters (1970:33), when they suggested that 'a
major book could be written solely round the problems raised by the emphasis or needs and interests'.
They actually specify a number of different ways in

which the term may be used to illustrate their
contention: diagnostic, eg. a poor person needs
more wealth; basic,eg. the need for a bed; biological, eg. the need for oxygen; psychological, eg.
the need for love and security; functional, eg. the
teacher needs his books. Clearly they have not ex-
hausted the possibilities and Bradshaw (1977)
specified four more types of need of which social
workers should be aware: normative, felt, expressed
and comparative needs. Halmos (1978) drew attention
to the distinction between primary and secondary
needs: the former referring to bodily requirements
while the latter are learned or acquired. Needs can
also be classified as individual, community or
societal. From the above discussion it can be appreciated that the concept of need is ill-defined
and, therefore, an inadequate basis for curriculum
development.

Educational analysis of the concept has revealed a number of other reasons why it may be a dubious
concept to employ in this context. Dearden (1972),
illustrated its weaknesses in a number of ways:
those needs diagnosed as such against a norm may be
rebutted by rejecting the validity of the norm,
since it is not absolute - perhaps the exception to
this is the basic learning need referred to in the
opening chapter; those expressions of need that
imply motivation may be rejected since learners may
not want what they actually need,and needs and wants
are not synonymous concepts; needs are not free
from value judgments despite their apparent objectivity; needs are not empirically based. Dearden
(1972:54-5) concedes that it 'might be said in con-
nexion with needs and the curriculum ..... that
there are certain general injunctions about needs
which do have a point in that they lay down something called "basic policy"'. Dearden's criticisms
may be less familiar to adult educators, however,
than that made by Wiltshire (1973) who rightly
claimed that the use of the term begged a number of
significant questions and he specifically noted that,
by giving adult education an ethic of service to the
needy, it drove a wedge between thinking and practice, which prevented practice from being fully
analysed. Lawson (1975), has also highlighted some
of the weaknesses of the concept, concentrating upon
the value judgment and the prescriptive issues.
While he (1975:37) maintains that needs statements
should not be abandoned he does appeal that they
should be recognised for what they are. Paterson
(1979:242), has also criticised the use of the word

233

because he claims that the idea implies that people have the right to achieve a specific level of educational attainment, whatever that might be, and this is patently not the case. Even more recently, Armstrong (1982) has suggested that needs meeting is both an element in liberal ideology and also a justification of compensatory education. Yet do such needs exist? Coates and Silburn (1967) claimed that no such needs exist. Illich (1977:22-23) noted the implicit ideological bias in the term and claimed that 'Need, used as a noun, becomes the fodder on which professions were fattened into dominance'. This suggests that the term is used in order to achieve power and that need is the creation of the power seeker. Illich's strictures are perhaps appropriate for continuing education since it will no doubt develop considerably in the next few years and continuing educators may seek to justify their existence. Perhaps, therefore, the need to learn, as recognised by the potential learner, is a better basis for the education of adults and that learning needs rather than educational needs are more significant.

Once a learning need is recognised by a potential student, then it reflects a want, an interest or a desire. The learner may, therefore, exert pressure upon an educational provider to respond to his demands. But 'wants', 'interests' and 'demands' are not words that occur so frequently in the vocabulary of adult educators, nor do they carry the same moral overtones as does the term 'need'. However, they are terms that are analytically more convincing and it has been argued the fact that demand may be one of the foundations of adult education curricula does not detract from the value of the education (Jarvis 1982a). It was also suggested that if adult education actually became demand orientated, it might conceivably break away from the ethos of middle class respectability that it carries at present.

However, it might be asked whether this analysis is only theoretical or has adult education managed to reach out and respond to people's demands. Mee and Wiltshire (1978:41) claimed that there 'seems to be some sort of national concensus that these are the things (their core curriculum) that institutions of adult education ought to be offering to the public and that there is something wrong if these subjects are not given something like their due place in the programme'. Commenting upon their work Keddie (1980:54) suggests that their findings

merely indicate that adult education has been op-
erating a provider's model rather than a needs model
of curriculum. If she is correct it is even less
likely that there has been a response to demand, nor
even tremendous attempts to discover it and the needs
meeting ideology has merely provided legitimation
for the retention of the status quo. Even if there
had been outreach to discover expressed learning
needs, or demands, they are not in themselves sufficient reason for the inclusion of the appropriate
learning activity in the curriculum. The demands
have to be considered within the overall scheme and
it is essential that curriculum planners ensure that
their response is not mindless. Perception of demand is, therefore, one factor in the planning of
a curriculum in adult and continuing education but
one that should perhaps play a larger part in the
future than it appears to have done in the past.

Psychological Factors: One of the strengths of
Knowles' formulation of andragogy is that it focused
upon some of the psychological factors that need to
be taken into consideration in planning adults'
learning. If adults are, for instance, problem-
centred rather than subject-based, then more courses
should be planned that have relevance to the everyday life environment: if they are going to respond
to the rapidly changing socio-cultural milieu with
active questioning, then the programme should include courses/sessions that provide opportunities
for them to seek answers: if some adults have developed an adversion to education as a result of
their experiences in initial education everything
must be done to overcome the problem from the outset,
including the employment of tutors able to put
adults at their ease, the way the accommodation is
used and the programme advertised. However, it is
appreciated that some of the psychological factors
may not be fully responded to in planning because
there may be limited resources available.

Resources: The above discussion has already indicated the inter-relationship between the different
elements of this curriculum planning model, since
it would be impossible to consider resources without
recognising that these depend upon policy decisions,
etc. Resources may be classified as financial,
accommodation and staff. Little more needs to be
written about the first of these since it plays a
self-evidently important part in curriculum planning.
Nevertheless, it must be recognised that many

education authorities make a financial grant to the educational institution and, thereafter, it is responsive to the market forces and fee income, except where such agencies as the Manpower Services Commission funds specific activities. However, response to market forces means that the curriculum of an institution will depend upon the ability of the educational providers to perceive demands accurately or else it will result in a form of traditionalism in curriculum planning - the continuation of successful courses. Once the institution depends on the market forces, then the course fees become a significant factor in which courses are actually included in the final programme.

Accommodation for adult education has been the subject of a report by ACACE (1982c) in which it is recognised that day schools should continue to form the main accommodation resource for adult education. Clearly it makes a good deal of sense to utilise premises for this purpose when they are not being used by children but it is necessary to recognise that such usage may inhibit some adults from participating in post-initial education because of their experiences when they attended school. Research needs to be conducted to investigate the effect of this 'poor cousin' image of adult education and it may be that if this is to remain a pattern for the future, then new schools should be built having more facilities for wider community use. The Advisory Council Report also recommends that every adult should have access to prime use accommodation, even though this may not be as close to their homes as the local school.

The main resource in education of most kinds is the tutor and there has been considerable discussion in this study about the tutor's role in the education of adults, so that it is unnecessary to cover this ground again. There are, however, two issues that should be mentioned here: the use of staff untrained in the art of teaching adults and the use of part-time staff to mount classes in minority subjects and interests. If there is a demand for a class in a specific topic and no tutor trained in the art of teaching adults, should the class be mounted? Since training is not mandatory then response to demand may necessitate use of untrained staff. By contrast, Hetherington (1980) suggests that part-time staff are occasionally asked by a principal of an adult education institute to mount a class in a minority interest topic. Having undertaken the commitment and a great deal of preparatory

work, the part-time tutors discover that the class
is closed after a few weeks because it has attracted
so few enrolments hence they lose their part-time
work. This might cause hardship and it certainly
would cause loss of job satisfaction. In order to
organise a wide and attractive programme it might
be necessary to employ tutors in this manner but the
extent to which the part-time tutors should be regarded as a reserve army of labour is another
matter. Indeed, loyalty by an institution to its
part-time staff from year to year might well result
in the tutors seeking additional training and
providing a better service to the students.

Advertised Programmes: Two major issues here that
need some discussion are the actual programme and
way that it is advertised and both will be discussed
in turn.
     In the preparation of the programme at least
three educational issues must be taken into consideration: scheduling, balance and level. The actual
time when courses are programmed is a major curriculum issue since potential students may not be free
to attend a class, even an in-service one, if it
clashes with their work. Hence, it may be necessary
for professional in-service education courses to be
mounted on days when the pressure on that specific
occupational groups is least. In adult education
classes it might be necessary to vary the time when
they commence, since some topics may be attractive
to those who commute to work and who might prefer a
Saturday morning class to an evening one. Clearly
it is impossible to satisfy every demand since a
mutually convenient time for all potential students
may be impossible to discover and, even if it were,
it may not be convenient for the caretaker! Hence,
it may be necessary for different approaches to
teaching and learning to be created if scheduling
cannot be satisfactorarily achieved, such as learning networks, individualised learning, etc.
     Mee and Wiltshire (1978:41) rightly point out
that much adult education seeks to respond to
several publics, so that when adult educators refer
to the idea of a balanced curriculum they may be
suggesting that the balance should suit the demand.
This is a different conception of balance to that in
compulsory education when it might refer to the
balance between different forms of knowledge or
between the cognitive disciplines and physical
skills, etc. Clearly, then, within the education of
adults these considerations should play a

significant part since the balance between supply
and demand is hardly sufficient educational rationale for producing a programme of courses. It may be
appropriate, therefore, to regard the concept of
balance as an ideal to be aimed at, so that a balance may be created between the market forces and
the minority interests. Hence, a variety of learning needs should be catered for but, however broad
the programme offered,it is certain that not everybody's interest can be included within it, so that
it may be necessary to organise an educational advisory service or learning networks in order to respond to these demands. Since these latter topics
are discussed later in this chapter no further reference is made to them here.

However, it is necessary to recognise that if
there is a learning need that should be responded to
in terms of human justice then there is sufficient
reason for organising an unbalanced programme.
Hence balance in a programme will ultimately depend
upon the philosophy of the curriculum designer and
balance in itself is not a phenomemon to be achieved
at all costs.

Mee and Wiltshire (1978:33) discovered that the
subject matter for courses in the programmes that
they analysed consisted of: 51% craft courses
(personal care, household and leisure);   24% physical
skills (maintenance of health, physical fitness and
leisure);   12% languages;   6% other intellectual
courses; 5% courses for disadvantaged groups. However, when the university extension classes were
included, the academic component was 25% of the actual
programme offered. It is clear that craft and
physical skill courses comprise the greater proportion of the advertised programme, so that it does
tend to reflect a recreational, demands orientated
approach to education rather than a compensatory
programme. But, it may be asked, to what extent
does the advertised programme actually reflect the
philosophy of the providers? Clearly, Mee and
Wiltshire's findings provide a valuable basis from
which to discuss the balance of the curriculum and
they, themselves, raise vital questions about this.
Perhaps, wisely, they refrain from suggesting answers and yet it is important that answers are
sought since only by undertaking research at this
level will the advertised programme ever relate to
other elements in the curriculum planning model.

The concept of 'level' may be considered within
a very similar theoretical framework, so that it
would be repetitious to elaborate upon it here. The

curriculum, because it seeks to respond to people with different educational interests and backgrounds, has to achieve a balance in levels suitable for a wide potential student body. Nevertheless, those who wish to pursue their studies in considerable depth may be disadvantaged if no, or few, advanced courses are offered. Hence, advanced courses may be viewed within the same perspective as minority interests and it may even be useful to consider a progression of level similar to that proposed by the Haycocks report for part-time tutor training, with the adult education institutes offering introductory and intermediate level courses and university (or polytechnic) extension offering advanced courses in the same subject but in fewer centres. However, this requires considerable planning and liaison between the various providers, which may not actually occur.

At this juncture it is necessary to draw attention to the fact that in the consideration of level of courses offered, psychological factors, programmes and advertising meet. If a programme is seen to offer all introductory courses, or all hobbies and skills type courses, then those who seek advanced intellectual stimulation may look elsewhere and tend to regard adult education as distinct from higher or advanced education. In contrast, if a programme apparently offers a lot of advanced courses then those who want introductory study may conclude that their level of proficiency is not sufficient to enrol in a course in an educational institution and they may, consequently, not actually bother to enrol anywhere.

Courses and programmes must be advertised and two issues need to be considered here: to advertise successfully is a professional undertaking but to advertise too successfully may be contrary to the high ideals of education itself. Rogers and Groombridge (1976:76) claim that adult education is 'a service needing constant promotion and visibility (but) it remains largely unpromoted and directly invisible; where sympathetic understanding of all modern media is needed, it continues hopelessly to rely on methods which would have looked out of place in the late nineteenth century'. They suggest a variety of approaches that might be employed, including: focused distribution; a supplement in a local newspaper; direct mailing; skilful cultivation of the local press in order to ensure good coverage of newsworthy items; militant publicity. Obviously post-compulsory education must reach out

239

to the wider populace and many of these suggestions
are now included in the advertising programmes of
many educational institutions. Yet advertising, as
an occupation, is often accused of employing
immoral, or at least questionable methods. While
the accusation is rarely substantiated it is important that education should not be seen to use methods
to promote its courses that create a sense of need
in, or manipulate, potential students. These techniques may be regarded as immoral and certainly fall
short of the high ideals of education. Hence, it is
important to prepare good publicity and to disseminate it widely but the means used to persuade
people to enrol on courses must always be in accord
with the ideals of education, other means do not
justify the ends.

Actual Demand: At the commencement of the academic
year is term, the enrolment period brings the
preparatory work into focus. The extent to which
the curriculum prepared by the educators actually
responds to the demands of the potential students
may now be revealed. Clearly the programme may not
respond to everybody's learning needs, so that there
has arisen in recent years educational advisory
services that can help potential students to find
another course in the prospectus that responds to
their interests or to discover another educational
institution offering the course that the student
requires. Adult education institutions are not the
sole providers of this service; public libraries,
citizens advice bureaux and careers service offices
have all contributed greatly to this, so that
liaison between providers and advisors is very necessary to ensure that an efficient advisory service
exists. In the Advisory Council for Adult and
Continuing Education's report on this topic, it
(ACACE 1979c:15) notes that, for instance, the
Guildford Adult Education Week held in the public
library was a 'collective effort involving many
agencies, including the University and the Women's
Institute'. In fact, over twenty agencies, either
advisors or providers, co-operate every year during
the enrolment period to inform the general public of
the courses that they can follow, offer advice about
where they can find the courses that they wish to
study and even to counsel enquirers about the educational requirements that they might need in order to
pursue certain careers or seek specific qualifications. This service has been made even more effective since the County Library Service has a

computerised record of the majority of adult courses
offered throughout Surrey. This is but one example
of how response to demand can be met and adult education offer a genuine service while it still seeks
to inform people about the proposed content of the
educational programmes of a number of providers. The
ACACE report (1979c:27) recommends that such educational services 'should be recognised as a crucial
link between the educational needs and demands of
adults and the learning opportunities offered by educational providers'.

However, it must be realized that the provision
of such a service may be motivated by the providers'
need to attract students, so that while it may be
viewed as an altruistic service, it may also be continued as part of an advertising campaign mounted by
adult education. Mixed motivation is obviously
present in the providers but the offer of such a
service is in keeping with the humanistic ideals of
adult education.

Courses that fail to enrol sufficient students
during that period may be closed immediately, or
allowed to run for a few weeks to see if student
enrolments increase. However, each year a number of
courses may be closed, so that the educational institution offers no course in specific topics. This
may be the place at which curriculum innovation may
commence; since the creation of learning networks,
self-help groups, etc. may find some support and if
cooperation between providers could be increased it
might be possible to employ peripatetic teachers
with self-help groups.

Actual Curriculum: The actual content of the teaching programme of any educational institution,
depending totally or partially upon voluntary participation, must, therefore, to some extent, rely on
the response to the prospectus. Yet it will be
recalled that demand itself is hardly sufficient
reason for inclusion in the curriculum of any particular topic, so that there must be a place for some
minority interests. Even so, the extent to which
economically unviable courses may be continued does
depend upon the philosophy underpinning the educational institution's curriculum and upon the social
policy factors that affect the funding arrangements
for specific courses.

The actual curriculum of an educational institution is more than its programme of courses, as
will be recognised from the discussion about the
way in which the term is employed. Since it can

refer to the total learning situation; the whole ethos of the institution, its hidden curriculum and the teaching and learning curriculum are all united at this point. Each of these points will be discussed later in this chapter but it may be seen that the curriculum planning model leads directly to the product of the actual curriculum, so that it is at this point in the model that the learning and teaching curricula could be inserted.

Evaluation: In Figure 8.3 it will be noted that the curriculum planning model demands that the educator of adults should evaluate many of the elements of the process. The basis of his evaluation must be his educational philosophy but even that may be called into question by other demands in the programme. In addition, there are certain factors that may be evaluated by other criteria, eg. the use of physical resources by financial criteria, the whole of the operation by criteria of organizational efficiency, since the educator of adults clearly plays an administrative and managerial role. Hence, it is necessary to utilise the criteria of management in evaluating the planning and implementation of the curriculum, but because the end-product is an educational curriculum the major criterion by which the whole is evaluated must remain the educational philosophy of the educators of adults.

The above discussion has sought to highlight some of the major elements in the curriculum planning model and it is clear that the curriculum, when employed in the context of the total learning situation provided by the educational institution, has connotations for organization and management that demand that those full-time staff employed in this role should have additional training if they require it. However, it was recognised that the majority of part-time staff are involved in a learning and teaching situation, so that it is now necessary to examine the elements of the model depicted in Figure 8.4.

A Learning and Teaching Process Model of the Curriculum:
Taba (1962:10) wrote:

> A curriculum usually contains a statement
> of aims and of specific objectives; it
> indicates some selection and organization
> of content; it either implies or manifests
> certain patterns of learning and teaching,
> whether because the objectives demand

them or because the content organization
requires them. Finally, it includes a
programme of evaluation of the outcomes

The above model may be applied to every course offered in an educational institution rather than to
the overall programme, so that there may be considerable variation with the elements of the curriculum between different courses. Hence, discussion
about the aforementioned elements must necessarily
still remain at the level of generality.

Aims and Objectives: British educators, claimed
Davies (1976:11) 'have been more interested in def-
ining aims than in studying objectives, while
American teachers have been more willing to think in
terms of concrete objectives'. Certainly this claim
would be true of the curriculum models of both
Verner and Houle that were identified earlier in
this chapter. By contrast, British theorists have
focused upon the broader philosophical issues for
both Griffin (1978) and Mee and Wiltshire (1978)
demonstrate, in their respective ways, the significance of aims in the education of adults. Yet the
broad philosophy of the educator of adults may also
affect his attitude towards the concept, and use, of
objectives within the design of a teaching and
learning situation. Curriculum theorists have
posited many types of objectives: instructional,
teaching, learning, behavioural, expressive, etc.
Davies (1976) discussed the whole area very thoroughly, so that there is no need to expand it here.
Even so, it is useful to examine the relationship
between aims and objectives and to see whether the
latter actually reflect the overall aims as even the
general philosophy of adult education. For instance,
in recent years there has been considerable
emphasis given to behavioural objectives and while
these might be quite valid on a skills-based course,
their usefulness in cognitive learning courses may
be more questionable and contrary to the overall
philosophy of adult learning. Objectives specified
in behavioural terms, tend to imply that the human
learner will learn and behave in a manner designated
by the teacher, like a pigeon or a rat! Another
implication of this approach is that the teacher
will adopt a didactic and authoritarian approach to
teaching and this is quite contrary to the philosophy of teaching adults, a point discussed in a
previous chapter. It is maintained here that any
approach to teaching that designates how a learner

will behave as a result of undergoing the teaching
and learning process undermines the dignity of the
learner and, consequently, the process of teaching
and learning falls short of the high ideals of education elaborated in this study. By contrast,
Eisner (1969) regards expressive objectives as
evocative rather than prescriptive, which is much
closer to the general philosophy of the education of
adults which is advocated here. Nevertheless, behavioural objectives have a valid place in some
forms of therapy but while therapy might involve
learning it is not education.

Subject Matter: The content of some courses,
especially those that are vocationally orientated
or award bearing is usually prescribed by the examining or the validating body. This reflects the
point that the curriculum may be regarded as a
selection of culture made by those who have status
or power within the profession or within education.
Elsewhere Jarvis (1983a:50-63) has outlined other
criteria for the selection of curriculum content in
professional education including the demands of
professional practice, the relevance of the topic,
and its worthwhileness. However, there are courses
in which the subject matter may actually be negotiated between tutor and students, but these courses
tend to be exceptions rather than everyday occurrences. In liberal adult education these occurrences
may be more frequent and the subject matter may depend upon the interests of the students and be
negotiated between tutor and students.
     Negotiated subject content may be much more
common in continuing professional education since
the practitioner, being aware of his strengths and
weaknesses in practice, will probably know what he
needs to learn during in-service education in order
to improve the quality of his practice. Diagnosis
of learning needs should have occurred prior to the
course, so that it is essential for the teacher to
join with the students in planning a teaching and
learning programme. Often in continuing professional education it is useful to spend a planning day,
a few weeks prior to the commencement of the course,
mapping out the areas of the subject matter that
should be covered during it. Diagnosis should
always precede learning and teaching.

Organization and Methods: The location of the
teaching, the organization of the room in which the
teaching and learning is to occur, the content of

244

the session and the methods to be employed and all
part of the educational process. They should all
relate to the learners, their learning needs or
wants and to their learning styles, but they are
also dependent upon the expertise of the tutorial
staff. The organization of the environment has been
referred to already and relates to the adulthood of
the learners and to the teaching methods to be
employed. Similarly, the actual methods employed by
the teacher are important considerations in the
educational process. Bourdieu and Passeron (1977:5)
claim that all 'pedagogic action is, objectively,
symbolic violence in so far as it is the imposition
of a cultural arbitrary by an arbitrary power'.
Hence, the methods employed are a significant factor
and relate not merely to the content but also to the
philosophy of the teacher. Teaching methods have
already been examined in a previous chapter so that
it is unnecessary to repeat any of that discussion
here. But it is important to recognise the symbolic
significance of the teaching method. Moreover, the
symbolism becomes an immoral reality if the teaching
methods employed in any teaching and learning transaction inhibit the development of, or undermine the
dignity and humanity, of the learners;but it becomes
moral, and good curriculum practice, when they
encourage the growth and expression of humanity of
the learners.

The philosophical issues involved in teaching
are important considerations, especially in the
education of adults, but the methods employed must
also relate to the ethos of the group and the
content of the session. Hence, the skill of the
teacher is not only in relation to techniques but
also in relation to human interaction and it is a
combination of these various factors that can lead
to teaching and learning becoming an effective and
stimulating process.

Evaluation: Clearly the aims and objectives that
have been set for any single teaching and learning
session or for a course as a whole provide one base
for its evaluation. Yet these may prove to be too
restrictive since the class may have deviated from
the selected aims and even from the content de-
cided upon because it followed up ideas that arose
during the process itself. This may have resulted
in effective learning and class satisfaction and all
the participants regarded it as successful. Hence,
if learning and understanding has occurred, within
a humanistic context, then the education may be

245

assessed as successful.

Yet evaluation should not be undertaken by the teacher by himself; in the education of adults the students should be full-participants in the process. In non-compulsory education this occurs in any case, since as Newman (1979:66) forcibly reminds his readers:

> Adult education is a cruel test of a tutor's skills. It is a sink or swim business. If the tutor does not have what it takes, people stop coming. His students vote with their feet, unobtrusively transferring to other classes or simply staying away. The class dwindles week by week, leaving him all too well aware that he has been found wanting ....

Perhaps this is a dramatic over-portrayal of the manner by which students are actually involved in the process of evaluation. Indeed, many students are very kind to their tutors and encourage inexperienced ones. Even so, students do evaluate their tutors and the process of teaching and learning that has occurred, so that it is beneficial to all concerned to involve them in the more formal process.

Two models of curriculum have been elaborated upon in this section but it was pointed out earlier that the total learning situation also involved the hidden curriculum.

The Hidden Curriculum: Every institution evolves its own procedures, many of which contain values that are recognised and intended but some of which may be unrecognised and unintended by those who formulate them. Some of these values have been highlighted in this chapter, such as those implicit in the teachers or students selecting the curriculum content, or in the use of various types of teaching. Yet there are others, and some of those that are unintended or unrecognised by the educators of adults may be apparent to the students who attend the institution and it may be some of these that are learned and which affect their attitudes towards adult or continuing education. Hence, for instance, the differing status accorded to different types of class may be very clear to students and those whose class is given low status may feel deprived. Examination classes may be given precedence over nonexaminable leisure time study, even though the latter may actually be more academic in some

instances! Courses that bring in funds to the
institution may be given preference to other forms
of education. There may be a profession of its
being an adult education institution but the
students may not be treated as adults either in the
organization or in teaching methods employed, or in
the evaluation of the life and work of the institution. By contrast, other institutions may create
such an ethos that the hidden curriculum purveys
the humanistic ideals of education itself. The
ethos of the institution is, therefore, the carrier
of a message that may be received and learned by
adult students who attend.

CONCLUDING DISCUSSION

It is perhaps not without significance to note that
the curricular models of progressive education
amongst children are valid and important in considering curriculum theory in adult and continuing
education. Many criticisms of initial education are
raised on issues of control and regard schools as
institutions processing children and moulding them
in such a manner as to take their place in the wider
society. These criticisms relate to the classical
model of curriculum in which children are controlled
and expected to learn accepted knowledge. Such an
approach is less easy with adults, especially those
who have developed confidence, experience and expertise in the wider world. Hence the progressive
curriculum model which allows freedom to the children appears to be more realistic. This clearly
raises some quite significant issues about the
difference between the education of adults and the
education of children: it asks questions about the
extent to which initial education dehumanizes
children and treats them as objects (Freire 1972b:
50) and it raises questions about there being any
distinction between the education of adults as described here and progressive education. Perhaps,
most significantly of all, it points to the fact
that within the wider society initial education is
instrumental and post-compulsory education is, in
part, expressive: in the former the end-product may
lie partially beyond the learner whereas in latter
the learner may be the end-product. Wherever there
is instrumantality the opportunity for control is
greater and it pervades the whole system. As continuing education becomes more systematised and institutionalised social control may become more

prevalent and the humanistic values epitomised in
this study may recede from aspects of adult and
continuing education and the high ideals of educa-
ation become less prevalent.

SUMMARY

This chapter has sought to draw together from a
variety of sources theoretical perspectives on the
curriculum that are relevant to the education of
adults. It commenced by pointing out that this
material is relatively sparse and this is, perhaps,
because adult education in the United Kingdom has
used the term programme rather than curriculum.
Having examined the terms course, programme and
total learning situation, a number of curriculum
models were then analysed. The work of two
American theorists, Verner and Houle, was examined
and it was recognised that while their formulations
were valuable they did not give sufficient explicit
reference to the wider sociological factors, so that
two other curriculum models were examined. Fourteen
different elements in these two models were expanded,
with especial reference being made to the concept of
need. It was recognised that Wiltshire's (1973)
criticism of the concept was fully justified since
it appears to offer a moral rationale rather than
theoretical justification for the education of
adults. Such a rationale, it is claimed, is unnec-
ssary because the educational process is valuable
in itself.
      Throughout this chapter the polarization
between the classical and romantic approaches to the
curriculum has been prevalent and as education is
regarded in this study as a humanistic process there
has been a tendency to claim that the latter approximates more closely to the ideals of education. It
was also recognised that this approach appears to be
closer to the theoretical perspectives of other
writers in adult education, so that a connection between progressive initial education and adult education is noted; their common ancestor being Dewey
who also had a humanistic and idealistic perspective
on education. However, the educational process is
not neutral and the chapter concluded with a recognition that where education is instrumental the
elements of social control become more significant.
      Having examined the curriculum in the education
of adults it is now necessary to look at the way in
which this education is organised in the wider

society and this constitutes the subject for the
next chapter.

SELECTED FURTHER READING

*Recurrent and Continuing Education - a curriculum model
approach   C Griffin 1978*

This brief paper is an excellent introduction to
curriculum analysis - perhaps the best paper on the
subject yet published. However, between the time
that this is written and its publication Dr Griffin's
own book *Curriculum Theory in Adult and Lifelong Education*
will have appeared.

The Design of Education.   C O Houle 1972

In keeping with everything that Houle writes, this
is an excellent and thorough analysis of the design
features in education. His models are clear and his
discussion important to any consideration of curriculum in adult education.

*Philosophical Concepts and Values in Adult Education
                    K H Lawson 1975*

This is a clear introduction to the philosophical
issues in adult education, with a clear discussion
on the concept of 'needs'. Nevertheless, Lawson
does not adopt quite the same humanistic perspective
as that adopted here, so that it offers another
approach to some of the issues.

*Structure and Performance in Adult Education
                    G Mee and H Wiltshire 1978*

A large survey in adult education in England and
Wales, financed by the Department of Education and
Science. This report contains a great deal of data
about the programmes mounted in the education of

adults, so that considerable raw material exists here for theorising about curriculum issues.

Adult Education   *C Verner 1964*

This book is a little dated now but the chapters on designing and managing the learning experience in adult education are thorough and contain a lot of ideas that are relevant to the study of curriculum in adult education.

Chapter Nine

THE PROVISION OF EDUCATION FOR ADULTS IN THE UNITED
KINGDOM

Since the 1944 Education Act it has been the duty of
the Secretary of State for Education and Science 'to
promote the education of the people of England and
Wales and the progressive development of institutions devoted to that purpose, and to secure effective execution by local authorities, under his
control and direction, of the national policy of
providing a varied and comprehensive educational
service in every area'. (cited from the Russell
Report 1973:25). Later in the same Act of
Parliament, the requirements are specified:

Section 4.1: Subject as hereinafter provided,
it shall be the duty of every local education
authority to secure the provision for their
area of adequate facilities for further
education, that is to say:
a. full-time and part-time education for
persons over compulsory school age; and
b. leisure time occupation, in such organised cultural training and recreative
activities as are suited to their requirements, for any persons over
compulsory school age who are able and
willing to profit by the facilities
provided for that purpose.

(cited from Stock 1982:12)

It is clear, from the above quotations that since
the 1944 Education Act it has been the duty of every
local education authority in the United Kingdom to
make provision for lifelong education, but it will
be recognised immediately that the educational model
implicit in this Act is a front-end model, so that
no consideration was given to the idea of an

integrated curriculum. Even so, the vision of the
1944 Act was long term and idealistic and this is as
significant as other parts, eg. the structure of
initial education, of this most influential statute.
During the prosperous period of the 1950s and 1960s
there was a considerable expansion in the provision
of education for adults. Yet this branch of education has remained marginal, so that recent economic
and policy decisions have merely re-inforced this
position. This has resulted in the failure of local
education authorities to fulfil completely the
ideals of those who framed this Act and who anticipated that they would 'contribute towards the
spiritual, moral, mental and physical development of
the community by securing that efficient education..
.. to meet the needs of the population of their
area'. (1944 Education Act: Section 7). By contrast to the forces to restrict the provision there
have been technological innovations that have resulted in the creation of new knowledge, so that
continuing education in the vocational sphere is
being recognised as an area of importance and resources are being given to it. Nevertheless, it
would be contrary to the ideals of the 1944
Education Act and to the nature of education itself
if the whole person were not taken into consideration in the provision of continuing education in the
future.

Since the education authorities have only had
limited budgets with which to provide an education
service for adults, their provision has been restricted and it has rarely been possible to offer
the comprehensive service that was envisaged.
Hence, the purpose of this chapter is to examine
the provision made for the education of adults and
some of the organizations that support the service.
Consequently, it will be recognised that less emphasis will be given to industrial and commercial
provision than to that of the local authorities.
The chapter contains four main sections: the
providers; recent developments in provision;
organizations that support the service; recent
research in the education of adults. This fourth
section is included here since much of the research
has been initiated by the organization that support
the education of adults. The chapter concludes
with a brief discussion and summary.

THE PROVIDERS OF EDUCATION FOR ADULTS

From the terms of the 1944 Education Act it might
be assumed that the problem of isolating the providers of education for adults would not be a difficult task and yet immediately it is undertaken it
becomes apparent that the number of providers is
multitudinous and that much of the provision is
covert rather than open and explicit. For instance,
the Guildford Adult Education Week, referred to in
the previous chapter (ACACE 1979c), has over twenty
different participant organizations each year,
including: the University of Surrey, the Guildford
College of Technology, the Workers Educational
Association, the Adult Education Institute, the
County Library Service, the Careers Service, the
Women's Institute, the Friends of Guildford House,
the French Circle etc. Yet this list, which is incomplete, does not make explicit the concept of a
provider of education for adults and Legge (1982)
makes it clear that this is a difficult undertaking.
It will be recalled that the definition of education
adopted here is 'any planned service of incidents
having a humanistic basis directed towards the
participants learning and understanding'. Hence any
provider, or facilitator, of a series of incidents
directed towards learning, provided that they have a
humanistic basis, may be considered within this discussion. But to isolate all of these providers
would be another task, and one that Legge (1982) has
already done most admirably, so that this discussion
is limited to the main providers: the local education authorities, the universities, the Workers
Educational Association and, finally, some of the
other providers are mentioned briefly.

The Local Education Authorities: The provision made by
local education authorities varies from one area to
another, so that it is difficult to summarise the
organization in simple terms and the following description seeks only to highlight some of the main
features. Four separate types of local authority
provision are noted here: higher education,
colleges of further education, adult education institutes and community colleges.
    It must be recognised from the outset that the
polytechnics and colleges of higher education
frequently provide both vocational and advanced
courses in general education for adults. There has
been considerable debate about the extent to which
polytechnics should play similar roles to

universities or whether they should retain the
function for which they were originally established
- to provide opportunities for adults to follow work
related education at an advanced level on either a
full-time or a part-time basis. If the polytechnics
and colleges of higher education were actually able
to provide this service then non-university higher
education would have the means of creating a lifelong system of education and Wood (1982:9-11) indicates that continuing education, at least, is being
seriously considered by many of these institutions.
Despite these considerations the pressure to respond to the demands of the young adults and to concentrate resources on initial education has resulted
in much of the work of such institutions being similar to university-type undergraduate education.
    Less advanced work related to the education of
adults is undertaken by the colleges of further education. The distinction between higher and further
education often appears to be blurred but advanced
further education is usually regarded as being that
education that is above the General Certificate in
Education (advanced level). Since many colleges of
further education offer courses that are generally
recognised as being advanced further education it is
difficult to differentiate between institutions
offering higher and those offering further education.
Many colleges, however, offer education for adults
in courses leading to: a vocational award;
General Certificate of Education; awards of other
validating agencies. In addition, many provide
short courses for vocational or general interest
that carry no academic qualifications upon com-
pletion. Nevertheless, many of these courses do
attract many adult students, so that the general
image of these colleges as catering exclusively for
young adults (16-19 years old) who are reaching the
end of their education is now misleading. However,
the change in the image may only be completed when
the front-end model of education has lost its
currency and a form of lifelong education is seen to
be the basis of education. Then these colleges may
be regarded as colleges of continuing or recurrent
education, although Illich and Verne (1976) do warn
of the dangers of too much institutionalisation of
lifelong education.
    More recently, some local education authorities
have established departments of adult education
within colleges of further education, so that
general adult education is being located in the
institutions that also provide vocational education.
254

This is, clearly, a movement in the direction mentioned above, that of creating colleges of continuing education. There are a number of advantages
to this, despite the warnings of Illich and Verne,
as the colleges of further education can become the
focal point for the local authority provision of
education for adults in a specific area; the distinction between vocational and non-vocational education, which is already blurred, becomes even less
apparent; the duplication of provision between the
colleges and the adult education institutes may be
avoided and the resources of the colleges may be
even more fully utilised. By contrast, there are a
number of potential problems in this policy including the exacerbation of the status differential between those staff whose main work is in teaching
advanced vocational courses and those whose work is
in general, non-vocational education, a point highlighted by Mee and Wiltshire (1978). However, a
general,non-vocational education class may actually
achieve a higher academic level than that of the
vocational one but since there may be no examination
to demonstrate it, the general, non-vocational education course may be accorded lower status. Other
potential disadvantages include: a greater likelihood to fail to respond to demand from small groups
of individuals since they may be less likely to
make their requests to employees of large bureaucratic organizations than they are to staff from
local adult education institutes and the likelihood
that examination courses will always be given precedence over liberal adult education. As this movement has occurred in some areas, as was mentioned
earlier, it will be interesting to see if there are
differences in the variety of provision between
authorities that have implemented it and those that
are retaining a distinction between the two branches.
        One of the more significant developments in
the education of adults that has occurred in recent
years has been the funding of courses, usually but
by no means exclusively, in colleges of further and
higher education, by the Manpower Services Commission, including: the Training Opportunities Scheme;
Youth Opportunities Programme; the New Training
Initiative. Hence, considerable government funding
for education is coming from a central government
agency that is not controlled by the Department of
Education and Science, so that state-provided education has itself become a complex phenomenon.
Woodhall (1980:16) notes that 'by 1978 the total
number of adults, including 16-18 year olds, who

benefited from government training schemes was about
150,000 (250,000 if all YOP participants are included), compared with 90,000 in 1970, and expenditure rose from under £30 million to well over
£300 million!

Other local education authorities have retained
separate institutions of adult education and these
tend to have a centre, with a small full-time staff,
and perhaps a little amount of prime use accommodation. The institutes utilise classrooms from local
schools and colleges on an evening, and occasionally on a day-time basis. Mee (1980) discusses how
adult education functions on this model. However,
when adult education and further education are separated, the curriculum of the former tends to be
mainly based upon leisure time and hobby activities,
not that there is anything wrong in this since these
activities may contribute to the growth and development of the students in a variety of ways. Perhaps
the content of the curriculum is, however, one of
the reasons why adult education has remained a low
status marginal activity. Even so, there is some
overlap between the educational programmes offered
by institutes of adult education and colleges of
further education, where both are in the same local
education area, and this occurs especially in
General Certificate of Education courses. Such
duplication is one reason why liaison between providers is necessary. However, there are some local
education authority areas in which there is an adult
education institute but not a college of further
education and in these instances the former may seek
to fulfil many of the functions of the latter, including offering courses sponsored by the Manpower
Services Commission.

While many adult education institutes were
formed after the 1944 Education Act, Kelly (1970:
383-384) states:

> The tradition of the non-residential centre
> can be traced back to the mechanics'
> institutes and working men's colleges of the
> nineteenth century, but few of these survived
> as educational institutions into the twentieth
> century. It was the Educational Settlements
> Associations (from 1946 the Educational Centres
> Association) which took the lead in developing
> the modern movement and at the same time
> provided a link with the historic past.

Perhaps Kelly underplays the degree of continuity

between the mechanics' institutes and the contemporary adult education institutes and Devereux
(1982) would appear to suggest that in London, at
least, this was more apparent than Kelly claims.
However, discussion upon this point will be pursued
no further here, since historical analyses as beyond
the scope of this study. Nevertheless, it may be
seen that the history of adult education has been
one in which institutes, rather than schools or
colleges, have been the location of the education
offered.

Perhaps the most well known of all the adult
education provision made by local education authorities are the community colleges, associated with
the name of Henry Morris. Morris who was chief
education officer for Cambridgeshire, had a passionate belief in lifelong education and an interest in
architecture. He had a vision of the educational
institution becoming the centre of the village
community in almost the same manner as the eccles-
iastical institution had been in a bygone age.
Morris (1956, cited in Fletcher 1980:16) claimed
'that the centre of gravity in education and the
culture it transmits should be in that part which
provides for youth and maturity .... Our main means
to this end is to group our local communities round
their colleges and secondary schools'. Under his
direction, in the 1930s, the first four village
colleges were opened and, after the Second World
War, other colleges were opened in Cambridgeshire
and elsewhere (Jennings - no date). The village
college incorporated the village hall, adult classrooms, rooms for òther public meetings and organizations and the secondary school. Fairbairn (1971)
actually provides a plan of the Countesthorpe school
which had a community education department within
a comprehensive school. However, the idea of util-
ising a large comprehensive school as the basis for
a community school has subsequently been adopted in
a number of places, such as the Sutton Centre in
Nottinghamshire (Wilson 1980), the Abraham Moss
Centre in Manchester and the model has been copied
in Grenoble in France. There appears to be tremendous advantages in providing all the community facilities on one campus but until Fletcher's study of
the Sutton Centre is actually published it would be
unwise to speculate about these.

The Universities: In 1867, James Stuart who was a
fellow of Trinity College, Cambridge, delivered a
course of lectures in various cities organised by

the North of England Council for Providing Higher Education for Women, and this is generally regarded as the start of the university extension movement (Kelly 1970:219). The movement was actually sanctioned by the University of Cambridge in 1873 with the first course commencing in Derby on 8th October of that year. Thereafter, the universities of Oxford and London offered classes and there are currently twenty five universities in England and Wales which have a department with extra-mural responsibility and provide a university extension service in their regions. These universities have the designation of Responsible Body, which entitles them to receive a grant from the Department of Education and Science towards the cost of organising adult education classes of a university standard in their designated area. This is the only aspect of the normal work of a university which is open to the scrutiny of Her Majesty's Inspectorate.

There is a danger in universities that extra-mural staff may be seen as tutor organizers who have a degree of expertise in a subject, other than adult education, so that their competence is judged by their peers in terms of the subject in which they were originally qualified rather than by their understanding of adult education. One of the reasons for this is that there are few universities that actually offer courses that lead to an academic qualification in the education of adults. Like American universities, however, there has been a gradual movement in this direction with a small number of universities currently offering courses of study that lead to a university post-graduate qualification in adult education. Once these are established, the academic status of the discipline may be raised.

The universities have also been involved with other aspects of adult education including tutor training, research and writing books and papers for publication. (Thornton and Stephens, 1977). Research and publication are normal functions of a university academic but tutor training is one that occurs less frequently. However, members of university extra-mural departments do often train the part-time staff that are employed to teach in their responsible body area. Even so, this initial preparation was not generally institutionalised, so that the universities received little mention in the recommendations of the Advisory Committee for the Supply and Training of Teachers on the part-time tutor training, which is unfortunate since the universities have always been heavily involved in initial teacher training.

Many of the classes provided by the universities are offered in their own centres but others are organized and mounted in conjunction with local authority, or Workers Educational Association, provision. A small staff of academics, often having the title 'staff tutor' and sometimes not being regarded as part of the university's academic staff, organize the extension service, but it may be seen from this statement that once again adult education tends to have low status compared to other branches of education. Few universities have yet actually offered part-time degree programmes for adults, despite the fact that the Open University demonstrated the extent of the demand (Tight 1982). However, most universities are willing to waive certain of their formal entry requirements to their full-time undergraduate courses for mature students. There has been one notable exception to this failure to respond to the demand for education at an advanced level by adults: Birkbeck College, a constituent college of the University of London is concerned exclusively with adult students. This college is named after Dr George Birkbeck who was professor of natural philosophy at Anderson's Institute in Glasgow when he offered courses of lectures to adults in that city at the start of the nineteenth century. Birkbeck College has offered a wide range of courses, including part-time masters degree programmes, for mature students for many years. The University of London has also offered part-time undergraduate level study at Goldsmith's College and it has also provided the opportunity for part-time mature students to take external degrees and diplomas. On a much more restricted scale the extramural department at the University of Hull and the School of Continuing Education at the University of Kent have been involved in organizing undergraduate courses for adults.(Tight 1982:7).

More recently, a major advance in the provision of part-time higher education for adults has been the establishment of the Open University. This is funded directly by the Department of Education and Science and offers a range of courses at undergraduate level, a smaller amount of post-graduate work and a programme of short courses. The undergraduate programme is modular in structure, with each module being equivalent to a year's part-time study. In addition, there are some half credit courses but these also span a year's study. Students are expected to accumulate six credits for the award of a degree and eight for an honours. Not all modules are regarded as being the same degree of difficulty, so that the courses are offered at four levels, foundation and three other. Students are expected to study two foundation courses for all degrees, unless they are granted exemptions. Additionally, in order to be awarded an honours degree students have to have gained at least two credits at the third and fourth levels. The Open University has now introduced a taught higher degree (B.Phil) and a small research degree programme; this latter innovation demonstrates that there is a demand from a number of people who would like to pursue academic research as a leisure time interest. Some of the Open University's undergraduate courses may be studied by associate students who are not registered for a degree and who may have no intention of registering for one. In addition, the Open University offers a programme of short courses in both continuing and community education. After a decade of existence the Open University began to offer courses in adult education itself, with both tutor training courses and a third level half credit course in education for adults which commence in 1984.

Distance teaching in its present form, especially that employed by the Open University using the media as an integral part of the course design, is a new development, although some of the larger established correspondence colleges might dispute this and regard it as merely a development in their own work. Nevertheless, since the establishment of the Open University it has acquired considerable significance and a number of established universities, eg. Surrey, and polytechnics are also experimenting with courses of study through distance learning. Hence, at the time of writing there seems a distinct possibility that more opportunities for adults to pursue their own academic interests, and even vocational continuing education, by this method will arise in the foreseeable future. While the Open University pioneered the idea of distance learning undergraduate programmes, other countries in the world have rapidly developed similar versions, as Rumble and Harry (1982) have clearly demonstrated.

The Workers' Education Association: Founded in 1903 by Albert Mansbridge but not by this name, the Workers' Educational Association also has Responsible Body status from the Department of Education and Science and since the Russell Report (1973) the Association has stressed its work with industry and the socially

disadvantaged, in accordance with the recommendations made in the Report. The Association is a
national voluntary body, divided into seventeen
districts in England and Wales, plus a further three
in Scotland and one in Northern Ireland. Each has
its own full-time secretary and a few full-time
tutor organizers who both teach on the programme
and are involved in its development.

However, each local branch is autonomous, so that
the members' interests constitute one of the basic
criteria for the content of the programme for any
one year. Often this programme is arranged in conjunction with a local university extra-mural department and the local education authority provider, so
that in such instances duplication in the programme
should not occur. While it is the members of the
local branches who contribute to the programme
planning, each branch offers its courses to the
general public so that it depends on the extent to
which members are aware of local interests whether
the classes actually attract many non-members of the
association. Since most branches do not have their
own premises, each programme is usually offered in
premises hired by the association and it is often
the same set of premises as the other providers use,
eg. a local school.

Some Other Providers of Education for Adults: It will be
recalled from the discussion at the outset of this
section that the concept of provider is difficult
to define, so that it would be possible to take the
broadest interpretation and examine the work of a
multitude of different educationally orientated
institutions, including museums and art galleries,
etc. However, only three main types of provision
are mentioned here: the residential colleges,
independent educational organizations and some
other voluntary associations. However, it must be
appreciated that even this is an arbitrary division
since some of the voluntary associations run their
own residential colleges eg, the Women's Institute
has its own college, Denman College, near Oxford.

Residential Colleges: There are basically two
types of residential college; those that run long
courses lasting about an academic year or more and
those that organize mostly short courses. There are
currently nine of the long-term colleges, Ruskin
College being the oldest while Northern College was
founded only a few years ago in 1977. The other
seven colleges are: Coleg Harlech, Co-operative
College, Fircroft, Hillcroft, Newbattle Abbey,
Plater and Woodbrooke. All the aforementioned

colleges offer courses for mature students of both
sexes, with the exception of Hillcroft which is for
female students only. Two of these colleges have a
religious foundation: Plater being a college of the
Church of Rome and Woodbrooke is organized by the
Society of Friends. Many of the students who attend
these colleges receive grant aid, although some
attend on scholarships awarded by the Trades Union
Movement; this being especially true for some
attending Ruskin and Northern colleges. Frequently
the courses studied by students at these colleges
lead to an award of a diploma, validated by a
university or the Council for National Academic
Awards, and while these courses are entities in
their own right they also provide sufficient qualification to enable their holders to proceed to a
university or polytechnic in order to read for a
degree.
    Apart from these nine long term residential
colleges there are, according to Legge (1982), about
fifty short-term residential colleges which organize
short, work-related courses. Often these courses
are organized by the college in conjunction with
specific companies for the latter's employees and
run during the weekdays, while at the weekend they
run liberal adult education courses for the general
public. Some of these colleges are owned by
universities, others by local education authorities,
whilst some are private enterprises. Many employ a
full-time principal, or warden, but use specialist
part-time staff on the specific courses that are
organised.

Independent Educational Organizations: Apart from
the independent short-term residential colleges
there are a number of other independent organisa-
tions offering a variety of educational services to
adults, eg. correspondence colleges, conference
centres, language schools, commercial schools and
industry's own shools and centres. Correspondence
colleges offer courses in a variety of areas,
especially in the sphere of the General Certificate
of Education but it is difficult to ascertain the
number of adult students enrolling with these
colleges each year. The private language schools
are flourishing at the time of writing since
English as a foreign language is becoming increasingly important for foreign nationals who wish to
reside in the United Kingdom and because it is used
so widely in international trade and commerce. It
would be difficult to describe all the different

types of education offered by these various independent organizations, indeed it is a study in
itself, but their existence is evidence of the demand for education that exists and which is often
met in an open market situation.

By contrast to these organizations, it is
probably true to claim that the largest providers of
information in the United Kingdom are the media and
it might be claimed that they constitute a major
element in the education of adults in the country.
Obviously the tabloid newspapers offer little in the
way of systematic education for their readers but
they do constitute a source of information regularly
provided for many people. Unlike these, the so-
called 'quality press' and many of the local newspapers offer regular financial and legal columns,
systematic analyses of the current political and
economic situations, and even columns about architecture and antiques. Indeed Rogers and Groombridge
(1976:171) record how some educational courses have
been offered through the newspapers. Radio and
television, likewise, provide a similar service to
their listeners and viewers and these have certainly
become a major instrument in the transmission of
culture. The Open University has utilised both in
a much more systematic manner than any other educational institution in the United Kingdom but in
other parts of the world they are also used for this
purpose and with the growth of local radio in the
United Kingdom these media will no doubt assume a
community education role in some instances. However,
to include the media, apart from when they are employed in a more systematic manner, raises a conceptual issue - do they actually provide education
as opposed to being media through which learning
occurs? Obviously they are the latter, but are they
also the former? For somebody following a series of
documentary programmes or who reads regularly the
analysis of the contemporary political scene, for
instance, they provide the material for a plannned
series of learning episodes on a self-directed
basis. Whether it is the editor or the viewer/
listener/reader who is the planner is irrelevant;
the fact remains that they are planned and systematic, so that they constitute the basis of a
curriculum.

Voluntary Organizations: The Workers' Educational
Association has already been mentioned but apart
from it there are many voluntary organizations which
provide education. The Women's Institute was

mentioned previously and it is one of the three
major providers of education for women, the others
being the Townswomens Guilds and the womens clubs.
The Women's Institute receives a grant from the
Department of Education and Science towards its educational activities and it has recently co-operated
with the Open University in mounting one of the
latter's courses. These associations may, in some
ways, be compared to the Workers' Educational
Association and should be regarded as major providers of education for adult women.

Among the voluntary organization that provide
education are the churches which are both at
national and local level have always sought this
role and while they are often regarded as only
promulgators of a spiritual message, they have always sought to enable their members to learn about
a wider variety of matters.

Education, then, occurs at work, at home and during
leisure, in an educational or an informal setting,
the amount provided is impossible to quantify but
it does mean that facilities for a life of learning
exist in the United Kindgom. Perhaps the fact that
it is neither institutionalised nor formal, that it
is not all provided by the state and that it is
often on an unplanned and unco-ordinated basis
means that the ideal of state provision of lifelong
education for all, on a voluntary basis for adults,
has not yet been achieved in the United Kingdom.
Nevertheless, the vast amount of provision for the
education of adults that has been documented above
does not exhaust the provision, as will be seen in
the following section of this chapter.

RECENT DEVELOPMENTS IN THE PROVISION OF EDUCATION
FOR ADULTS

There have been a variety of recent developments in
this field and it is not intended to provide an exhaustive documentation of all of these changes in
this section but rather to illustrate the directions into which this branch of education is being
influenced. The areas highlighted here are discussed briefly and related to the conceptual framework
suggested earlier and they are: the increasing
involvement of the further and higher education
sectors in the education of adults; the implementation of return to study courses; adult basic education; pre-retirement education. It would have

been possible to focus upon many other issues such as community education, distance learning, flexi-study, women's education etc. but discussion of these selected areas is considered sufficient to provide an overview of the developments and trends in the education of adults.

The Increasing Involvement of the Further and Higher Education Sectors in the Education of Adults: It was argued in the opening chapter that the social and technological changes in industrial society are such that some forms of lifelong education or continuing education is becoming a greater necessity for the health of the nation and its people. Hence, adult education with its liberal image, is bound to remain on the periphery of the concerns of central govern-ment, while other facets of the education of adults are more likely to assume a greater significance; a danger in this trend is that liberal adult education will be subsumed in the avalanche of demands from industry and the professions for continuing educa-tion. While the national needs are of tremendous importance they must be balanced against the demands of individuals for a liberal education beyond initial education. Therefore, it is hoped that the latter will not be totally swamped by the former. Meanwhile, there is an increasing demand for voca-tional continuing education from industry and the professions and much of the responsibility for re-sponding to these appears to be resting with inst-itutions of further and higher education. It is indicative of this trend that both the University Grants Committee and the National Advisory Body are taking a close scrutiny at continuing education, that the Further Education Curriculum Review and Development Unit has instituted curriculum research projects in the education of adults and the Advisory Council for Adult and Continuing Education has recommended that a National Development Body for Continuing Education in England and Wales should be established (ACACE 1982 e).

Hence it is anticipated that there will be greater recognition given to the education of adults within the formal organization of further and higher education and that continuing education will become institutionalised within these spheres within the foreseeable future. This suggests that a completely new system of education will evolve and, perhaps, with it is a new category of educational specialist - the continuing education professional. There are certain dangers attached to this movement and these

have already been referred to in this study, so that
they will not be repeated here.

Return to Study Courses: Two types of return to study
courses are mentioned here: the first is the full-
time courses that some colleges mount that enable
adults to take a new direction in their lives and
the second refers to those courses that are organised, usually on a part-time basis, to prepare
people to return to the student role on either a
full-time or a part-time basis.
    There is a sense in which the long term resid-
ential colleges mentioned earlier in this chapter
organize courses that could be classified within
this category since they mount courses lasting for
at least one academic year for mature students,
usually in the sphere of the humanities or the
social sciences, but that might help people prepare
for a new career. However, most of these colleges
would not claim that their courses have a vocational
aim and yet they would recognise that the academic
award that their students gain may well be of vocational assistance. Since 1966, the City Literary
Institute in London has provided a similar opportunity, initially on a part-time but since 1973
on a full-time basis. Once these courses were
implemented full-time students became eligible for
maintenance grants in the same manner as the full-
time students in the long term residential colleges.
Such was the success of the City Literary
Institute's venture that the Inner London Education
Authority approved the commencement of similar
courses in 1975 at Paddington College.
    Since the start of the London courses there has
been another important step in the provision of education of this nature for adults with the emergence
of the Open College, initially in Nelson and Colne
but more recently elsewhere in the United Kingdom.
One of the most significant features of the open
college system was the recognition that General
Certificate of Education courses, the usual pre-
requisite for entry into higher education, were not
designed to allow adults to demonstrate their ability, so that new introductory courses have been
prepared for mature students which have enabled the
successful ones to proceed to higher education.
Initially, the open college system was a liaison
between Nelson and Colne College and Preston
Polytechnic but within a few years the provision
was increased as a number of institutions of higher
education were prepared to accept students that had

followed the new courses. Even more recently the
'Open Tech' has been launched and since its development is in the early stages its contribution to the
education of adults is awaited with interest.

One factor that has been recognised is that as
mature students return to study, often after a long
absence from it, they frequently require help in the
techniques of studying. Hence, the Open College
courses have contained units on study skills and
scientific method. Similarly, the Hutchinsons
(1978:85) note the importance of teaching study
skills on *Fresh Horizon* courses. Since the inaug-
uration of the Open University many colleges of
further education have also commenced study techniques courses for adults. These courses,being
specifically orientated towards new recruits to the
Open University,are often run in the term preceding the commencement of the Open University
academic year. Gradually courses of this nature are
also being introduced into the school curriculum
(Tabberer and Allman 1981,Mannion Watson 1982) but
this provision will probably not affect the demand
for return to study courses in the adult education
curriculum for many years to come. Indeed, with the
development of distance learning, the demand for this
type of course may esculate over the next few years.

Adult Basic Education: Despite all of these developments in the education of adults it must be recognised that it is not that many years ago that the
prevalence of adult illiteracy in the United
Kingdom, thought to have been eradicated by the introduction of compulsory education, was first,
recognised. Indeed,Cardy and Wells (1981:5) point
out that provision to cope with adult illiteracy
only began this century in 1975 and that this was
initially organized by the Adult Literacy Resource
Agency, established as a specialist division under
the auspices of the National Institute of Adult
Education. This agency disbursed grants from
central government to the local education authorities in order to stimulate an awareness of the problem. As a result of the British Broadcasting
Corporation's involvement in the field with the
television programme *On the Move*, the demand for
basic education grew enormously, so that from
1 April 1980, the government established the Adult
Literacy and Basic Skills Unit, as an agency of the
National Institute of Adult Education, with an
initial grant for a period of three years and with
a remit to develop:

provision designed to improve the standards
of proficiency for adults, whose first or
second language is English, in the area of
literacy, numeracy, and those related basic
communication and coping skills without which
people are impeded from applying or being
considered for employment
  (Albsu - Guidelines for Special Development
  Projects para 1.1).

It will be noticed that both numeracy and life skills
have been included in this remit, which makes it far
broader than the original area of concern. The
remit is in accordance with the recommendations of
the Advisory Council for Adult and Continuing
Education (1979b) which also specified that adult
basic education should include language, number and
life skills. Among the other recommendations of
this report were that the Department of Education and
Science and the Welsh Office should establish a
strategic plan for adult basic education over the
next decade and that an Adult Basic Education Unit
should be established. Even so, it did appeal that
the increased provision of adult basic education
should not be made at the expense of other adult and
further education provision. It is also quite significant that the New Training Initiative, which has
been initiated by central government and funded by
the Manpower Services Commission, has included some
of the main aspects of adult basic education within
its recommended curriculum. In addition, the
Advisory Council for Adult and Continuing Education
recommended that it should be included in courses
for the unemployed (ACACE 1982d). While Little et
al (1982) note that, while adult education provision for the black communities in the United Kingdom
tends not to consider their needs very adequately,
adult basic education is still needed by many of
them.

Pre and Post Retirement Education: It will be noted in the
remit given to the Adult Literacy and Basic Skills
Unit that the reason why adults should receive basic
education is because without these skills they are
unable to apply for or unlikely to be considered for
employment, rather than because it might actually
help the individuals develop and grow. It is this
interface between work and non-work that constitutes
the theme for much of the discussion about the final
recent development in the education of adults that
is being examined here. Pre-retirement education

268

has been among the most rapidly expanding areas of education for adults in the United Kingdom in the latter half of the twentieth century and Coleman (1982:7) claims that:

> The foundations of the pre-retirement education movement in the United Kingdom were laid during the years 1955-1959, in Scotland by the efforts of the late Dr Andrew Hood when he was Lord Provost of Glasgow; and in England and Wales through the work of the late Mr W A Sanderson, secretary of the Gulbenkian Foundation.

Much pre-retirement education is organized by local authority adult education provision although industry and commerce also mounts its own courses. However, many of the courses appear to be rather instrumental in terms of these aims and it has been argued elsewhere that they should include a much greater emphasis upon the individual and his own perspectives upon his approaching retirement (Jarvis 1980). Curriculum development is clearly a very important issue in this form of education and Coleman (1982:60-72) records a course which he conducted during his own research. This is a useful inclusion since it both demonstrates an educator of adults at work and shows the type of content that the participants themselves considered that they needed.

One of Coleman's (1982-95-6) recommendations was that:

> the Department of Education and Science along with the industrial and voluntary sectors supports the establishment of a national organization which shall be recognised as the focus for pre-retirement education in England and Wales.

In an important post-script to the research the chairman of the Pre-Retirement Association wrote, 'that the Department of Education and Science was recognising the Pre-Retirement Association as the appropriate national body. Funds were being made available on an initial three year basis, to enable the PRA to create an educational development group' (cited in Coleman 1982:99). Hence, it may be seen that this is another area in the education of adults which central government has viewed as significant enough to recent years to invest monies, so that more development in this area can be confidently anticipated in the future.

By contrast to pre-retirement education, the education of the elderly after retirement is also gaining an important place in the education of adults, which is not surprising since there are now so many more adults who have retired. Indeed, the mid year estimate for 1976 showed that the Office of Population and Consensus showed that 9.6 million adults out of a population of 56.0 million in the United Kingdom had retired, a proportion of 17.1% of the total population. Hence, there is a duty laid upon local education authorities to cater for this large preportion of the population. In America, the elderly have been attending university summer schools and Zimmerman (1979) records the enthusiasm with which they tackle their studies. The 'université du troisième age' has been widely acknowledged as an exciting venture in France and now the University of the Third Age is being started in the United Kingdom. But the education of the elderly does not have to carry a university label to be popular; some holiday camps are now filled in out of season times with elderly adults seeking to learn etc., so that another element in the education of adults is emerging. Indeed, it will be recalled that Label (1978) actually suggested that this area was becoming a separate branch of education and that it should be called gerogogy. However, this suggestion has not been widely accepted and the term remains as little more than a remainder of the place of the elderly in the education of adults.

Some recent trends in the education of adults have been examined in this section, although it is acknowledged that the choice was somewhat arbitrary. It would have been possible to have included many others but the reason for choosing these developments has been in order to illustrate that while adult education remains marginal, elements in the education of adults are assuming a greater significance and that central government is beginning to play a greater role in this provision. If this trend continues then, as Cantor (1974) suggested, the rudiments of a policy of recurrent education are appearing in a piecemeal fashion, but the term being employed is continuing education.

Having examined some of the recent trends in the education of adults, the main organizations and associations in the field will now be considered.

ORGANIZATIONS INVOLVED IN THE EDUCATION OF ADULTS

The Department of Education and Science is, naturally, involved in the provision of education for adults since the 1944 Education Act placed this responsibility firmly in the sphere of the local education authorities. However, there is little discussion on the role of the Department here since this might better be undertaken within the context of the organization and administration of education in the United Kingdom. Cantor and Roberts (1972) give a good description of the work of the Department and its relationship to the Regional Advisory Councils, which are also playing an increasingly significant role in the education of adults as it is becoming a more important element in the further and higher education sectors. However, there are members of Her Majesty's Inspectorate who have responsiblity for adult education and their sphere of influence is extensive. In addition, many local authorities have advisors in adult education, although their post may be on a part-time basis and they may also have responsibility for other spheres of education. Leaving aside the central and local government's involvement in the education of adults which is the same as it is for all branches of education, the purpose of this section is to examine some of those organizations and associations whose remit is specifically in the area of the education of adults, especially: the National Institute of Adult Education, the Advisory Council for Adult and Continuing Education, the Universities Council for Adult and Continuing Education, the Standing Conference on University Teaching and Research in the Education of Adults, the Educational Centres Association and the Association of Recurrent Education.

The National Institute of Adult Continuing Education which was formerly the National Foundation of Adult Education was founded in 1946 and in 1949 this new body merged with a much older one, the British Institute of Adult Education (established in 1921), to become the National Institute of Adult Education. However, the term 'national' is a little misleading because it refers only to England and Wales, since Scotland has its own Institute and Northern Ireland its own National Association. The National Institute for Adult Education was originally located in London but it is currently based in Leicester. The Institute has a small professional staff and its main function is

to promote the study and general advancement of
adult education. Legge (1982:183-4) suggests that
it seeks to achieve this by: facilitating the ex-
change of experiences by conferences and meetings,
especially its annual study conference; acting as
a clearing house for the collection and dissemina-
tion of information about adult education through
the publication of books, journals and research
reports, perhaps the most well known journal being
Adult Education; seeking to encourage and conduct
research into adult education; developing co-
operative relations with other bodies concerned with
adult education throughout the world.

The Advisory Council for Adult and Continuing Education: The
Russell Report (1973:54) recommended that the
Secretary of State should establish a Development
Council for Adult Education for England and Wales.
However, in 1977 an Advisory Council was established
and the actual change in the wording of the title is
significant. The Council was initially established
for three years and it was subsequently granted a
three year extension. During the final year of this
latter period the Advisory Council concluded that it
had fulfilled its remit and it proposed that its
successor should be a completely new body which
might be called the Continuing Education and Training Services Commission (ACACE 1982e:3). Before
this recommendation is examined, it is necessary to
recall the original terms of reference of the
Advisory Council, which were:

> To advise generally on matters relevant to
> the provision of education for adults in
> England and Wales, and in particular:
> a)   to promote co-operation between the
>   various bodies in adult education and
>   review current practice, organization
>   and priorities, with a view to the
>   most effective deployment of the
>   available resources;   and
> b)   to promote the development of future
>   policies and priorities, with full
>   regard to the concept of education as a
>   process continuing throughout life
>
> (cited from Taylor 1978:209-210)

The membership of the Council was the perogative of
the Secretary of State who nominated individuals to
serve as members in a personal rather than in a

epresentative capacity and, as Taylor pointed out,
ts brief was extremely wide and had few limitations
laced upon it. In the Council's own review of its
ork, it pointed out that it had: published reports
n enquiries into policy and organizations,
urriculum and programme development and fact find-
ng; provided written statements and provided oral
vidence in response to policy and consultative
apers published by other bodies; made public
tatements on educational matters. At the time
his report was published the Council had
ublished five discussion papers, twenty-three
eports (with up to thirteen more to appear in its
inal year) and had prepared and submitted thirty
wo written responses to policy and consultative
apers published by other bodies. (ACACE 1982e:7).
hese publications have provided the most extensive
nd comprehensive analysis of adult and continuing
ducation ever produced in the United Kingdom and
ave focused the minds of many upon this aspect of
ducation. However, the Council considered that it
ad fulfilled its remit and recommended to the
ecretary of State that a Continuing Education and
raining Services Commission should be established.
owever, this is an ambitious proposal, as the Council
ecognised, so that it proposed that an interim body
hould be established, having three main purposes:

1)   To review regularly the facilities avail-
        able in England and Wales for the con-
        tinuing education and training of adults
2)   To initiate, and respond to requests for,
        advice and help in the development of all
        aspects of continuing education and
        training
3)   To identify areas of provision in need of
        specific development and to undertake or
        sponsor innovative and experimental work
        so as to encourage and enable the most
        effective country-wide provision
        appropriate to particular local circum-
        stances

   (ACACE 1982e:3)

he Council recommended that this new body should
ave five years in which to demonstrate its worth
ut considered that the establishment of some such
ody is necessary in England and Wales, so that it
roposed that an annual budget of £1.75 million
hould be allocated to it by the third year of its
xistence. However, the Secretary of State did not
ccept these proposals and the National Institute of

Adult Continuing Education has been given additiona
grant aid in order to fulfill some of these functio
which the Advisory Council has discontinued.

The Universities Council for Adult and Continuing Education:
Prior to 1947 the universities liaised with each
other through the Universities Extra-Mural Consultative Committee but, in that year the Universities
Council for Adult Education was formed. More recen
ly, it has inserted the element of continuing educa
tion.   Universities having an extra-mural responsibility have a seat on this council and its function
consist in disseminating information about the
universities' involvement in extra-mural adult educ
ation, which is done both through an annual conference and through the establishment of occasional
working parties.

Standing Conference on University Teaching and Research in th
Education of Adults: This organization is one of more
recent origin than the Universities Council and, as
its name suggests, it has wider interests and concerns in the education of adults. Universities whic
have either a teaching or a research function, or
both, in the education of adults may have membership. Like the other bodies mentioned, this organiz
ation has established an annual conference and it ha
also established a number of working groups in
various disciplines in order to bring together
academics who have interests in specific areas of th
education of adults, such as the sociology of the ec
ucation of adults, psychology of adult learning etc

The Educational Centres Association: This association was
established in 1947 as a result of a decision of the
Educational Settlements Association to change its
name and to broaden its membership (Allaway 1977:41
42); it is a national, voluntary body which seeks tc
represent all those centres which cater specificall
for the education of adults. Allaway (1977:106)
estimated that one-third of all adult education
centres were in membership with the association in
the mid-1970s and, in addition, there is also a cat
egory of individual membership. Since the association grew out of the Educational Settlements Associa
tion, it is hardly surprising that it has a democratic philosophy and seeks to support the educational centres in a national context. Like other
associations, it organizes conferences for its
members and also seeks to disseminate information
about adult education as widely as possible.

The Association of Recurrent Education: The association is
of more recent origin than the older associations
mentioned above and seeks to provide a focus for

ll who are concerned about recurrent education,
laiming to act as a national pressure group to en-
ure that the principle of recurrency is taken into
onsideration in educational policy making. It seeks
o disseminate information to all its members
hrough a regular newsletter. In addition, it
ublishes discussion and occasional papers on sig-
ificant issues within lifelong education and, like
ost of the bodies thus far mentioned, it organizes
egular conferences and workshops.

variety of other associations could also have
een examined here including the Association for
dult and Continuing Education, formerly called the
ssociation of Adult Education, which also organ-
zes its own conference but is less active in the
roduction of published material. In addition,
here are tutors' associations, principals'
ssociations and various other interest groups that
eet to provide a forum for their own members. There
re also some regional associations that meet on a
egular basis. Nevertheless, there is no one single
ational body that draws together all who are in-
olved in adult and continuing education in either
n individual or corporate capacity, or which
peaks for all whose occupation is in the field of
he education for adults. The National Institute
s obviously the association that comes closest to
erforming this function but it has tended to be
ore active in the areas of liberal adult education
nd education of the socially disadvantaged than in
he wider sphere of the education of adults.

Apart from the associations already discussed
here are a number of other associations whose role
n the world of adult education impinge upon the
ork of adult educators in the United Kingdom; four
f which are mentioned here. The International
ouncil of Adult Education is located in Ontario,
anada. This council publishes a quarterly journal
onvergence which provides a basis for compara-
ive adult education. In the United States, the
merican Association of Adult and Continuing
ducation was created in 1982, as a result of a
erger between the National Association of Public
ontinuing and Adult Education and the Adult
ssociation of the United States of America. The
ssociation is based in Washington and publishes two
ournals, *Adult Education* quarterly and *Lifelong
earning - the Adult Years* appears ten times per annum.
aturally, there are other associations in America
oncerned with the topic but this is noted here not

275

only because of its journals, but because it has
initiated many other studies that are useful to adu
educators in the United Kingdom. In Europe, the
European Bureau of Adult Education is based in the
Netherlands and has membership from the United
Kingdom and, finally, UNESCO has a lifelong education unit based in Paris and another centre in
Hamburg, both of which initiate publications on
adult education. Naturally, this is only a selection of the organizations that either provide or seek
to support education for adults, but these are mentioned to indicate some of the more influential one
in respect to adult education in the United Kingdom
    One of the most significant elements in the wor
of many of the associations mentioned above has bee
their support for research into adult education, so
that the final section of this chapter focuses upon
this important topic.

RESEARCH IN ADULT AND CONTINUING EDUCATION

Some of the organizations mentioned above have spon
sored considerable research in this field but clear
ly the research reports from the Advisory Council
for Adult and Continuing Education will remain one
of its most outstanding contributions to the development of this branch of education. Certainly ther
has never been a period in the history of the
education of adults in the United Kingdom when as
many research publications of such significance hav
appeared in such a brief span of time. Since the
final reports of ACACE had not been published at th
time when this chapter was completed it would be
unwise to list the variety of reports thus far published, suffice to note that they include policy an
organization, curriculum and programme development
and the publication of factual surveys. Many of th
reports have been referred to in this study, so tha
many titles appear in the bibliography at the end.
Additionally, the National Institute of Adult
Education has either co-operated in or initiated a
number of major research projects and it has also
sought to become a national resource centre for
adult education by storing and computerising adult
education material and producing a number of research reviews. The Further Education Curriculum
Review and Development Unit has also recently
sponsored a small number of projects in adult educa
tion and if this policy continues the field of
education for adults will be enriched by a diversit

of studies from a variety of perspectives.

As previously mentioned, some universities have also awarded higher degrees and diplomas for research in adult education and while many of the studies remain in university shelves it is possible to obtain them through the inter-library loan service. In addition to these these, a number of universities have published their own series of research monographs. The University of Manchester has an influential series of Manchester Monographs; the University of Nottingham has published a number of influential books and booklets; Leeds, Surrey and other universities have also produced their own literature; the Open University is also producing a course in the education of adults. Hence, it may be seen that adult and continuing education is becoming the focus of much more research attention than ever before.

CONCLUDING DISCUSSION

Adult education has been the 'poor cousin' (Newman 1979) of the education service since its inception but as Cantor (1974) has suggested there are very gradual policy changes occurring and continuing education is beginning to assume a place of importance within the education service. It may be significant, however, that while continuing education is becoming an acceptable form of education, the term adult education appears to be declining in significance. Naturally, in an industrial society where the speed of change is so rapid vocational continuing education is of paramount importance, but to lose the liberal adult education tradition would be tragic for education as a whole. Thus the human needs of the learners must be taken into consideration in the provision of education for adults as are the demands of the wider society. It might be argued that ultimately there is no difference between the two and that professional development should also result in personal development. While this may occur, it need not always be the case, nor need personal growth result in professional development. Ultimately, the quality of education provided for adults must relate to the learners and their needs as well as to society and its demands.

One further point that needs to be noted here is that the growth and development of research in the education of adults is of significance in as much as it is adding to the body of knowledge about

277

this branch of education, and this continues
to construct the foundations of an academic discipline in adult and continuing education and this,
in its turn, provides a theoretical basis upon which
the occupation of adult educator is established.

SUMMARY

This chapter has indicated that adult and continuing
education, at least in the form of continuing education, is emerging as a significant branch of the
education service as a whole. Continuing education,
especially in its vocational form, may emerge as a
branch of education that is far from the 'poor
cousin' of education but a question mark must hang
over the future of traditional liberal adult education. Apart from noting this change in the education of adults, this chapter has recognised the
foresight of those who framed the 1944 Education
Act and the provisions that were made for the establishment of an adult education service. In addition, some of the multitude of providers of adult
education were mentioned and it was recognised that
independent adult education provision is quite extensive especially in the area of the short-term
residential colleges. The place of entrepreneurial
provision has not been fully discussed here but
there are clearly a number of problems with it, such
as the entrepreneur seeking financial gain for the
sale of his commodity either caters for a mass
audience or he prices his commodity so highly
that the mass audience cannot afford to purchase it.
Hence, entrepreneurial education for adults, which
may appear attractive in some ways, may also have
disastrous results in the long term, so that it is
important that the spirit of the 1944 Education Act
should continue to be implemented by local education
authority provision.
　　Among the trends in the education of adults
mentioned was that education is occurring at both
the stage of the preparation for work and at the
stage of preparation for leisure. Pre-retirement
education is beginning to be recognised as an important new provision, one which may assume additional significance if the age of retirement is
lowered. Additionally, it may be shown that returning to study, for whatever purpose, has resulted in
adult learners learning how to study as well as what
to study. Finally, some of the organizations that
are involved in the provision of and support of

278

adult education were discussed, especially in relation to the research and publication of material.
This leads to a final question that needs to be
posed: to what extent in the study of education for
adults a separate discipline? The epilogue focuses
upon this topic.

SELECTED FURTHER READING

Adult Learning Today   *C Ellwood 1976*

Although this book is now a little dated, it does
provide an account of the universities' involvement
in the education of adults. Its discussion extends
beyond the extra-mural involvement of the universities and, as such, it provides a useful overview of
some of the developments in the 1970s.

The Education of Adults in Britain   *Derek Legge 1982*

This book is written by an adult educator whose
involvement in the education of adults has spanned
many years and the depth and breadth of his experience is apparent throughout. The author has un-
ravelled much of the complexity of adult education
provision in Britain and this book provides a fine
source of reference for anyone interested in this
aspect of adult education.

Adult Education in the United Kingdom   *A Stock 1982*
                                                        (edition)

This provides a brief introduction of some of the
main aspects of adult education in the United
Kingdom but since this purports to be no more than
a summary statement it is more superficial than the
account provided by Derek Legge.

279

Chapter Ten

EPILOGUE

As the education of adults appears to be assuming a
more significant place within mainstream education,
even if it is in the continuing rather than the
liberal form, then one question remains to be raised
in this study: to what extent is the study of the
education of adults a discipline in its own right?
    There are at least two ways of seeking to re-
spond to this question: the first starts with the
traditional disciplines which are employed in the
study of education eg. philosophy, sociology, psychology and approaches the educational processes
from these different perspectives. Then the study of
the education of adults may be viewed as a multi-
disciplined perspective, eg. the philosophy of the
education of adults, but the study of the education
of adults itself would not be regarded as an
academic discipline in its own right.
    However, this approach assumes that the struct-
ure of knowledge is a static phenomenon and that its
branches remain unchanging from one decade to another. Yet this study actually began with the recognition that some branches of knowledge change at
a very rapid rate, so that it would be quite inconsistent to conclude with implications that it is
actually unchanging. Clearly there are tremendous
changes, not only in the amount of knowledge in existence but also in the way that it is structured.
Berger and Luckmann (1967:95) relate the growth and
change in the structure of knowledge to the emergence of specific roles. They claim that in order to
'accumulate role-specific knowledge a society must
be so organised that certain individuals must concentrate on their specialities' and that specialists
arise who become administrators of the stock of
knowledge that relates to this specialism. This
raises at least two points relevant to the topic

under discussion: that there is an emergence of a
specific role of educator of adults and the fact
that a body of knowledge about that role is emerging
both from the practice and from the research into
it.

Once the role of educator of adults exists and
the process of the education of adults is established, it automatically creates new sub-disciplines of
each of the major disciplines. Hence, the prob-
ability of a philosophy of adult education and a
sociology of the education of adults exists etc. As
these sub-disciplines develop so it is recognised
that they may be useful to the adult educator or to
the prospective adult educator. Hence, a knowledge
about the practice and process evolves. At the same
time a knowledge how to practise emerges and this is
also included in the training of new recruits to the
occupation. In the first instance, the knowledge
how to practise is regarded as most significant and
is taught in induction courses, but as the training
of new recruits is extended knowledge about the
practice and the process may be included in the
training. Hence gradually a body of knowledge about
the education of adults may become formalised, which
may be taught to students, possibly those in training.

Recent developments in training, therefore, and
the upsurge in the amount of research that has been
conducted in adult and continuing education have
both contributed to the emergence of a body of role-
specific knowledge and as training becomes a more
frequent occurrence it is very likely that this
knowledge will become codified in some way and will
form some part of the curriculum that new recruits
to teaching in adult education will be expected to
master. The establishment of role-specific knowledge is, it is maintained, one step in the process
of professionalization and it is one that is
currently occurring in adult education.

However, it must be recognised that as the discipline is emerging and its boundaries are being
established, there is a process of inclusion and exclusion. This raises one significant issue, at
least. To what extent should the body of knowledge
about the education of children be included as excluded from the body of knowledge about the education of adults? Hence the debate about andragogy
and pedagogy is not an irrelevant exercise since it
is also about the constitution of academic disciplines and sub disciplines. Questions about similarities and differences in the learning process for
children and for adults, about the extent to which

there are similarities in the selection of curriculum content etc., all need to be posed. Clearly
there are some similarities between the two processes, so that it would be quite wrong to draw a clear
boundary between them. Yet there are times when the
processes are different. Hence, it is suggested
here that education should be regarded as the
academic discipline and that it has a number of
branches, or sub-disciplines, one of which is the
study of the education of adults.

But what should it be called? The name of the
sub-discipline may not be particularly important but
there are indications that the term 'andragogy' is
gaining a wide degree of acceptance throughout the
world of adult education, even though it may have
been used by Knowles in an ideological manner.
Hence, it may be that this would be an acceptable
title for the sub-discipline and, while it has the
disadvantage just mentioned, it has the advantage of
overcoming the implications contained in the terms
adult education, education of adults etc. Even if
it were to be used in this way, andragogy should not
be regarded as totally distinct from pedagogy, but
at one end of a continuum, pedagogy being at the
other since both are about human beings teaching and
learning and learning and teaching.

BIBLIOGRAPHY

Adult Literacy and Basic Skills Unit (no date)
    Guidelines for Special Development Projects
    Adult Literacy and Basic Skills Unit.   London.
Advisory Council for Adult and Continuing Education,
    (1978) *The Training of Adult Education and Part Time
    Further Education Teachers – a formal response from the
    Advisory Council for Adult and Continuing Education.*
    ACACE.   Leicester.
  - (1979a) *Towards Continuing Education.*   ACACE.
    Leicester.
  - (1979b) *A Strategy for the Basic Education of Adults.*
    ACACE.   Leicester.
  - (1979c) *Links to Learning.* ACACE.   Leicester.
  - (1980)   *Regional Provision for the Training of Part Time
    Adult Education Staff.* ACACE.'   Leicester.
  - (1981)   *Protecting the Future for Adult Education.*
    ACACE.   Leicester.
  - (1982a) *Continuing Education From Policies to Practice.*
    ACACE.   Leicester.
  - (1982b) *Adults: Their Educational.Experience and Needs.*
    ACACE.   Leicester.
  - (1982c) *Prime Use Accommodation for Adult Education.*
    ACACE.   Leicester.
  - (1982d) *Education for Unemployed Adults.*   ACACE.
    Leicester.
  - (1982e) *The Case for a National Development Body for
    Continuing Education in England and Wales.*   ACACE.
    Leicester.
Alford, H. J. (ed) (1980)   *Power and Conflict in
    Continuing Education.* Wadsworth Publishing Co.,
    Belmont, California.
Allaway, A. J. (1977) *The Educational Centres Movement,
    1909-1977.*   National Institute of Adult Education
    in association with the Educational Centres
    Association.
Allman, P. (1982) "New Perspectives on the Adult:

An Argument for Lifelong Education in" *The
International Journal of Lifelong Education* Vol 1 No 1,
The Falmer Press.

Apps, J. W. (1979) *Problems in Continuing Education*.
McGraw Hill Book Co. New York.

Argyle, M. (1974) *The Social Psychology of Work*. Penguin
Books. Harmondsworth.

Armstrong, P. F. (1982) "The'Needs Meeting'
Ideology in Liberal Adult Education" in *The
International Journal of Lifelong Education* Vol 1 No 4.

Aslanian, C. B. and Brickell, H. H. (1980)
"Americans in Transition: Life Changes and
Reasons for Adult Learning" in *Future Directions for
a Learning Society*. College Board, New York.

Beard, R. (1976 - 3rd Edition) *Teaching and Learning in
Higher Education*. Penguin Books. Harmondsworth.

Belbin, C. and Belbin, R. M. (1972) *Problems in Adult
Retraining*. Heinemann. London.

Berger, P. L. and Luckmann, T. (1967) *The Social
Construction of Reality*. Allen Lane, The Penguin
Press. London.

Bergevin, P., Morris, D. and Smith, R. M. (1963)
Adult Education Procedures. Seabury Press. New York.

Bestwick, D. and Chadwick, A. (1977) "A Co-operative
Training Scheme for Part-Time Teachers of Adults"
in *Adult Education* Vol 50 No 4. N.I.A.E.
Leicester.

Bligh, D. A. (1971) *What's the Use of Lectures?*
D. A. and B. Bligh. Briar House. Exeter.

Bloom, B. (ed) (1956) *Taxonomy of Educational Objectives -
Book I. The Cognitive Domain*. Longman. London.

Boone, E. J., Shearon, R. W., White, E. E. et al
(1980) *Serving Personal and Community Needs through
Adult Education*. Jossey Bass Publishers.
San Francisco.

Borger, R. and Seeborne, A.E.M. (1966) *The Psychology
of Learning*. Penguin Books. Harmondsworth.

Boshier, R. (1980) *Towards a Learning Society*. Learning
Press Ltd. Vancouver.

Boud, D. and Bridge, W. (1974) *Keller Plan: A Case
Study in Individualized Learning*. Institute of
Educational Technology. University of Surrey.

Boud, D. J., Bridge, W. A. and Willoughby, L. (1975)
"P.S.I. Now - A Review of Progress and Problems"
in *Journal of Educational Technology* Vol 6 No 2

Bourdieu, P. and Passeron, J-C. (1977) *Reproduction
in Education, Society and Culture*. Sage Publication Ltd.
London.

Bowles, S. and Gintis, H. (1976) *Schooling in
Capitalist America*. Routledge and Kegan Paul Ltd.

London.
Boyle, C. (1982) "Reflections on Recurrent Education"
in *International Journal of Lifelong Education* Vol 1
No 1. The Falmer Press.
Bradshaw, J. (1977) "The Concept of Social Need"
in Fitzgerald et al *op cit.*
Brookfield, S. (1979) "Supporting Autonomous Adult
Learning Groups" in *Adult Education* Vol 51 No 6.
N.I.A.E. Leicester.
Brundage, D. H. and Mackeracher. D. (1980) *Adult
Learning Principles and their Application to Program
Planning.* The Ontario Institute for Studies in
Education. Toronto.
Bruner, J. S. (1968) *Towards a Theory of Instruction.*
W. W. Norton and Co. New York.
Brunner, E. da S., Nicholls, W. L. and Sieber, S. D.
(1959) *The Role of a National Organization in Adult
Education.* Bureau of Applied Social Research,
Columbia University. New York.
Bryant, I. (1983) "Paid Educational Leave in
Scotland" in *International Journal of Lifelong
Education.* Vol 2 No 1. The Falmer Press
Burgess, P. D. (1974) *The Educational Orientations of
Adult Participants in Group Educational Activities.*
Unpublished doctoral thesis, University of
Chicago. Cited in Houle (1979) *op cit.*

Caldwell, P. A. (1981) "Preservice Training for
Instructors of Adults" in Grabowski et ·al *op cit.*
Campbell, D. D. (1977) *Adult Education as a Field of
Study and Practice.* Centre for Continuing Educa-
tion, University of British Columbia. Vancouver.
Candy, P. C. (1981) *Mirrors of the Mind.* Manchester
Monographs 16, Department of Adult and Higher
Education. University of Manchester.
Cantor, L. M. (1974) *Recurrent Education - Policy and
Developments in OECD Member Countries: United Kingdom.*
OECD. Paris.
Cantor, L. M. and Roberts, I. F. (1972 - 2nd Edition)
Further Education in England and Wales. Routledge and
Kegan Paul. London.
Caplow, T. (1954) *The Sociology of Work.* University of
Minnesota Press. Minneapolis.
Cardy, E. and Wells, A. (1981) *Adult Literacy Unit:
Development Projects 1978-80.* Adult Literacy and
Basic Skills Unit. London.
Carp, A., Peterson, R and Roelfs, P. (1974). "Adult
Learning Interests and Experiences". cited in
Cross (1981) *op cit.*
Cashdown, A. and Whitehead, J. (eds) (1971)
Personality, Growth and Learning. Longman. London

Chadwick, A. F. (1980) *The Role of the Museum and Art Gallery in Community Education*. Department of Adult Education, University of Nottingham.

Charnley, A., Osborn, M and Withnall, A. (1980) *Review of Existing Research in Adult and Continuing Education: Vol I - Mature Students*. National Institute of Adult Education. Leicester.

- (1982) *Review of Existing Research in Adult and Continuing Education: Vol VIII - Training the Educators of Adults*. National Institute of Adult Education. Leicester.

Charters, A. N. et al. (1981) *Comparing Adult Education Worldwide*. Jossey Bass Publishers. San Francisco.

Child, D. (1977 - 2nd Edition) *Psychology and the Teacher*. Holt, Rinehart and Winston. London. New York.

- (1981 - 3rd Edition) *Psychology and the Teacher*. Holt, Rinehart and Winston. New York.

Child, J. (1977) *Organization - A Guide to Problems and Practice*. Harper and Row. London.

City and Guilds of London Institute. (1978) *730 Further Education Teachers' Certificate*. CGLI. London.

Coates, K. and Silburn, R. (1967) *St Ann's: poverty, deprivation and morale in a Nottingham Community*. Department of Adult Education. University of Nottingham.

Coleman, A. (1982) *Preparation for Retirement in England and Wales*. National Institute of Adult Education. Leicester.

Collin's *Dictionary of the English Language*. (1979). Collins. London and Glasgow.

Cooper, C. L. (ed) (1975) *Theories of Group Processes* John Wiley and Sons. London.

Courtney, S. (1981) "The Factors Affecting Participation in Adult Education: An Analysis of some Literature" in *Studies in Adult Education* Vol 13 No 2. N.I.A.E. Leicester.

Crane, J. M. (1982) *Individualized Learning: an analysis of the theoretical principles with illuminative references from the experientially-evolved practices of an Individualized Learning System developed in an Adult Basic Academic Upgrading Programme*. Unpublished MSc dissertation. University of Surrey.

Cross, K. P. (1981) *Adults as Learners*. Jossey Bass Publishers. San Francisco.

Dadswell, G. (1978) "The Adult Independent Learner and Public Libraries" in *Adult Education* Vol 51 No 1 N.I.A.E. Leicester.

Dale, S. M. (1980) Another Way Forward for Adult

Learners: the Public Library and Independent Study
in *Studies in Adult Education* Vol 12 No 1.   N.I.A.E.
Leicester.
Dave, R. H. (ed) (1976) *Foundations of Lifelong
Education*. Published for the UNESCO institute for
education by Pergamon Press. Oxford.
Davies, I. K. (1971) *The Management of Learning*.
McGraw Hill Book Co. London.
- (1976) *Objectives in Curriculum Design* . McGraw Hill
Books Co. London.
Day, C. and Baskett, H. K. (1982)"Discrepancies be-
tween Intentions and Practice: Re-examining
Some Basic Assumptions about Adult and Continuing
Professional Education"in *International Journal of
Lifelong Education* Vol 1 No 2. The Falmer Press.
Dearden, R. F. (1972) "'Needs' in Education" in
Dearden, Hirst and Peters (eds) *op cit.*
Dearden, R. F., Hirst, P. H. and Peters, R. S. (eds)
(1972) *A Critique of Current Educational Aims (Part I
of Education and the Development of Reason)*. Routledge
and Kegan Paul. London.
Devereux, W. (1982) *Adult Education in Inner London
1870-1980*. Shepheard-Welwyn in collaboration with
Inner London Education Authority.
Dewey, J. (1916) *Education and Democracy*. The Free
Press. MacMillan Publishing Co. New York.
- (1938) *Experience and Education*. Collier MacMillian
Publishers. London.
Draves, B. (1979) "The Free University Network" in
Lifelong Learning - The Adult Years Vol 3 No 4.
- (1980) *The Free University - a model for lifelong
learning*. Association Press. Follett Publishing
Co. Chicago.
Durkheim, E. (1956) *Education and Sociology* (translated
S.D. Fox) The Free Press. New York.

Eisner, E. W. (1969)"Instructional and Expressive
Educational Objectives"in Popham et al *op cit.*
Elias, J. L. (1979)"Andragogy Revisited"in *Adult
Education* Vol 29 pp 252-6. Washington.
Elias, J. L. and Merriam, S. (1980) *Philosophical
Foundation of Adult Education*. Robert E Krieger
Publishing Co. Malabar, Florida.
Ellwood, C. (1976) *Adult Learning Today*. Sage Pub-
lications. London.
Elsdon, K. T. (1970) The East Midlands Scheme in
Adult Education Vol 46 No 4. N.I.A.E. Leicester.
- (1975) *Training for Adult Education*. Department of
of Adult Education. University of Nottingham
in conjunction with N.I.A.E.
- (1981) *New Directions: Adult Education in the Context*

of Continuing Education. Department of Education
and Science. London.

Elsey, B. (1980) Volunteer Tutors in Adult Education
in *Studies in Adult Education* Vol 12 No 2. N.I.A.E.

Fairbairn, A. N. (1971) *The Leicestershire Community
Colleges*. N.I.A.E. London.
- (1978) *The Leicestershire Community Colleges and Centres*.
Department of Adult Education. University of
Nottingham.

Faure, E. (Chairman) (1972) *Learning to Be*. UNESCO.
Paris.

Fitzgerald, M., Halmos, P., Muncie, J. and
Zeldin, D. (1977) *Welfare in Action*. Routledge
and Kegan Paul in association with the Open
University Press. London.

Fletcher, C. (1979) "The Theory of Community
Education and its relation to adult education" in
Thompson, J. L. (ed) *op cit*.
- (1980) "Community Studies as Practical Adult
Education" in *Adult Education* Vol 53 No 2. N.I.A.E.
Leicester.
- (1982) "Adults in a Community Education Centre"
in *The International Journal of Lifelong Education* Vol 1
No 3. The Falmer Press.

Fletcher, C. and Thompson, N. (1980) *Issues in
Community Education*. Falmer Press. Lewes, Sussex.

Flude, R. A. (1978) "A Course in Rural Community
Action" in *Adult Education* Vol 51 No 3. N.I.A.E.
Leicester.

Flude, R. and Parrott, A. (1979) *Education and the
Challenge of Change - a recurrent education strategy for
Britain*. The Open University Press.
Milton Keynes.

Fordham, P., Poulton, G. and Randle, L. (1979)
Learning Networks in Adult Education. Routledge and
Kegan Paul. London.

Freire, P. (1971) "A Few Notions about the word
'concientization'" in *Hard Cheese* No 1. Reprinted
in *Schooling and Capitalism* (1976). Routledge and
Kegan Paul in association with the Open
University. London.
- (1972a) *Cultural Action for Freedom*. Penguin.
Harmondsworth.
- (1972b) *Pedagogy of the Oppressed* translated by
M. B. Ramer. Penguin. Harmondsworth.
- (1973a) *Education for Critical Consciousness*. Sheed
and Ward. London. Reprinted under the title
Education: the Practice of Freedom. Writers and
Readers Publishing Co-operative. London.
- (1973b) "Education, Liberation and the Church"
in *Study Encounter* Vol 9 No 1. World Council of

Churches.
- (1973c) **By Learning they can Teach** in *Convergence* Vol 6 No 1.
- (1978) *Pedagogy in Process. The Letters to Guinea-Bissau.* Writers and Readers Publishing Co-operative. London.

Gagné, R. M. (1977 - 3rd Edition) *The Conditions of Learning.* Holt, Rinehart and Winston. New York.

Gelpi, E. (1979) *A Future for Lifelong Education* (2 Vols) translated by Ruddock, R. Manchester Monographs 13. The University, Manchester.

Gibbs, G. (1981) *Teaching Students to Learn.* The Open University Press. Milton Keynes.

Gibbs, G. and Durbridge, N. (1976) "Characteristics of Open University Tutors (Part 2): Tutors in Action" in *Teaching at a Distance* No 7. Open University. Milton Keynes.

Giles, H. H., McCutcheon, S. P. and Zechriel, A. N. (1942) *Exploring the Curriculum.* Harper. New York.

Gould, A. (1979) *Towards Equality of Occupational Opportunity.* Association of Recurrent Education. Discussion Paper 5. Centre for Research into Education for Adults. University of Nottingham.

Grabowski, S. H. et al (1981) *Preparing Educators of Adults.* Jossey Bass. San Francisco.

Graham, T. B., Daines, J. H., Sullivan, T., Harris, P. and Baum, F. E. (1982) *The Training of Part-Time Teachers of Adults.* Department of Adult Education. University of Nottingham.

Greenwood, E. (1957) "Attributes of a Profession" in *Social Work* Vol 2 pp44-55.

Griffin, C. (1978) *Recurrent and Continuing Education - a curriculum model approach.* Association of Recurrent Education, School of Education. University of Nottingham.
- (1979) "Continuing Education and the Adult Curriculum" in *Adult Education* Vol 52 No 2. N.I.A.E. Leicester.
- (1982) "Curriculum Analysis of Adult and Lifelong Education" in *International Journal of Lifelong Education* Vol 1 No 2. The Falmer Press.

Groombridge, B. (1972) *Television and the People.* Penguin Books Ltd. Harmondsworth.

Gross, R. (1977) *The Lifelong Leaner.* Touchstone Books, Simon and Schuster. New York.

Hall, R. H. (1969) *Occupations and the Social Structure.* Prentice Hall Inc. Englewood Cliffs, New Jersey.

Halmos, P. (1978) "The Concept of Social Problem" in *Social Work and Community Work Course DE206,* Block 1

Open University. Milton Keynes.

Handley, J. (1981) *An Investigation into the Training Needs of Part-Time Tutors, with particular reference to the development of courses at ACSTT Stage II level*. Unpublished MSc dissertation. University of Surrey.

Harper, K. (1982) "Colleges warned against 'politics' in YOP courses" in *Guardian Newspaper* 29.11.82. p22.

Harries-Jenkins, G. (1982) "The Role of the Adult Student" in *International Journal of Lifelong Education* Vol 1 No 1. The Falmer Press.

Harris, W.J.A. (1980) *Comparative Adult Education - practice, purpose and theory*. Longman. London and New York.

Harvey, B., Daines, J., Jones, D. and Wallis, J. (1981) *Policy and Research Adult Education*. Department of Adult Education. University of Nottingham.

Haycocks, J. N. (Chairman) (1978) *The Training of Adult Education and Part-Time Further Education Teachers*. Advisory Committee on the Supply and Training of Teachers. London.

Head, D. (1977) "Education at the Bottom" in *Studies in Adult Education* Vol 9 No 2. N.I.A.E. Leicester.

Hegarty, T. B. (1976) "Education for the Legal Profession" in Turner and Rushton (eds) *op cit*.

Hetherington, J. (1980) "Professionalism and Part-Time Staff in Adult Education" in *Adult Education* Vol 52 No 5. N.I.A.E. Leicester.

Hilgard, E. R. and Atkinson, R. C. (1967 - 4th Edition) *Introduction to Psychology*. Harcourt, Brace and World, Inc. New York.

Hirst, P. H. and Peters, R. S. (1970) *The Logic of Education*. Routledge and Kegan Paul. London.

Holmberg, B. (1981) *Status and Trends of Distance Education*. Kogan Page. London.

Holt, R. (1982) "An Alternative to Mentorship" in *Adult Education* Vol 55 No 2. N.I.A.E. Leicester.

Hopper, E. and Osborn, M. (1975) *Adult Students: Education, Selection and Social Control*. Frances Pinter. London.

Hostler, J. (1977) "The Education of Adults" in *Studies in Adult Education* Vol 9 No 1. N.I.A.E. Leicester.

- (1978) "Liberal Adult Education" in *Studies in Adult Education* Vol 10 No 2. N.I.A.E. Leicester.

Houghton, V. (1974) "Recurrent Education: a plea for lifelong learning" in Houghton, V. and Richardson, K. *op cit*.

Houghton, V. and Richardson, K. (eds) (1974) *Recurrent Education: a plea for lifelong learning*.

Ward Lock Educational in conjunction with the
Association of Recurrent Education.   London.

Houle, C. O. (1961) *The Inquiring Mind*. University of
Winsconsin Press.   Madison.

- (1972) *The Design of Education*. Jossey Bass Publishers
San Francisco.

- (1979) "Motivation and Participation with special
reference to non-traditional forms of study" in
OECD 1977 Vol 3 (published 1979)   *op cit*.

- (1980) *Continuing Learning in the Professions*.   Jossey
Bass Publishers.   San Francisco.

Houston, R. P., Bee, H., Hatfield, E. and Rimm, D.C.
(1979) *Invitation to Psychology*.   Academic Press.
New York.

Howe, M. J. A. (1977) *Adult Learning*.   John Wiley and
Sons.   Chichester.

Hoy, J. D. (1933) "An Enquiry as to Interests and
Motives for Study among Adult Evening Students"
British Journal of Educational Psychology Vol 3 No 1.

Hughes, M. (1977)   "Adult Education on the Cheap:
an extension of adult education provision into
the school classroom," in *Adult Education* Vol 50
No 4.   NIAE.   Leicester.

Husén, T. (1974) *The Learning Society*. Methuen and Co
Ltd.   London

Hutchins, R. M. (1970) *The Learning Society*.   Penguin.
Harmondsworth.

Hutchinson, E. M. (ed) (1970)   "Adult Education –
Adequacy of Provision". *Adult Education* Vol 42 No 6
N.I.A.E.   Leicester.

Hutchinson, E. and E.M.(1978)   *Learning Later*. Routledge
and Kegan Paul.   London.

Illich, I. (1973a) *Deschooling Society*. Penguin Books.
Harmondsworth.

- (1973b) *After Deschooling, What?* Writers and Readers
Publishing Corporation, London.

- (1977) Disabling Professions in Illich et al
op cit.

Illich, I. and Verne, E. (1976) *Imprisoned in a Global
Classroom*. Writers and Readers Publishing Co-
operative. London.

Illich, I., Zola, I. K., McKnight, J. Caplan, J.
and Shanken, R.   (1977) *Disabling Professions*.
Marion Boyars.   London.

Jarvis, P. (1975) "The Parish Ministry as a Semi-
Profession" in *Sociological Review* Vol 23 pp 911–922.
University of Keele.

- (1978a) "Students' Learning and Tutors' Marking"
in *Teaching at a Distance* No 13.   Open University.

Milton Keynes.
- (1978b) "Knowledge and the Curriculum in Adult Education: a sociological approach" in *Adult Education* Vol 51 No 4. N.I.A.E. Leicester.
- (1980) "Pre-Retirement Education: Design and Analysis" in *Adult Education* Vol 53 No 1 N.I.A.E. Leicester.
- (1981) "The Open University Unit: andragogy or pedagogy?" in *Teaching at a Distance No 20*. Open University. Milton Keynes.
- (1982a) "What's the Value of Adult Education?" in *Adult Education* Vol 54 No 4.
- (1982b) *Adult Education in a Small Centre: a case study in the village of Lingfield*. Department of Adult Education. University of Surrey.
- (1983a) *Professional Education*. Croom Helm. London.
- (1983b) "Education and the Elderly" in *Adult Education* Vol 55 No 4. N.I.A.E. Leicester.
- (1983c) "The Lifelong Religious Development of the Individual and the Place of Adult Education" in *Lifelong Learning: The adult years* Vol 6 No. 9.
- (forthcoming) "Continuing Professional Education, Study Tours Abroad and Adult Education"in *Adult Education*. N.I.A.E. Leicester.
Jennings, B. (ed) (No date) *Community Colleges in England and Wales*. N.I.A.E. Leicester.
Jessup, F. W. (ed) (1969) *Lifelong Learning - a symposium on Continuing Education*. Pergamon Press. Oxford.
Johnstone, J. W. C. and Rivera, R. J. (1965). *Volunteers for Learning*. Aldine Publishing. Chicago.

Kagan, J. (1971) "Developmental Studies in Reflection and Analysis" in *Perceptual Development in Children* eds. A. H. Kidd and J. E. Rivoire. International Universities Press. New York. Reprinted in Cashdan and Whitehead (eds) *op cit*.
Kallen, D. (1979) *Recurrent Education and Lifelong Learning: definitions and distinctions* in Schuller and Megarry (1979) *op cit*.
Katz, D. (1960) "The Functional Approach to the Study of Attitudes" in *Public Opinion Quarterly* Vol 24 pp 163-177.
Keddie, N. (1980) "Adult Education: an ideology individualism" in Thompson,J. C. (ed) *op cit*.
Keller, F. S. (1968) "Good-bye, Teacher ..." in *Journal of Applied Behaviour Analysis* Vol No 1.
Kelly, A. V. (1977) *The Curriculum: Theory and Practice*. Harper and Row. London.
Kelly, G. A. (1955) *The Psychology of Personal Constructs*.

Norton. New York.

Kelly, T. (1970) *A History of Adult Education in Great Britain.* Liverpool University Press.

Kidd, J. R. (1973 Revised Edition) *How Adults Learn.* Association Press, Follett Publishing Co. Chicago.

Killeen, J. and Bird, M. (1981) *Education and Work.* National Institute of Adult Education. Leicester.

Kirk, P. (1976) "The Loneliness of the Long Distance Tutor" in *Teaching at a Distance* No 7. Open University, Milton Keynes.

Kirkwood, C. (1978) "Adult Education and the Concept of Community" in *Adult Education* Vol 51 No 3. N.I.A.E. Leicester.

Knowles, M. S. (1978 - 2nd Edition) *The Adult Learner: A Neglected Species.* Gulf Publishing Co. Houston.
 - 1979 "Andragogy Revisited II" in *Adult Education* Vol 3 pp 52-3. Washington.
 - (1980 - Revisited and uptdated) *The Modern Practice of Adult Education.* Association Press. Follett Publishing Co. Chicago.

Knox, A. B. (1977) *Adult Development and Learning.* Jossey Bass Publishers Ltd. San Francisco.

Knudson, R. S. (1979) "Andragogy Revisited: Humanagogy Anyone?" in *Adult Education* . Vol 29 pp 261-4. Washington.

Köhler, W. (1947) *Gestalt Psychology.* Liveright Publishing Corporation. New York.

Kolb, D. A. and Fry, R. (1975) "Towards an Applied Theory of Experiential Learning" in Cooper C. L. (ed) , *op cit.*

Krech, D., Crutchfield, R. S. and Ballachery, E. L. (1962) *Individual in Society.* McGraw-Hill Book Co. Ltd. New York.

Kulich, J. (Ed) (1977) *Training of Adult Educators in East Europe.* Centre for Continuing Education , University of British Columbia.
 - (1982a) *Adult Education in Continental Europe: an annotated bibliography of English language materials 1975-9.* Centre for Continuing Education, University of British Columbia. Vancouver.
 - (1982b) "Lifelong Education and the Universities: a Canadian Perspective" in *International Journal of Lifelong Education* Vol 1 No 2. The Falmer Press

Kumar, K. (1978) *Prophecy and Progress.* Penguin Books Ltd. Harmondsworth.

Label, J. (1978) "Beyond Andragogy to Gerogogy" in *Lifelong Learning: the Adult Years.* No 1. Washington.

Labouvie-Vief, G. (1978) "Models of Cognitive Functtioning in the Old Adult: Research Needs in

Educational Gerontology" in Sherron and Lumsdon (eds) 1978 *op cit.*

Lawson, K. H. (1975) *Philosophical Concepts and Values in Adult Education*. Department of Adult Education. University of Nottingham. Reprinted in a 2nd edition and published by the Open University Press.

- (1977) "Community Education: a critical assessment" in *Adult Education* Vol 50 No 1. N.I.A.E. Leicester.

- (1982) "Lifelong Education: Concept or Policy?" in *International Journal of Lifelong Education* Vol 1 No 2. The Falmer Press

Lawton, D. (1973) *Social Change, Educational Theory and Curriculum Planning*. Hodder and Stoughton. London.

Legge, D. (1968) "Training Adult Educators in the United Kingdom" in *Convergence* Vol 1 No 1.

- (1971a) "The Use of the Talk in Adult Classes" in Stephens, M. D. and Roderick, G. W. (eds) 1971 *op cit.*

- (1971b) "Discussion Methods" in Stephens and Roderick 1971 *op cit.*

- (1981) "The Training of Teachers of Adults" in Harvey et al *op cit.*

- (1982) *The Education of Adults in Britain*. The Open University Press. Milton Keynes.

Lengrand, P. (1975) *An Introduction to Lifelong Education*. Croom Helm. London.

Lester-Smith, W. O. (1966) *Education - An Introductory Survey*. Penguin Books. Harmondsworth.

Leytham, G. (1971)"The Principles of Programmed Learning"in Stephens, M. D. and Roderick, G. W. *op cit.*

Lindeman, E. (1961 - first published 1926) *The Meaning of Adult Education*. Harvester House. Montreal.

Lippitt, R. and White, R. K. (1958) An Experimental Study of Leadership and Group Life in Maccoby et al *op cit.*

Little, A.,Willey, R. and Gundara, J. (1982) *Adult Education and the Black Communities*. ACACE. Leicester.

London, J. (1973)"Reflections upon the relevance of Paulo Freire for American Adult Education"in *Convergence* Vol 6 No 1.

Lovell, B. R. (1980) *Adults Learning*. Croom Helm. London.

Lovett, T. (1975) *Adult Education, Community Development and the Working Class*. Ward Lock Educational. London.

- (1979) "Adult Education and Community Action" in Thompson, J. L. *op cit.*

Bibliography

Lovett, T. and Mackay, L (1978) "Community Based
Study Groups" in *Adult Education* Vol 51 No 1.
N.I.A.E. Leicester.
Luckmann, T. (1967) *The Invisible Religion.* Collier-
MacMillan Ltd. London.
Lusterman, S. (1977)"Education in Industry"in
Vermilye, D. W. *op cit.*

Maccoby, E. E., Newcomb, T. M. and Hartley, E. L.
(Eds) (1958 - 3rd Edition) *Readings in Social
Psychology.* Holt. New York.
Macfarlane, T. (1978) "Curriculum Innovation in
Adult Literacy: the cost of insularity" in
Studies in Adult Education Vol 10 No 2. N.I.A.E.
Leicester.
McGregor, D. (1960) *The Human Side of Enterprise.*
McGraw Hill. New York.
McIntosh, N. (1974)"The Open University Student" in
Turnstall, J. *op cit.*
McIntosh, N. E. (1979) "To Make Continuing Education
a Reality" in *Oxford Review of Education* Vol 5 No 2
and republished by ACACE. Leicester.
McKenzie, L. (1977) "The Issue of Andragogy" in
Adult Education Vol 27 pp 225-229. Washington.
 - (1979) "Andragogy Revisited: Response to Elias"
in *Adult Education* Vol 29 pp 256-261. Washington.
McLagan, P. A. (1978 - Revised Edition) *Helping Others
Learn.* Addison-Wasley Publishing Co.
Massachusetts.
Mannion-Watson, C. (1982) *An Evaluation of a Pilot
Course on the Teaching of Study Skills to Sixth Form
Students.* Unpublished MSc dissertation.
University of Surrey.
Martin, B. (1981) *A Sociology of Contemporary Cultural
Change.* Basil Blackwell. Oxford.
Martin, L. C. (1981) "A Survey of the Training
Needs of Part-Time Tutors in a Region" in *Studies
In Adult Education* Vol 13 No 2. N.I.A.E.
Leicester.
Maslow, A. H. (1968 - 2nd Edition) *Towards a Psychology
of Being.* D. Van Nostrand Company. New York.
Mee, G. (1980) *Organisation for Adult Education.* Longman.
London.
Mee, G. and Wiltshire, H. (1978) *Structure and
Performance in Adult Education.* Longman. London.
Merton, R. K. (1968 - Edition) *Social Theory and Social
Structure.* The Free Press. New York.
Mezirow, J. (1977)"Perspective Transformation"in
Studies in Adult Education Vol 9 No 2. N.I.A.E.
Leicester.
 - (1981) "A Critical Theory of Adult Learning and

Education" in *Adult Education* Vol 32 No 1.
Washington.

Midwinter, E. (1975) *Education and the Community*.
George Allen and Unwin Ltd. London.

Mocker, D. W. and Noble, E. (1981) "Training Part-
Time Instructional Staff" in Grabowski et al
op cit.

Moemeka, A. A. (1981) *Local Radio - community education
for development*. Ahmodu Bello University Press Ltd
Zaria. Nigeria.

Morris, H. (1956) "Architecture, Humanism and the
Local Community" in Fletcher, C. and Thompson, N.
op cit.

Mortain, B. R. and Smart, J. C. (1974) "Reasons for
Participation in Adult Education Courses: A
Multivariate Analysis of Group Difference" in
Adult Education Vol 24 No 2. Washington.

Newman, M.   (1973) *Adult Education and Community Action*.
Writers and Readers Publishing Co-operative.
London.
 - (1979) *The Poor Cousin*.   George Allen and Unwin.
London.

OECD (1971) *Equal Educational Opportunity: A Statement of
the Problem with Special Reference to Recurrent Education*.
OECD.   Paris.

OECD/CERI (1973) *Recurrent Education: A Strategy for
Lifelong Education*. OECD.   Paris.
 - (1975) *Recurrent Education: Trends and Issues*. OECD.
Paris.

OECD (1977) *Learning Opportunities for Adults (4 volumes)*.
OECD. Paris.

Open University (1982) *The Training of Adult Educators
(3 volumes and 2 video cassettes)* Open University.
Milton Keynes.

Parker, S. (1976)   *The Sociology of Leisure*.   George
Allen and Unwin. London.

Paterson, R. W. K. (1979) *Values, Education and the
Adult*. Routledge and Kegan Paul. London.

Pavlov, I. P. (1927) *Conditioned Reflexes*. Oxford
University Press. New York.

Peers, R. (1958) *Adult Education - a comparative
perspective*. Routledge and Kegan Paul. London.

Peters, J. M. and Gordon, S. (1974) *Adult Learning
Projects: a study of adult learning in urban and rural
Tennessee*. University of Tennessee. Knoxville.

Peters, R. S. (1966) *Ethics and Education*. George
Allan and Unwin Ltd. London.
 - (1972) "Education and the Educated Man",

in   D. F. Deaden, P. H. Hirst and R. S Peters 1972 *op cit*.

Peterson, R. E. et al (1979) *Lifelong Learning in America*. Jossey Bass Publishers. San Francisco.

Piaget, J. (1929) *The Child's Conception of the World*. Routledge and Kegan Paul. London.

Popham, W. J., Eisner, E. W., Sullivan, H. J. and Tyler, L. L. (1969) *Instructional Objectives*. Rand McNally. Chicago.

Richardson, M. et al (1979) *Preparing to Study*. The Open University Press. Milton Keynes.

Riesman, D. (1950) *The Lonely Crowd: a Study of Changing American Character*. Yale University Press. New Haven.

Roderick, G. W., Bell, J., Dickenson, R., Turner, R. and Wellings, A. (1981) *Mature Students in Further and Higher Education*. Division of Continuing Education. University of Sheffield.

Rogers, A. (ed) (1976) *The Spirit and the Form*. University of Nottingham, Department of Adult Education.

Rogers, C. R. (1969) *Freedom to Learn*. Charles, E. Merrill Publishing Co. Columbus,Ohio.

Rogers, E. M. (1962) *Diffusion of Innovations*. The Free Press. Glencoe.

Rogers, J. (ed) (1973) *Adults in Education*. British Broadcasting Corporation. London.

- (1977 - 2nd Edition) *Adults Learning*. Open University Press. Milton Keynes.

Rogers, J. and Groombridge, B. (1976) *Right to Learn*. Arrow Books. London.

Rumble, G. (1982) *The Open University of the United Kingdom*. Distance Education Research Group. The Open University. Milton Keynes.

Rumble, G. and Harry, K. (1982) *The Distance Teaching Universities*. Croom Helm. London and Canberra.

Russell, L. (Chairman) (1973) *Adult Education: A Plan for Development*. Her Majesty's Stationery Office. London.

Scheler, M. (1926) *Die Wissens former and die Gessellschaft*. Der Neue-Guist Verlag, Leipzig cited in Merton *op cit*.

Schuler, T. and Megarry, J. (eds) (1979) *World Yearbook on Education 1979: Recurrent Education and Lifelong Learning*. Kogan Page. London.

Schutz, A. and Luckmann, T. (1974) *The Structures of the Life World*. Heinemann. London.

Sherron, R. H. and Lumsden, D. B. (eds) (1978)

Bibliography

Introduction to Educational Gerontology. Hemisphere
Publishing Company. Washington.
Sidwell, D. (1980) "A Survey of Modern Language
Classes" in *Adult Education* Vol 52 No 5. N.I.A.E.
Leicester.
Skinner, B. F. (1951) "How to Teach Animals" in
Scientific American Vol 185 No 6.
- (1971) *Beyond Freedom and Dignity*. Penguin Books.
Harmondsworth.
Sless, D. (1981) *Learning and Visual Communication*.
Croom Helm. London.
Smith, A. L. (Chairman) (1919) "Adult Education
Committee Final Report". Reprinted in"The 1919
Report". Department of Adult Education,
University of Nottingham.
Sockett, H. (1981) "Editorial Introduction" in
Educational Analysis. Vol 3 No 1. The Falmer Press
Srinivasan, L. (1977) *Perspectives on Non formal Adult
Learning*. World Education. New York.
Stephens, M. D. (1981) The Future of Continuing
Education in *Adult Education* Vol 54 No 2. N.I.A.E.
Leicester.
Stephens, M. D. and Roderick, G. W. (eds) (1971)
Teaching Techniques in Adult Education. David and
Charles. Newton Abbot.
Stock, A. (1971) "Role Playing and Simulation
Techniques" in Stephens,M. D. and Roderick, G. W.
op cit.
- (1982 - Edition) *Adult Education in the United
Kingdom*. N.I.A.E. Leicester.
Surridge, R. and Bowen, J. (1977) *The Independant
Learning Project: A Study of Changing Attitudes in
American Public Libraries*. Public Libraries Research
Group.

Taba, H. (1962) *Curriculum Development: Theory and
Practice*. Harcourt, Brace and World. New York.
Tabberer, R. and Allman, J. (1981) *Study Skills at
16 Plus*. National Foundation for Educational
Research. Slough.
Talyor, J. (1978) "The Advisory Council for Adult
and Continuing Education" in *Adult Education* Vol 51
No 4. N.I.A.E. Leicester.
Thompson, J. L. (ed)(1980) *Adult Education for a Change*.
Heinemann. London.
Thorndike, E. L. (1928) *Adult Learning*. MacMillan.
London.
Thornton, A. H. and Stephens, M. D. (eds) (1977)
The University in its Region. Department of Adult
Education. University of Nottingham.
Tight, M. (1982) *Part-Time Degree Level Study in the*

United Kingdom. ACACE. Leicester.

Titmus, C. (1981) *Strategies for Adult Education - practices in Western Europe*. Open University Press. Milton Keynes.

Toennies, F. (1957) *Community and Society* (translated C. P. Loomis). Michigan State University Press. Michigan. Published in the United Kingdom as *Community and Association* by Routledge and Kegan Paul. London.

Tough, A. (1979 - 2nd Edition) *The Adult's Learning Projects*. Ontario Institute for Studies in Education. Toranto.

Tough, A. (1981 - 3rd Edition) *Learning Without a Teacher*. Ontario Institue for Studies in Education. Educational Research Series No 3. Toronto.

Tunstall, J. (ed) (1974) *The Open University Opens*. Routledge and Kegan Paul Ltd. London.

Turner, J. R. and Rushton, J. (eds) (1976) *Education for the Professions*. Manchester University Press. Manchester.

Tyler, R. W. (1949) *Basic Principles of Curriculum and Instruction*. University of Chicago Press. Chicago.

Venables, P. (Chairman) (1976) *Report of the Committee on Continuing Education*. Open University. Milton Keynes.

Vermilye, D. W. (ed) (1977) *Relating Work and Education*. Jossey Bass Publishers. San Francisco.

Verner, C. (with assistance from C.Booth) (1964) *Adult Education*. Center for Applied Research in Education, Inc. Washington.

Westwood, S. (1980) "Adult Education and the Sociology of Education: an exploration" in Thompson, J. L. *op cit*.

Wilensky, H. A. L. (1964) "The Professionalization of Everyone?" in *American Journal of Sociology* Vol LXX pp 137-158.

Williams, E. and Heath, A. E. (1936) *Learn and Live*. Methuen. London.

Williams, G. (1977) *Towards Lifelong Education: a new role for higher education institutes*. UNESCO. Paris.

Williams, G. L. (1980) "Adults Learning about Adult Learning" in *Adult Education* Vol 52 No 6. N.I.A.E. Leicester.

Wilson, S. (1980) "The School and the Community" in Fletcher, C. and Thompson, N. *op cit*.

Wiltshire, H. (1973) "The Concepts of Learning and Need in Adult Education" in *Studies in Adult Education* Vol 5 No 1. N.I.A.E. Leicester.

Reprinted in Rogers, A. (ed) *op cit*.
- (1976) "The Nature and Uses of Adult Education" in Rogers, A. *op cit*.
- (1981) "Changing Concepts of Adult Education" in Elsdon, K. *op cit*.
Witkin, H. A. (1971) Psychological Differentiations in *Journal of Abnormal Psychology* Vol 70, 1965, reprinted in Cashdan and Whitehead (eds)*op cit*.
Wood, D. (1982) *Continuing Education in Polytechnics and Colleges*. Department of Adult Education. University of Nottingham.
Woodhall, M. (1980) *The Scope and Costs of the Education and Training of Adults in Britain*. ACACE. Leicester.
Workers' Education Association. (1982) *The Robert Tressell Papers: Exploring 'The Ragged Trousered Philanthropists'* obtainable from Robert Tressell Workshop, c/o Robert Tressell House, 25 Wellington Square, Hastings, East Sussex.

Yarrington, R. (1979) "Lifelong Education Trends in Community Colleges" in *Convergence* Vol XII Nos 1-2.
Yeaxlee, B. A. (1929) *Lifelong Education*. Cassell Co. Ltd. London.
Young, M. F. D. (1971) "Curricula as Socially Organized Knowledge" in Young, M.F.D. *op cit*.
- (ed) 1971 *Knowledge and Control*. Collier-MacMillan Publishers. London.

Zimmerman, F. E. (1979) "Elder hostel '78 at Adelphi University" in *Lifelong Learning: the Adult Years*. Vol III No 3.

301

ADULT AND CONTINUING EDUCATION

UNIVERSITY OF
WOLVERHAMPTON
KNOWLEDGE · INNOVATION · ENTERPRISE

Harrison Learning Centre
City Campus
University of Wolverhampton
St. Peter's Square
Wolverhampton
WV1 1RH
Telephone: 0845 408 1631
Online Renewals: www.wlv.ac.uk/lib/myaccount